The Cosmopolitan Vision

What is enlightenment? To have the courage to make use of one's cosmopolitan vision and to acknowledge one's multiple identities – to combine forms of life founded on language, skin colour, nationality or religion with the awareness that, in a radically insecure world, all are equal and everyone is different.

The Cosmopolitan Vision

By Ulrich Beck

Translated by Ciaran Cronin

polity

First published in German in 2004 by Suhrkamp Verlag as *Der kosmopolitische Blick oder: Krieg ist Frieden* and © Suhrkamp Verlag Frankfurt am Main 2004

This English translation © Polity Press, 2006

First published in 2006 by Polity Press

Polity Press
65 Bridge Street
Cambridge CB2 1UR, UK

Polity Press
350 Main Street
Malden, MA 02148, USA

ISBN: 0-7456-3398-6
ISBN: 0-7456-3399-4 (pb)

A catalogue record for this book is available from the British Library.

Typeset in Stempel Garamond 10 on 12pt
by Servis Filmsetting Ltd, Manchester
Printed and bound in Great Britain by TJ International Ltd, Padstow, Cornwall

The publisher has used its best endeavours to ensure that the URLs for external websites referred to in this book are correct and active at the time of going to press. However, the publisher has no responsibility for the websites and can make no guarantee that a site will remain live or that the content is or will remain appropriate.

For further information on Polity, visit our website: www.polity.co.uk

Contents

Detailed Contents

Acknowledgements

This book developed out of an intense conversation and exchange of ideas with Daniel Levy and Natan Sznaider, whose numerous promptings I have accepted and who consistently provided very valuable comments on drafts. Thus this book also presents results of our joint research project (funded by the Deutsche Forschungsgesellschaft) with a specific focus on 'Reflexive Modernization' (see, in addition, Beck, Levy and Sznaider 2004). This research project itself exemplifies the topic of the book: Daniel Levy teaches sociology at the State University of New York, Stonybrook, Natan Sznaider at the Academic College of Tel Aviv and I in Munich and London. Without this international network of exchange and cooperation, which also includes Michael Pollak, a sociologist and editor in New York, and numerous colleagues at the London School of Economics and Political Science, this book would not have been possible. In addition, Edgar Grande, Boris Holzer and Angelika Poferl have carefully read individual chapters and made highly stimulating comments on them, for which I offer them my sincere thanks. Finally, this book benefited greatly from what Elisabeth Beck-Gernsheim was writing concurrently in her book *Wir und die Anderen*. The larger research project of which this book is a part will be documented in the volume *Entgrenzung und Entscheidung*, edited by myself and Christoph Lau.

My work has been generously supported by the Volkswagen-Stiftung, for which I am very grateful.

Introduction

What is 'Cosmopolitan' about the Cosmopolitan Vision

What makes the cosmopolitan outlook 'cosmopolitan'? What do we mean by 'cosmopolitanism'? This word evokes at once the most marvellous and the most terrible histories.

The greatest and most productive controversies of the European Enlightenment are connected with it, but they have long since been forgotten. Some, such as Heinrich Laube in the middle of the nineteenth century, invoked the therapeutic value of the fatherland against the allegedly excessive demands of cosmopolitanism: 'Patriotism is one-sided and petty, but it is practical, useful, joyous and comforting; cosmopolitanism is splendid, large, but for a human being almost too large; the idea is beautiful, but the result in this life is inner anguish' (1973: 88). Cosmopolitanism is in the end just a beautiful idea: 'Nowadays in our concern for humanity we tend to lose sight of human beings; and in this time of conflagrations, cannons and fiery speeches this is abject. The idea is a beautiful thing, too large for almost everybody, and it remains a mere idea. If it does not take on a concrete individual form, it might as well have never existed' (ibid.: 131).

Heinrich Heine, by contrast, who regarded himself as an embodiment of cosmopolitanism, prophesied around the same time 'that in the end this will become the universal conviction among Europeans, and . . . it has a greater future than our German chauvinists, these mere mortals who belong to the past' (1997: 710). He criticized German patriotism, which in his view involved 'a narrowing of the heart, which contracts like leather in the cold, and hatred of all things foreign – a desire no longer to be a world citizen or a European but merely a narrow German.' He excoriated 'the shabby, coarse, unwashed opposition to a sentiment which is the most splendid and sacred thing Germany has produced, that is, opposition to the humanity, the universal brotherhood of man, the cosmopolitanism to which our great minds, Lessing, Herder, Schiller, Goethe, Jean Paul and all educated people in Germany have always paid homage' (ibid.: 379). (These quotations, like many others in this introduction, are taken from Thielking 2000.)

Nowadays there is no point in arguing over whether patriotism, although practical, is too petty, whereas cosmopolitanism, by contrast, is splendid, but cold and unliveable. The important fact now is that the human condition has itself become cosmopolitan. To illustrate this thesis we need only highlight the fact that the most recent avatar in the genealogy of global risks, the threat of terror, also knows no borders. The same is true of the protest against the war in Iraq. For the first time a war was treated as an event in global domestic politics, with the whole of humanity participating simultaneously through the mass media, even as it threatened to shatter the Atlantic alliance. More generally, the paradox that resistance against globalization itself produces political globalization has been apparent for some time. The globalization of politics, economic relations, law, culture, and communication and interaction networks spurs controversy; indeed, the shock generated by global risks continually gives rise to worldwide political publics.

In this way cosmopolitanism has ceased to be merely a controversial rational idea; in however distorted a form, it has left the realm of philosophical castles in the air and has entered reality. Indeed, it has become the defining feature of a new era, the era of reflexive modernity, in which national borders and differences are dissolving and must be renegotiated in accordance with the logic of a 'politics of politics'. This is why a world that has become cosmopolitan urgently demands a new standpoint, the cosmopolitan outlook, from which we can grasp the social and political realities in which we live and act. Thus the cosmopolitan outlook is both the presupposition and the result of a conceptual reconfiguration of our modes of perception.

The national outlook – or, in technical terms, methodological nationalism – opposes this structural transformation. Until now it has been dominant in sociology and in the other social sciences, such as history, political science and economics, which analysed societies on the assumption that they are nationally structured. The result was a system of nation-states and corresponding national sociologies that define their specific societies in terms of concepts associated with the nation-state. For the national outlook, the nation-state creates and controls the 'container' of society, and thereby at the same time prescribes the limits of 'sociology'.

Cosmopolitanism which has taken up residence in reality is a vital theme of European civilization and European consciousness and beyond that of global experience. For in the cosmopolitan outlook, methodologically understood, there resides the latent potential to break out of the self-centred narcissism of the national outlook and the dull incomprehension with which it infects thought and action, and thereby enlighten human beings concerning the real, internal cosmopolitanization of their lifeworlds and institutions.

What enables and empowers the concept of cosmopolitanism to perform this task? Paradoxically, two contradictory tendencies: the fact that it represents an age-old, untapped and unexhausted tradition, and the fact that it has had a long and painful history. That cosmopolitanism has been forgotten, that it has been transformed and debased into a pejorative concept, is to be ascribed to its involuntary association with the Holocaust and the Stalinist Gulag. In the collective symbolic system of the Nazis, 'cosmopolitan' was synonymous with a death sentence. All victims of the planned mass murder were portrayed as 'cosmopolitans'; and this death sentence was extended to the word, which in its own way succumbed to the same fate. The Nazis said 'Jew' and meant 'cosmopolitan'; the Stalinists said 'cosmopolitan' and meant 'Jew'. Consequently, 'cosmopolitans' are to this day regarded in many countries as something between vagabonds, enemies and insects who can or even must be banished, demonized or destroyed.

Adorno thought that one cannot write poems after Auschwitz. However, the contrary also holds: all poems speak or remain silent about Auschwitz.

Which contemporary author is not an author of the Holocaust? What I mean is that the Holocaust does not have to be made an explicit theme for us to sense the undercurrent of trauma that has haunted modern European art for decades. I would go even further: I know of no genuinely good and authentic art in which one cannot discern such a rupture, like someone shattered and disoriented after sleep haunted by nightmares. For me the Holocaust represents the human situation, the terminus of the great adventure at which Europeans have arrived after two thousand years of ethical and moral culture.

Imre Kertész also stresses the power of this negative experience to found new traditions: 'In my view, when I consider the traumatic impact of Auschwitz I touch on the fundamental question of the viability and creative energy of present-day humanity; which means that, in reflecting on Auschwitz, I am, perhaps paradoxically, thinking about the future rather than the past' (Kertész 2003: 2, 51, 255).

To paraphrase Gottfried Benn – 'Words, words – names! They need only take wing and the millennia fall away with their flight' – the name 'cosmopolitanism' need only take wing and the European trauma will fall away with its flight. This lends it a sober seriousness and lightness, a sharpness and penetration, by which it may succeed in breaking open the iron conceptual cage of methodological nationalism and reveal how, and to what extent, global reality can become cosmopolitan, thereby rendering it visible, comprehensible and even liveable.

What do we mean, then, by the 'cosmopolitan outlook'? Global sense, a sense of boundarylessness. An everyday, historically alert, reflexive awareness of ambivalences in a milieu of blurring differentiations and cultural contradictions. It reveals not just the 'anguish' but also the possibility of shaping one's life and social relations under conditions of cultural mixture. It is simultaneously a sceptical, disillusioned, self-critical outlook. Nothing can show this better than a couple of examples.

Cosmopolitan identities, or the logic of inclusive differentiation

In sociological research there is currently much talk of new identities, including the demonstrative reassertion of national, ethnic and local identities all over the world. What is new about them becomes clear when we examine their peculiarities. They are identities which are perhaps too quickly labelled as 'neonational' but which, in contrast to the explosive fascistic nationalisms of the twentieth century, do not aim at ideological and military conquests beyond their own borders. These are *introverted* forms of nationalism which oppose the 'invasion' of the global world by turning inwards, though 'introverted' here should not be confused with 'harmless'. For these domestic nationalisms do in fact foster an aggressive intolerance which is capable of turning on anybody or anything. Their novelty consists in the fact that they involve usually conscious resistance to the cosmopolitanization of their lifeworlds, to globalization and globalizers who are perceived as threatening the local form of life of the 'natives'. Those involved seek refuge in a strategic 'as-if' essentialism of ethnicity in an attempt to fix the blurred and shifting boundaries between internal and external, us and them. Two things follow. First, these nationalisms also presuppose the daily experience of globalization. And, second, without a proper understanding of how globality overcomes and reconfigures differentiations, hence without a cosmopolitan outlook, the new topographies of identity and memory, and the introverted nationalisms they potentially foster, remain utterly incomprehensible.

Some time ago on a flight to Helsinki the passenger next to me, a Danish businessman, irritated me by repeatedly emphasizing how advantageous the European Union is for his business dealings. Less out of curiosity than finally to get a word in edgeways, I asked him whether he felt more Danish or more European. He responded with barely disguised amazement that he saw himself as neither the one nor the other but as a cosmopolitan citizen, a 'global citizen'. He is at home in all countries in the world. Wherever he goes he speaks English, in which he is fluent. Everywhere a hotel bed is waiting for him. He chooses the well-known hotel chains where he can be sure of uniform standards regardless of the location. In China he eats Indian food, in India French. His business partners see things from a similar viewpoint. Experienced as he is, he knows whom he can trust and whom he can't, whether in business or in choosing a taxi. By the same token, he is Danish born and bred, lives in Denmark and feels Danish. At Christmas he is a Christian, at election time a social democrat. Recently, however, he joined a civic movement supporting a restrictive immigration policy. God knows he is in favour of foreigners, he added without a glimmer of embarrassment, but the flood of immigrants has to stop! And so on, and so forth. After a brief pause he returned to my question: no, he is not a European – the idea never even occurred to him.

This is without doubt a paradigm example of a determination of identity that has replaced the either/or logic with the both/and logic of inclusive differentiation. One constructs a model of one's identity by dipping freely into the Lego set of globally available identities and building a progressively inclusive self-image. The result is the proud affirmation of a patchwork, quasi-cosmopolitan, but simultaneously provincial, identity whose central characteristic is its rejection of traditional relations of responsibility. That this is not necessarily synonymous with the cosmopolitan humanitarianism one usually associates with the label 'world citizen' should be clear from the fact that, although politics is a matter for election day for our 'global manager', at the same time he is campaigning against immigrants.

Here things are being yoked together that do not fit. For the invoked attachments do not fit into the fragmentary composition which is presented with a ring of inner conviction. It is like a painting of Picasso or Braque in which the naïve viewer looks for familiar traces of a coherent landscape or a group of people, whereas the work is playing with tokens of reality. This is a valid comparison, for our Danish world business citizen with his xenophobic outbursts is drawing freely on the historical refuse of formerly exclusive identities and lived identity-formations, just as cubism and expressionism drew on the ruins of realism and classicism.

Cosmopolitan empathy

Thinking in either/or categories prevails not just in classical sociology but also in sociobiology and in ethnological theories of aggression and conflict. The practice of exclusive differentiation is seen as a necessary principle of anthropology, biology, political theory and logic which, all false idealism aside, compels us to differentiate between all kinds of groups, be they tribes, nations, religions, classes or families. Whoever is naïve enough to disregard this 'logic' promotes aggression – that is the argument. Accordingly, to this day the myth that defining and demarcating ourselves over against what is foreign is a precondition of identity, politics, society, community and democracy preserves its bloody power in the core domains of the social sciences. Let us call this the 'territorial either/or' theory of identity. It assumes that a space defended by (mental) fences is an indispensable precondition for the formation of self-consciousness and for social integration.

This metatheory of identity, society and politics is empirically false. It arose in the context of the mutually delimiting territorial societies and states of the first modernity and generalizes this historical experience, in the shape of methodological nationalism, into the 'logic' of the social and the political. But the suffering of human beings in other global regions and cultures, for example, no longer conforms to the friend–foe schema. Whoever asks from a cosmopolitan perspective what fuelled the global protest against the war in Iraq in many major cities across the world finds an answer in *cosmopolitan empathy*. The protests were driven by what one might call the 'gobalization of emotions'. Everyone knows that the twentieth century witnessed an incredible refinement of weapons systems and we have learnt that the killing and dying continued unabated long after the peace treaties were signed. And once television images of war and its victims are broadcast all over the world it becomes clear that violence in one corner of the globe incites the readiness to resort to violence in many others, so that the resulting military chain reactions can easily spin out of control. This realization goes hand in hand with the capacity and the willingness to put oneself in the position of the victims, something which is also in large part a product of the mass media. The tears we guiltily wipe from our eyes before the television or in the cinema are no doubt consciously produced by Hollywood trickery and by how the news is stage-managed. But that in no way alters the fact that the spaces of our emotional imagination have expanded in a transnational sense. When civilians and children in Israel, Palestine, Iraq or Africa suffer and die and this suffering is presented in compelling images in the mass media, this produces cosmopolitan pity which forces us to act.

'For the first time in human history and with the help of major political and technological changes', writes Howard V. Perlmutter,

we have the possibility of a real time, simultaneously-experienced global civilization with almost daily global events, where global cooperation is in a more horizontal than vertical mode. This is why we now see the possibility of the emergence of one single world civilization with great diversity in its constituent cultures and interdependence among poles. From this historical perspective, there is but one human civilization which is seamless and global in its character but with a magnificent variety of indigenous variations on the life experience. (Perlmutter 1992: 103)

However, it would be a fatal error to conclude that cosmopolitan empathy is replacing national empathy. Instead, they permeate, enhance, transform and colour each other. A false opposition between the national and the transnational would generate an endless chain of misunderstandings. In fact, the transnational and the cosmopolitan should be understood as the summation of the redefinitions of the national and the local. This in no way alters the fact that the territorial theory of identity is a bloody error that might be called the 'prison error' of identity. It is not necessary to isolate and organize human beings into antagonistic groups, not even within the broad expanses of the nation, for them to become self-aware and capable of political action.

The social image of frozen, separate worlds and identities that dominated the first modernity of separate nationally organized societies can be completely overcome only when one contrasts exclusive differentiation with the inclusive differentiation that has been investigated and developed in the sociology of the second modernity (Beck, Bonss and Lau 2001, 2004). By way of explanation, consider the emergence of transnational forms of life promoted by the mass media (Robins and Aksoy 2001). Here too the framework of the nation is not overcome. But the foundations of the industries and cultures of the mass media have changed dramatically and concomitantly all kinds of transnational connections and confrontations have emerged. The result is that cultural ties, loyalties and identities have expanded beyond national borders and systems of control. Individuals and groups who surf transnational television channels and programmes simultaneously inhabit different worlds. How should sociologists describe Turkish- and German-speaking transmigrants who live in Berlin, though not only in Berlin, because they also inhabit transnational networks, horizons of expectation, ambitions and contradictions? Under the presuppositions of methodological nationalism, German-Turkish both/and identities are located and analysed in either one or the other national frame of reference, and are thereby stripped of their both/and character. Hence they appear as 'uprooted', 'disintegrated', 'homeless', living 'between cultural stools', and are seen as deficient or negative from the unitary mononational point of view (Beck-Gernsheim 2004).

As a counter-image to the territorial prison theory of identity, society and politics we can provisionally distinguish five interconnected constitutive principles of the cosmopolitan outlook:

- first, the principle of *the experience of crisis in world society*: the awareness of interdependence and the resulting 'civilizational community of fate' induced by global risks and crises, which overcomes the boundaries between internal and external, us and them, the national and the international;
- second, the principle of *recognition of cosmopolitan differences* and the resulting *cosmopolitan conflict character*, and the (limited) curiosity concerning differences of culture and identity;
- third, the principle of *cosmopolitan empathy* and of *perspective-taking* and the virtual interchangeability of situations (as both an opportunity and a threat);
- fourth, the principle of the *impossibility of living in a world society* without borders and the resulting compulsion to redraw old boundaries and rebuild old walls;
- fifth, *the mélange principle*: the principle that local, national, ethnic, religious *and* cosmopolitan cultures and traditions interpenetrate, interconnect and intermingle – cosmopolitanism without provincialism is empty, provincialism without cosmopolitanism is blind.

One can understand these principles in a normative-philosophical sense; but one can also understand them in an empirical-sociological sense, uncover their internal contradictions and investigate their concrete manifestations. In a certain sense, Alexis de Tocqueville already made a start in this direction, though only with reference to the post-hierarchical, democratic America of his day; however, his observations can be applied to postnational empathy. In the age of the cosmopolitan outlook when all men think and feel in nearly the same manner, each of them may judge in a moment of the sensations of all the others; he casts a rapid glance upon himself, and that is enough. There is no wretchedness into which he cannot readily enter, and a secret instinct reveals to him its extent. It signifies not that strangers or foes are the sufferers; imagination puts him in their place; something like a personal feeling is mingled with his pity and makes himself suffer while the body of his fellow-creature is in torture. (Tocqueville 1945: 2.175–6)

Natan Sznaider applies these observations to the transnational world. Imagined pity plays a key role in the development of Western humanism:

We are compassionate, and if we are not we ought to be. Only in a democratic setting can compassion be almost substitutive for representation. Public compassion is not only an individual manifestation of human conduct and care for others. Such episodes of human conduct occur everywhere and at all times. A sociology of public compassion addresses a social and collective pattern of conduct in which substantial numbers of people believe that to alleviate the sufferings, pains, and humiliations of others is the right thing to do. (Sznaider 1998: 128–9)

The world of the cosmopolitan outlook is in a certain sense a glass world. Differences, contrasts and boundaries must be fixed and defined in an awareness of the sameness in principle of others. The boundaries separating us from others are no longer blocked and obscured by ontological difference but have become transparent. This irreversible sameness opens up a space of both empathy and aggression which it is difficult to contain. This is a consequence both of pity and of hatred – pity, because the (no longer heterogeneous) other becomes present in one's feelings and experience, and observing oneself and observing others are no longer mutually exclusive activities; hatred, because the walls of institutionalized ignorance and hostility that protected my world are collapsing.

Both of these sentiments, pity and hatred – the sense of boundarylessness and the longing for the re-establishment of the old boundary-lines – prove that the cosmopolitan outlook is a politically ambivalent, *reflexive* outlook. When apparently fixed differentiations and dichotomies become sterile, no longer provide orientation, dissolve and intermingle, when the world has mutated into a 'Babylonian madhouse' (Robert Musil), when the historical fetishes of the state and the nation can no longer order and control the lives and interactions of human beings, they must themselves find a way to redefine their interests and interrelations among the ruins of former certainties in whatever way makes continued coexistence possible.

On the distinction between globalization and cosmopolitanization

In charting the conceptual topography of the cosmopolitan outlook, it makes sense to distinguish between globalization (or globalism) and cosmopolitanization.

In public discourse the fashionable political term 'globalization' is understood primarily in a one-dimensional sense as *economic* globalization, and is closely connected with what can be called 'globalism' (Beck 2005). *Globalism* promotes the idea of the global market, defends the virtues of neoliberal economic growth and the utility of allowing capital, commodities and labour to move freely across borders. This is also what economists and large sections of the public have in mind when they speak of 'globalization'. It is argued that globalism is responsible for economic growth in the last two decades all across the globe, and in particular in the so-called developing countries, because it promoted the 'deregulation' of markets during the 1980s. Even opposition to globalization remains fixated on this view when it presupposes and defends the power of the autonomous nation-state, which was a feature of the first but not the second modernity.

Cosmopolitanization, by contrast, must be interpreted as a *multidimensional* process which has irreversibly changed the historical 'nature' of social worlds and the standing of states in these worlds. Cosmopolitanization, thus understood, comprises the development of multiple loyalties as well as the increase in diverse transnational forms of life, the emergence of non-state political actors (from Amnesty International to the World Trade Organization), the development of global protest movements against (neoliberal) globalism and in support of a different kind of (cosmopolitan) globalization. People campaign for the worldwide recognition of human rights, for the right to work, for global protection of the environment, for the reduction of poverty, etc. To this extent there are the beginnings (however deformed) of an *institutionalized* cosmopolitanism, for example, in the paradoxical shape of the anti-globalization movement, the International Court of Justice and the United Nations. When the Security Council makes a resolution it is received as though it speaks for the whole of humanity.

But, one might object, isn't 'cosmopolitanization' simply a new word for what used to be called 'globalization'? The answer is 'no' and it is provided by this book as a whole. To anticipate: precisely the opposite is true, for what takes centre stage is the historically irreversible fact that people, from Moscow to Paris, from Rio to Tokyo, have long since been living in *really existing relations of interdependence*; they are as much responsible for the intensification of these relations through their production and consumption as are the resulting global risks that impinge on their everyday lives.

If we ask who are the intellectual progenitors of this internal cosmopolitanization of national societies, Adam Smith, Alexis de Tocqueville and John Dewey come to mind, as well as such classical German thinkers as Kant, Goethe, Herder, Humboldt, Nietzsche, Marx and Simmel. All of them construed the modern period as a transition from early conditions of relatively closed societies to 'universal eras' [*universellen Epochen*] (Goethe) of interdependent societies, a transition that essentially involved the expansion of commerce and the dissemination of the principle of republicanism.

For Kant, even more so for Marx and in different ways also for Adam Smith and Georg Simmel, the dissolution of small territorial communities and the spread of universal social and economic interdependence (though not yet of risks) was the essential mark, and even the law, of world history. Their preoccupation with long lines of historical development made them sceptical towards the idea that state and society in their nationally homogeneous manifestations could constitute the *non plus ultra* of world history.

The experience of delimitation and interdependence has in the meantime condensed and become normalized into a 'banal cosmopolitanism', not unlike the 'banal nationalism' characteristic of the first modernity (expressed in the waving of national flags, for instance). A small example, which nonetheless speaks volumes, can clarify what is at stake here: the modern odyssey of 'authentic' Indian cuisine. Anyone who thinks that the trademark 'Indian restaurant' implies that Indian cuisine comes from India is sorely mistaken. Indians in India have no tradition of public restaurants. As the British sociologist Sami Zubaida has shown, the 'Indian restaurant' is an invention of Bengalis living in London, as are the 'exotic dishes' which are now celebrated and consumed all over the world as ambassadors of Indian traditions. In the course of its march to globalization, the Indian restaurant and its characteristic menu were also ultimately exported to India, which stimulated Indian households to cook Indian food in accordance with the London inventions. Thus it came to pass that today one can eat 'Indian' food even in India, thereby confirming the myth of origins.

Banal cosmopolitanism is manifested in concrete, everyday ways by the fact that differentiations between us and them are becoming confused, both at the national and at international level. The modest, familiar, local, circumscribed and stable, our protective shell is becoming the playground of universal experiences; place, whether it be Manhattan or East Prussia, Malmö or Munich, becomes the locus of encounters and interminglings or, alternatively, of anonymous coexistence and the overlapping of possible worlds and global dangers, all of which requires us to rethink the relation between place and world.

Cosmopolitan Munich

I happen to live in Munich. If it is true that the cosmopolitan outlook reveals the cosmopolitan potentialities of the provinces, then it should be possible to show that this is also true of Munich. What does cosmopolitan Munich signify? In the first place, and in the spirit of banal cosmopolitanism, Bayern Munich soccer club.

Thomas Mann wrote: 'Munich is radiant.' If I may trivialize Mann somewhat: Bayern Munich is radiant, at least when the professional footballers of this world-famous soccer club score beautiful goals. Does Bayern Munich stand for Bavaria? Without a doubt. Does it stand for 'we are who we are' or, in Bavarian dialect, *'mir san mir'*? No! Absolutely not! Who scores the goals? Often a Brazilian whose wizardry lends the Bavarian football club a touch of world class. Bayern Munich players, of course, are neither from Bavaria nor from Munich; they are of many different nationalities, speak many different languages and have many different passports. What is so dear to many Bavarian hearts – 'we are who we are' and the others are others – does not hold when Bavarian hearts are beating fastest. Bayern Munich stands for a profane cosmopolitan 'We' in which the boundaries between internal and external, between the national and the international, have long since been transcended. Bayern Munich symbolizes a cosmopolitan Bavaria that officially cannot and must not exist in Bavaria, but which exists nonetheless. Indeed, without this taken-for-granted cosmopolitanism, Bayern Munich, hence Bavaria, would not exist.

Three authors who, among other things, also wrote about Munich and won fame far beyond Munich – Thomas Mann, Lion Feuchtwanger and Oskar Maria Graf – embody in their persons and works three distinct traditions of 'rooted cosmopolitanism', cosmopolitanism which has both 'roots' and 'wings', namely, national cosmopolitanism (Thomas Mann), German-Jewish cosmopolitanism (Lion Feuchtwanger) and Catholic cosmopolitanism (Oskar Maria Graf).

In *Reflections of a Nonpolitical Man*, written in the shadow of the First World War, Thomas Mann struggles with the question: what does cosmopolitanism mean? He finds words connoting demarcation – 'non-polyglot facility and sophisticated dilettantism', 'non-pacified Esperanto-world' – but also positive terms: 'encounters', 'intermingling', even 'global sense', and, anticipating the globalization debate, 'sense of boundarylessness'. He rejects the alternative 'nationalism versus internationalism' and formulates the position of a national cosmopolitanism of intellectual Germany, although he is well aware of the in-built ambivalences. Accordingly, he emphasizes that 'it is almost part of German humanity to act in a non-German, or even anti-German, fashion; it is commonly assumed that a sympathy for the cosmopolitan that is corrosive of national sensibility is inseparable from German nationality; that one may have to lose one's Germanness in order to find it; that without an addition of the foreign it may be impossible to achieve a higher Germanness' (Mann 1983a: 71).

Mann also stresses the mélange principle, the both/and of cosmopolitanism and nationalism. By the same token, he draws a problematic distinction between 'German world citizenship' and 'democratic internationalism'. He considers 'whether German world citizenship is not something different from democratic internationalism, and whether being a German world citizen is not indeed compatible with a deep love for one's nation' (Mann 1983a: 152). How easily this bourgeois-intellectual nationalist-cosmopolitanism can mutate into ignorance and conceit can be seen when Mann identifies philosophy with German philosophy: 'Can one be a philosopher without being German?' (ibid.: 92).

In his novel *Success: Three Years in the History of a Province* (1930), Lion Feuchtwanger revives a piece of Bavarian and Munich cosmopolitanism, for example in the character of the Munich functionary Sebastian von Gruber, founder of the Munich Museum for Technology, who is described as follows: 'He was both a Bavarian and a cosmopolitan, someone who could serve as an example for the education of a whole generation, if only you could cure him of his obstinate fixation on his stupid provincialism' (1993: 505). *Success* is written from a cosmopolitan perspective in the sense that, first, the characters are represented retrospectively, from the future perspective of the narrator, and, second, it is harshly critical of the blinkered and aggressive nationalism that was on the rise in the Weimar Republic:

The population of the planet at that time was 1800 million, of which 700 million were white-skinned. The culture of white-skinned peoples was regarded as superior to that of the others, and Europe as the best part of the earth. The whites had erected all manner of extremely arbitrary boundaries between themselves and spoke different languages. For example, they waged war on each other for national reasons, in other words, for no other reason than that they were born in different parts of the earth. They manipulated collective emotions and declared it a virtue to regard people who happened to be born outside the officially defined frontiers of their own country as inferior and to shoot them. These and similar virtues inculcated in children from a young age were collected together under the term 'patriotism'. (ibid.: 203)

Here again we have a textbook critique of the national prison theory of human existence. Which side of a completely arbitrary administrative boundary you were born on determines who are your friends and who are your enemies, what language you speak, whether you identify with the fate of one nation or another, and, when you are ordered, whether you make common cause with your neighbours or shoot them down (and are declared a hero for doing so!).

Feuchtwanger emphasizes the superiority of the nomadic existence of the Jewish diaspora over fixation on place:

Everywhere today the nomad has become the more important, more vital type of human being and is displacing the dull peasants. What the enemies of the Jews used to reproach them with as their most contemptible characteristic transpires all of a sudden to be a huge advantage. The fact that they were driven from one country to another for centuries and had to adapt constantly to new peoples and surroundings, makes them superior to those who can only function in their own locality at a time of rapidly changing and accelerating interactions. (Feuchtwanger 1984: 465)

Conversely, fanatical national isolation leads to desolation, narrowness, impoverishment and weakening, and hence is ultimately anti-national.

Already during the Second World War, between 1942 and 1943, the expatriate Bavarian Oskar Maria Graf, who was living in New York at the time, drafted a rather strange science fiction novel which originally bore different titles – among others, *The Conquest of the World* – but whose second edition appeared under the title *The Survivors of the Catastrophe*. In this novel, a complete catastrophe, an existential tabula rasa, becomes the precondition for a cosmopolitan global order:

From hopelessness and unheard of horror came other wandering hordes and everywhere made a new beginning . . . slowly, like honeycombs, the millions of pariahs from all countries came together on the endless plains of the continents. What was it that a much-ridiculed man once said a long, long time ago? 'Hunger, hands and earth are there! All three are there from the beginning!' Something decisive had occurred. Those who were saved had found their way back to the earth, the cradle of all beginnings from time immemorial. And all at once the whole world was home! (Graf 1982: 44f.)

Graf, who described himself as a 'religious socialist', envisaged a form of Catholicism that would be both democratic and cosmopolitan: 'Out of the destruction and hopelessness Catholicism also emerged fundamentally changed and the Church had lost its narrow, dogmatic character. In a fundamental break with the past, the faithful now elected the Pope, the bishops and the priests from their midst' (Graf 1982: 362). Graf's own outlook is reflected in his favourite quotation from Tolstoy's treatise *Christianity and Patriotism*: 'If men would only finally grasp that they are not children of some fatherland but of God the father!' As he put it elsewhere: 'The world must become provincial. Only then will it become human' (ibid.: 578).

Thus in Munich alone one can find not just one cosmopolitanism, but many different conceptions of cosmopolitanism, specifically, conceptions of cosmopolitanism mixed with local ethnic, religious and national traditions.

It is no accident that these three cosmopolitan writers with roots in Munich became (or were forced to become) expatriate writers. The foundations of cosmopolitan Munich were laid not in Munich, but in exile, at a time when Munich had become the anti-cosmopolitan 'capital of the movement' out of which a state-organized racist insanity emerged. Cosmopolitan Munich stands for the institutional memory of this madness and for the readiness to adopt the perspectives of others. It is the historically aware Munich, the Munich that lives in an awareness of a break with its past, which draws its identity from the discontinuity of its history. Cosmopolitan Munich stands in a relation of reflexive distance to itself from which it wins its openness to the world, and hence welcomes and celebrates the richness of the one hundred and eighty nations which live alongside each other in Munich and which make it what it is and lend it its radiance.

What, then, does the cosmopolitan outlook signify? It does not herald the first rays of universal brotherly love among peoples, or the dawn of the world republic, or a free-floating global outlook, or compulsory xenophilia. Nor is cosmopolitanism a kind of supplement that is supposed to replace nationalism and provincialism, for the very good reason that the ideas of human rights and democracy need a national base. Rather, the cosmopolitan outlook means that, in a world of global crises and dangers produced by civilization, the old differentiations between internal and external, national and international, us and them, lose their validity and a new cosmopolitan realism becomes essential to survival.

Part I

Cosmopolitan Realism

1

Global Sense, Sense of Boundarylessness: The Distinction between Philosophical and Social Scientific Cosmopolitanism

1   What is novel about the cosmopolitan outlook?

We can distinguish three phases in how the code word 'globalization' has been used in the social sciences: first, denial, second, conceptual refinement and empirical research, and, third, epistemological shift. The first reaction of the mainstream was to deny the reality or relevance of (economic) globalization and to declare that nothing that fell under the heading 'globalization' on the social scientific agenda was historically new. This explaining away of the phenomenon began to lose credibility during the second phase when social scientists in the most diverse disciplines began to subject phenomena of globalization to conceptual analysis and to situate them in the theoretical and empirical thematics of the social sciences (e.g., among many others, Held et al. 1999; Beisheim, Zürn et al. 1999; Beck 2000a; Randeria 2001; Sassen 2003).

   To the extent that this was successful, the third phase witnessed an *epistemological shift*. The insight began to gain ground that the units of research of the various social scientific disciplines become arbitrary when the distinctions between internal and external, national and international, local and global, lose their sharp contours (Gille and O'Riain 2002; Brenner 2000; Schmitt 1963; Beck 2003, 2005; and many others). The question for globalization research following the epistemological turn is: what happens when the premises and boundaries that define these units disintegrate? The answer provided by the present book is that the whole conceptual world of the 'national outlook' becomes disenchanted, that is, de-ontologized, historicized and stripped of its inner necessity. However, it is only possible to justify this and think it through to its logical conclusion within the framework of an interpretive alternative which replaces *ontology* with *methodology*, that is, which replaces the currently prevailing ontology and imaginary of the nation-state with what I propose to call 'methodological cosmopolitanism'.

   The foundations of this perspective will be laid in the present chapter in three steps. In the first part, I will distinguish between different types of 'cosmopolitanism'; most widespread is the reading which pleads for harmony beyond national and cultural boundaries ('normative' or 'philosophical cosmopolitanism'). This normative conception must be distinguished from a descriptive-analytical perspective in the social sciences which liberates itself from national categories (the 'cosmopolitan outlook' or 'analytical-empirical cosmopolitanism'). The increase in interdependence among social actors across national borders can be observed from this perspective, whereby the peculiarity consists in the fact that this 'cosmopolitanization' occurs as the unwanted and unobserved *side effect* of actions that are not intended as 'cosmopolitan' in the normative sense ('really existing cosmopolitanism' or 'the cosmopolitanization of reality'). Under certain circumstances the last type of 'cosmopolitanization' leads to the emergence of global discussion forums, with the result that global regimes concerned with transnational conflicts develop ('institutionalized cosmopolitanism'). In the second part, I will focus on the growing contradiction between 'methodological nationalism' and real cosmopolitanization.

The third part sketches a 'new grammar', the theoretical and empirical programme of a 'cosmopolitan social science', and develops by way of example four thematic complexes on which this shift in perspectives should concentrate on its path towards a 'methodological cosmopolitanism'. The risks of modern society are, as a matter of their internal logic, transnational and all attempts to control them unleash global conflicts and debates. Moreover, the cosmopolitan outlook also enables us to analyse interdependencies not only between states but also between other actors at different levels. Beyond that, denationalized social science can throw new light on global ('glocal') injustices. Finally, we can distinguish between different forms of more or less 'banal cosmopolitanism' and ask under what conditions awareness of them as such arises.[1]

1.1   *The distinction between philosophical cosmopolitanism and social scientific cosmopolitanization*

Focusing on analytical-empirical cosmopolitanism, on demonstrating the epistemological necessity of the cosmopolitan outlook in a world without boundaries, opens up a new field of research and controversy, that of cosmopolitan reality at the beginning of the twenty-first century. It demands not only that we develop new categories, but that we revise the grammar of the social and the political. The challenge is to devise a new syntax, the syntax of cosmopolitan reality.[2]

The national outlook, together with its associated grammar, is becoming false. It fails to grasp that political, economic and cultural action and their (intended and unintended) consequences know no borders; indeed, it is completely blind to the fact that, even when nationalism is reignited by the collision with globality, this can only be conceptualized from the cosmopolitan perspective. The cosmopolitan outlook is a prerequisite for analysing the real process of overcoming boundaries that triggers the neonational reflex to re-erect fences and walls. The 'why' and 'whither' questions which haunt stubborn and inert nations can only be answered through connection and cooperation. But cosmopolitan realism also includes a sense for the inexorability and bleakness, the horror, the malevolence and the sheer inhumanity which find violent expression when the boundaries between us and them lose their sharp contours.

During the national phase of modernity cosmopolitanism could only be grasped intellectually, in the head, but could not be felt as a living experience. Nationalism, by contrast, took possession of people's hearts. This head–heart dualism is turned upside down in the second modernity. Everyday life has become cosmopolitan in banal ways; yet the insidious concepts of nationalism continue to haunt people's minds almost unabated, not to speak of the theories and research practices of the advanced social sciences.

Taking my orientation from the distinction between philosophy and praxis, I distinguish in this book between *cosmopolitanism* and *really existing cosmopolitanization*. This distinction turns on the rejection of the claim that cosmopolitanism is a conscious and voluntary choice, and often that of an elite. The concept 'cosmopolitanization' is designed to draw attention to the fact that the becoming cosmopolitan of reality is also, and even primarily, a function of coerced choices or a side effect of unconscious decisions.[3] The choice to become or remain an 'alien' or a 'non-national' is not as a general rule voluntary, but a response to acute need, political repression or the threat of starvation. Or cosmopolitanization crosses frontiers like a stowaway, as an unforeseen consequence of mundane market decisions: people develop a taste for a particular kind of pop music or for 'Indian' food; or they respond to global risks by sorting their rubbish or changing their diet; or they invest their money in states whose policies conform to the neoliberal ideal of responsiveness to the imperatives of the global market. 'Cosmopolitanization' in this sense means latent cosmopolitanism, *unconscious* cosmopolitanism, *passive* cosmopolitanism which shapes reality as side effects of global trade or global threats such as climate change, terrorism or financial crises. My life, my body, my 'individual existence' become part of another world, of foreign cultures, religions, histories and global interdependencies, without my realizing or expressly wishing it.

A 'banal' cosmopolitanism in this sense unfolds beneath the surface or behind the façade of persisting national spaces, jurisdictions and labellings, while national flags continue to be hoisted and national attitudes, identities and consciousness remain dominant. Judged by the lofty standards of ethical and academic morality, this latent character renders cosmopolitanism 'trivial', unworthy of comment, even suspect. An idea that formerly strutted the stage of world history as an ornament of the elite cannot possibly slink into social and political reality by the back door. That simply won't do! Isn't it a straightforward contradiction to claim that the unconscious or half-conscious, coerced, migratory or minority cosmopolitanism, the cosmopolitanism of globalized production and consumption, of global movements and civilizational risks, are infiltrating the world of nation-states from below and transforming it from within?

No, really existing cosmopolitanism is deformed cosmopolitanism. As Scott L. Malcomson argues, it is sustained by individuals who have very few opportunities to identify with something greater than what is dictated by their circumstances.

The decision to enter a political realm larger than the local may sometimes be taken at leisure, but is more often made under force of circumstances. More narrowly market-driven choices usually derive from a desire not to be poor, or simply not to die. Entertainment choices are based on a range of options frequently beyond the control of the individual consumer. Such compulsions may explain in part why the mass of real cosmopolitanisms rarely enters into scholarly discussions of cosmopolitanism: to argue that the choice of cosmopolitanism is in some sense self-betraying and made under duress takes away much of its ethical attractiveness. If cosmopolitanism is both indeterminate and inescapable, it becomes difficult to theorize. Yet such is, I think, normally the case. (Malcomson 1998: 240)

In other words, cosmopolitanism in Kant's sense means something active, a task, namely, that of imposing an order on the world. Cosmopolitanization, by contrast, sharpens our gaze for uncontrollable events that merely befall us. This tends to nourish the view that globalization is a scourge of humanity, and hence the temptation to cast oneself in the role of victim – as the victim of the United States, of the West, of capitalism, of neoliberalism, etc. The paradoxical impression arises that everyone is in some sense suffering the fate of minorities, of species threatened with extinction. Even majorities feel like uprooted aliens in their own land.

This is because all communities and cultures have a sense that they are up against others stronger than they, a feeling that they can no longer keep their heritage safe. Looked at from the South and the East, it is the West that dominates. Looked at from Paris, it is America that hold sway. But if you go to the United States, then what do you see? You see minorities reflecting all the diversity in the world, all needing to assert their original allegiances. And when you have met all these minorities and been told a hundred times that power is in the hands of white males, or of Anglo-Saxon Protestants, you suddenly hear the sound of a huge explosion in Oklahoma City. And who are the people responsible? Some white male Anglo-Saxon Protestants who regard themselves as members of the most neglected and despised of minorities, and who believe that globalization is sounding the knell of 'their' America. (Maalouf 2000: 124)

But the practice of this conspiracy theory is terrorism.

There can be no doubt that a cosmopolitanism that is passively and unwillingly suffered is a *deformed* cosmopolitanism. The fact that really existing cosmopolitanism is not achieved through struggle, that it is not chosen, that

it does not come into the world as progress with the reflected moral authority of the Enlightenment, but as something deformed and profane, cloaked
in the anonymity of a side effect – this is an essential founding insight of cosmopolitan realism in the social sciences. A non-deformed cosmopolitanism,
by contrast, results from the sense of partaking in the great human experiment in civilization – with one's own language and cultural symbols and the
means to counter global threats – and hence of making a contribution to
world culture.

1.2   The distinction between (latent) cosmopolitanization and the cosmopolitan outlook

While reality is becoming thoroughly cosmopolitan, our habits of thought
and consciousness, like the well-worn paths of academic teaching and
research, disguise the growing unreality of the world of nation-states. A critique of the science of unreality of the national, which presents itself in
universalist garb but can neither deny nor shake off its national origins,
presupposes the cosmopolitan outlook and its methodological elaboration.
But what is the difference between (latent) cosmopolitanization and the cosmopolitan outlook? That is a difficult question which we will approach from
different angles during the course of this book. But essentially it can be
answered thus: the (forced) mixing of cultures is not anything new in world
history but, on the contrary, the rule; one need only think of wars of rapine
and conquest, mass migrations, the slave trade and colonization, world wars,
ethnic cleansing and forced repatriation and expulsion. From the very beginning, the emerging global market required the mixing of peoples and
imposed it by force if necessary, as the opening up of Japan and China in the
nineteenth century demonstrate. Capital tears down all national boundaries
and jumbles together the 'native' with the 'foreign'. What is new is not forced
mixing but awareness of it, its self-conscious political affirmation, its reflection and recognition before a global public via the mass media, in the news
and in the global social movements of blacks, women and minorities, and in
the current vogue for such venerable concepts as 'diaspora' in the cultural sciences. It is this at once social and social scientific reflexivity that makes the
'cosmopolitan outlook' the key concept and topic of the reflexive second
modernity.[4]

1.3   The distinction between cosmopolitanization and institutionalized cosmopolitanism

Ultimately, not only is the distinction between cosmopolitanization and the
cosmopolitan outlook important but also that between cosmopolitanization

and *institutionalized cosmopolitanism*. Under what conditions, subject to what limits and by which actors are certain cosmopolitan principles nevertheless translated into practice, and thereby acquire enduring reality? This question can be posed and answered in a paradigmatic fashion within the theory of world risk society. As recognition of the risks springing from global interdependencies increases, so too do the compulsion, the opportunity, but also resistance – stemming, for example, from environmental politics and the politics of human rights – to arriving at cosmopolitan solutions.

Some time in the not-too-distant past a qualitative transformation in the perception of social order took place. The latter was no longer perceived primarily in terms of conflict over the production and distribution of 'goods'; rather, it is the production and distribution of 'bads' that contradict the steering role claimed by the established institutions of the nation-state. This category shift in self-perception precipitated an interdependency crisis in the way modern societies organized their institutions and functions, a crisis which found quite diverse expressions: climate change ('risk of ultraviolet radiation'), global poverty, transnational terrorism, the BSE crisis, AIDS, etc. I call this interdependency crisis 'world risk society'. It also precipitates a crisis in the social sciences and political theory, which follow Marx and Weber in construing modern societies as capitalistic and rational. The truly epoch-making difference consists in the expansion of culturally produced, interdependent insecurities and dangers, and the resulting dominance of the public perception of risk as staged by the mass media. In world risk society what is at stake at all levels is accordingly the compulsive pretence of control over the uncontrollable, whether in politics, law, science, the economy or everyday life.

In the *spatial* dimension we are confronted with risks that disregard the borders of the nation-state, and indeed boundaries as such; climate change, pollution and the hole in the ozone layer affect everyone (though not to the same degree). Something similar holds for *temporal* disembedding. The long latency period of problems, such as the disposal of nuclear waste or the long-term effects of genetically modified foodstuffs, escapes the fixed routines for dealing with industrial dangers. Finally, in the *social* dimension, the attribution of responsibility for potential threats, and hence the question of who is liable, becomes problematic: who in a legally relevant sense 'causes' pollution, or a financial crisis, is difficult to determine, since these events are the result of interactions among many individuals. Thus civilizational threats are to a large extent deterritorialized, and hence it is difficult to pin the blame for them on anyone in particular or to control them within the framework of the nation-state.

We need to distinguish between at least three different axes of conflict in world risk society: first, *ecological* interdependency crises, which have their own global dynamic; second, *economic* interdependency crises, which are initially individualized and nationalized; and, third, the threat produced by *terrorist* interdependency crises.

Despite their differences, however, ecological, economic and terrorist inter-dependency crises share one essential feature: they cannot be construed as external environmental crises but must be conceived as culturally manu-factured actions, effects and insecurities. In this sense, civilizational risks can sharpen global normative consciousness, generate global publics and promote a cosmopolitan outlook. In world risk society – this is my thesis, at least – the question concerning the causes and agencies of global threats sparks new political conflicts, which in turn promote an institutional cosmopolitanism in struggles over definitions and jurisdictions.

Conflicts over civilizational risks arise, for example, in debates over the extent to which industrialized countries can legitimately demand that devel-oping countries protect important global resources such as rainforests, while simultaneously claiming the lion's share of energy resources for themselves. One might be tempted to conclude that we are not dealing here with a form of global socialization at all; but this makes a false equation between society and consensus. On the contrary, these very conflicts perform an integrating function in that they make clear that cosmopolitan solutions have to be found. Such solutions can scarcely be envisaged without new global institutions and rules, and hence without a certain degree of convergence. Questions con-cerning long-term transnational impacts and expectations of the unexpected found transnational risk communities, 'effect-publics', which lead to an *involuntary* politicization of world risk society.

The everyday experience of cosmopolitan interdependence is not a love affair of everyone with everyone. It arises in a climate of heightened global threats, which create an unavoidable pressure to cooperate. With the concep-tualization and recognition of threats on a cosmopolitan scale, a shared space of responsibility and agency bridging all national frontiers and divides is created that can (though it need not) found political action among strangers in ways analogous to national politics. This is the case when recognition of the scale of the common threats leads to cosmopolitan norms and agreements, and hence to an institutionalized cosmopolitanism.

However, existing research on the emergence of corresponding supra- and transnational organizations and regimes has shown how difficult it is to make the transition from agreement on the definition of the threats to agreement on what form the required response should take. Ongoing communication con-cerning threats is an important component of informal cosmopolitan norm-formation. The socializing effect of world risk society is not adequately grasped if we restrict its potential to new and yet to be founded institutions of successful global coordination. Already prior to any cosmopolitan institution-formation, global norms are produced by outrage over circumstances that are felt to be intolerable. The emergence of global norms is not necessarily con-tingent on the conscious efforts of 'positive' norm-formation but can be fuelled 'negatively' by the evaluation of global crises and threats. This can already be seen from the fact that, even when conflicts explode, the lines of conflict cannot be drawn in a straightforward regional manner. Rather, new lines of conflict emerge which in part circumvent geographical differentiations (e.g., between the First and the Third World).[5]

Thus analytical-empirical cosmopolitanism delimits itself from normative-political cosmopolitanism. This distinction not only promotes a 'value-free' approach to everyday experience and to the epistemology of world risk society in the social sciences; it compels us to demarcate, though not to neglect, normative and political cosmopolitanism in a world that has become a danger to itself. In fact, this distinction first makes it possible to pose the question of the relation between the categories and cognitions of the cosmopolitan outlook (or the critique of the national outlook), on the one hand, and the topics of cosmopolitan ethics and politics, on the other. How are cosmopolitan democracy, justice, solidarity, law, politics, state, etc., possible?

The cosmopolitan change in outlook gives rise to the possibility of a non-nostalgic critique of the national – of international law, of international institutions, of the trend towards new wars which loom with the eclipse of the guiding dualisms of the national and international – on the model of a *cosmopolitan critical theory* (Beck 2003). This involves two stages of argument: first, the critique of the national outlook and, second, preliminary reflections on the cosmopolitan grammar of social and political reality.

2   Critique of the national outlook and methodological nationalism

The cosmopolitan outlook calls into question one of the most powerful convictions concerning society and politics, which finds expression in the claim that 'modern society' and 'modern politics' can only be organized in the form of national states. Society is equated with society organized in nationally and territorially delimited states. When social actors subscribe to this belief, I speak of a 'national outlook'; when it determines the perspective of the scientific observer, I speak of 'methodological nationalism'. This distinction between the perspectives of social actors and social scientists is important because there is only a historical connection between the two, not a logical one. The rise of sociology coincided with the rise of the nation-state, nationalism and the system of international politics. This historical connection alone gives rise to the axiomatics of methodological nationalism according to which the nation, the state and society are the 'natural' social and political forms of the modern world.

The world which is being shaken to its foundations by the problems produced by the triumph of its civilization cannot be adequately grasped, investigated or explained within the national outlook (of agents) or within the framework of methodological nationalism (the perspective of the scientific observer).

2.1   Principles and errors of methodological nationalism

What is wrong with the national outlook – its clinical loss of reality – can be shown by the example of the so-called where-are-you-from-originally dialogue. As Elisabeth Beck-Gernsheim writes:

Someone named Michael Schmid or Petra Paulhuber who has blue eyes and blond or brown hair is automatically treated as a native when he or she appears in shops, schools, discotheques or other public places in Germany; he or she fits the picture of the normal German. It's very different with those who perhaps have a German passport but a strange-sounding name, dark skin colour or somewhat unusual facial features. Because they deviate from the standard German format they are regularly confronted with the question: 'Where do you come from?' This is the signal to begin what Santina Battaglia – herself someone with a foreign-sounding name – calls the 'where-are-you-from-originally' dialogue. It unfolds ritualistically, always along the same lines. For example:
  'Where do you come from?' – 'From Essen.'
  'No, I mean originally?' – 'I was born in Essen.'
  'But your parents?' – 'My mother comes from Essen.'
  'But your father?' – 'My father is Italian.'
  'A-ha . . .!'
  'Is that an Italian name?' – 'Yes.'
  'So what part of Italy do you come from?' – 'I don't come from Italy.'
  'But your parents?'. . .
  Such conversations always unfold along similar, predictable lines, yet the perceptions of the participants are very different. The 'native' (the normal German, the white US American or Briton) finds someone in front of him who does not correspond to the assumed mononational, monocultural image. He responds to his interlocutor with curiosity, even, as he sees it, with openness and interest. But the latter often feels embarrassed, discriminated against and excluded. It is no coincidence that Battaglia calls the where-are-you-from-originally dialogue a 'negotiation of rootedness'. It always involves a compulsion to justify oneself: you have to justify where you belong and why, contrary to appearance, this could nevertheless be Germany. You have to provide intimate details of your family background, then continually add others, getting dragged in ever deeper. In this way the chain of questions draws the person interrogated into a double-bind situation which presents her with an invidious alternative: 'If the person interrogated sets limits the questioners feel impolitely rebuffed. But if she lets herself be drawn in, she is forced to expose herself in a one-sided fashion.' (2004: 171)

People with strange-sounding names find themselves repeatedly subjected to such cross-examination. This reflects the territorial social ontology of the national outlook, of what I earlier called the prison error of identity (p. 6). According to this view of the world, each human being has one native country, which he cannot choose; he is born into it and it conforms to the either/or logic of nations and the associated stereotypes. Thus when you meet someone who looks Asiatic but speaks German without an accent your social ontology produces cognitive dissonance and the person must be 'grilled' for as long as it takes to re-establish the appearance of consonance with the assumed nation-state unity of passport, skin colour and place of origin – 'appearance', because in the growing turmoil of globalized lifestyles the imaginary world of self-enclosed cultural totalities is not only misleading but also involves a striking loss of reality.

For,

to the question 'Who am I? Where do I belong?' there is no longer a single answer that remains the same throughout one's life. Instead, there are a variety of possible answers, just as there are a variety of modes of belonging and layers of identity. Which answer is chosen and which identity is prioritized in a given case depends on external circumstances and on the desires and inclinations of the agent in question. Situational, in particular political, factors rather than stages in one's personal development play an important role here. Someone who grew up in Munich as the child of Greek immigrants may enjoy the warmth of the Greek summer and his extended Greek family during the holidays in Thessalonica, and may even feel longing for his Greek roots; when he returns to Munich he again becomes an enthusiastic supporter of 1860 Munich . . .; at work he is neither a Greek nor a Bavarian but a computer specialist or part of the Siemens workforce; and should he ever happen to travel to Africa he certainly would not feel Greek or German but something else again: a white European. (Beck-Gernsheim 2004: 103f.)

And yet the territorial social ontology of the national outlook is not just 'at home' in the everyday world of political parties, the mass media and politics, but even more so in law and especially in the social sciences. The founding duality of the national outlook – foreigner–native – no longer adequately reflects reality. 'All methods of enquiry that operate with statistical concepts such as 'foreigner' and 'native' are unprepared for the realities of life in a world that is becoming increasingly transnational and involves plural attachments that transcend the boundaries of countries and nationality. The data produced using such research methods are thus at best irrelevant, at worst misleading, even false' (Beck-Gernsheim 2004: 106; for evidence of this, see the book as a whole). Thinking and research in terms of exclusive differentiations is not designed to capture the both/and reality that conforms to principles of inclusive differentiation in many areas (Beck, Bonss and Lau 2004).

Although one can find partial arguments in the classics that point beyond methodological nationalism (see above, pp. 9f.), nevertheless it is mainly research on transnationalization over the past decade (less in sociology than in cultural studies, ethnology, ethnography, geography, etc.) that has effectively questioned the empirical and methodological assumptions of mainstream methodological nationalism (see chapter 3).

Empirical-analytical cosmopolitanism takes aim at methodological nationalism, but it does not engage in polemics against political cosmopolitanism (with such derogatory epithets as 'grand hotel cosmopolitanism', 'business lounge cosmopolitanism' or 'vulgar patriotism'). Nor does it focus (initially) on the normative-political issue of how cosmopolitan democracy is possible. Instead it is simply concerned with comprehending social and political conditions at the beginning of the twenty-first century. The critique of methodological nationalism within the cosmopolitan outlook is directed at the perspective of the social scientific observer. The accusation of *methodological* nationalism is not meant to imply that some or all social scientists are nationalists. Even non-nationalists and anti-nationalists think and conduct research within the framework of methodological nationalism insofar as they use the grammar of the social sciences as the basis for how they pose problems. As long as they employ the concepts of the social sciences, they take for granted the dogmas of methodological nationalism. Let us examine the principles of methodological nationalism.[6]

Society is subordinated to the state

The first principle asserts that the nation-state defines the national society, not the converse. Society does not choose the state; rather, the state promises security, strengthens borders and creates administrative apparatuses which enable it to shape and control 'national society'. It follows that there is not just one but many societies – or, to be more precise, there are as many national societies as there are national states and national sociologies. Methodological nationalism implies societies in the plural. It imposes a *territorial* understanding of society based upon state-constructed and state-controlled borders. This 'container model' of mutually delimiting national societies is reinforced by the principle of the reciprocal determination of state and society. The territorial national state is both creator and guarantor of civil rights, and citizens organize themselves through political parties to influence and legitimate the actions of the state.

This axiomatic system may be found in unadulterated form in the social theories of Emile Durkheim or Talcott Parsons, for example, but also in John Rawls (1993: 40f.). Rawls defines his theory of justice in terms of 'political society', which he understands as 'a complete and closed social system'. 'It is complete, in that it is self-sufficient and has place for all the purposes of human life. It is also closed, in that entry into it is only by birth and exit from it is only by death. . . . For the moment we leave aside entirely relations with other societies.' This conception of a nationally closed society and democracy axiomatically excludes all the increasingly explosive questions generated by the uncoupling of nation, state and society. How, for instance, in the age of 'liquid modernity' (Zygmunt Bauman), of flows and networks, can distinctions be drawn between foreigners and nationals, citizens and non-citizens, human rights and civil rights, in concrete social contexts – who should and should not be permitted to vote, and on what basis? – if even the understanding of the constitution is inextricably bound up with the concept of the nation, which for its part is becoming ever more fictitious and is even in open conflict with the fact that transnational realities and causalities are becoming the universal norm?[7]

Martin Shaw has proposed the metaphor of a stamp collection for the research practice of social sciences that conform to the principle of methodological nationalism. Stamps are issued by national institutions. They are symbols of the state and bear its 'stamp'. Someone who collects them behaves like someone collecting 'social facts': he or she follows the logic of the national outlook. Both stamps and social facts are sorted by symbols and dates according to the distinction between intra-national and inter-national communication. Social relations and symbols that escape or cut across this harmonization of territory and state remain invisible within this perceptual framework. Like a stamp collector, the social scientist starts from the assumption that social boundaries coincide with state boundaries and hence that the boundaries of research can and must also be fixed by the borders of the state.

The image of the world in the social sciences is determined by the opposition between the national and the international

Both for theory and the imagination, as well as for social scientific research practice, the opposition between national and international is fundamental. There is not just an internal national, but also an external international, recognition of societies and states. A single national society is a meaningless concept. There can only be a plurality of national societies which come into and remain in existence through reciprocal, international recognition. Consequently, the principles of legality, democracy, etc., that apply within nation-states cannot be transferred directly to relations between states. The national presupposes the international and vice versa.

The universalist fallacy involved in inferring from particular national society to universal society

There is an inner affinity between the national and universal perspectives. One's own society serves as the model for society in general, from which it follows that the basic characteristics of universal society can be derived from an analysis of *this* society. Thus Marx discovered British capitalism in British society, which he then generalized to the capitalism of modern society as such. Weber universalized the experience of the Prussian bureaucracy into the ideal type of modern rationality. And in criticizing the 'power elites', C. Wright Mills was criticizing not just American society but modern society as such.

This false inference from national to universal society was criticized and corrected from the beginning by the method of international comparison for which single case studies are necessary but not sufficient to make general statements about modern society. However, this approach is conceived and practised in the form of comparison between national societies; hence it too presupposes nation-states as the basic units, and hence all of the other assumptions of methodological nationalism. The possibility that the unity of state and nation might dissolve, disintegrate or undergo a complete transformation remains beyond the purview of the social sciences.

Anyone who takes for granted the mutually reinforcing differentiation between the national and the international must construe the global as the maximum intensification of the national. The world systems theory of Immanuel Wallerstein proceeds in this way from the differentiation of the national and the international. The result is a global perspective that analyses the relationship between nation-states within the 'world system'. In another variant of the global outlook, John Meyer and his research group have investigated the spread of global norms. Here too the national–international duality is not overcome but serves as a foil for studies and prognoses concerning the global homogenization of national domains of experience and action.

The territorial misunderstanding of cultural plurality: either universal homogenization or incommensurability of perspectives

Methodological nationalism involves and intensifies a territorial (mis)understanding of culture and cultural plurality. If culture is conceived as territorially circumscribed, then the question of plurality leads to a sterile false alternative: either universal sameness ('McDonaldization') or perspectives that resist comparison ('incommensurability').

Many critics view cosmopolitan culture accordingly as a natural successor to, or even as the product of, postmodern culture. In this view, the link between postmodernism and postnationalism gives rise to a variety of movements of cultural eclecticism and ambivalence and ultimately a general cultural plasticity; people use various styles, symbols and concepts stemming from older historical cultures, now playfully, now satirically, in literature, music, painting or architecture, reprocessing them for the mass media. Upon closer inspection, however, this ostensible plurality is continually trimmed and merged into an undifferentiated universalism. This shallow cosmopolitanism of quotation and montage can indeed exploit the past to renew itself continually and try to pass it off as a fashionable invention. But it is widely thought that it cannot locate itself in history or dispel the basic fact that cultures and cultural imagination are historically specific and rooted, and hence territorial, phenomena.

In short, a timeless culture answers to no living needs and conjures no memories. If memory is central to identity, we can discern no global identity-in-the-making, nor aspiration for one, nor any collective amnesia to replace existing 'deep' cultures with a cosmopolitan 'flat' culture. The latter remains a dream confined to some intellectuals. It strikes no chord among the vast mass of peoples divided into their habitual communities of class, gender, religion, and culture. (A. D. Smith 1995: 24)[8]

That is *not* what the cosmopolitan outlook dreams of. Smith invokes the hostile caricature of cosmopolitanism that reaffirms the premises and the errors of methodological nationalism. This humanistic universalism affirms that the actual tendency is towards greater sameness, and hence the elimination of plurality. To embrace this universalism would ultimately be to advocate cultural suicide. Cosmopolitanism, by contrast, means the exact opposite: recognition of difference, beyond the misunderstandings of territoriality and homogenization.

If difference is universalized out of existence in humanistic universalism, in methodological nationalism the territorial ontology of difference is given a new lease of life. The result is that culture in the national outlook is understood in terms of self-enclosed territorially demarcated units; and at the extreme the (uneasy) silence of incommensurable perspectives reigns between cultures. Such a belief frees us from the labour of dialogue, leading almost inevitably to imperialism, cultural conflict and the clash of civilizations. The absurdity of this container model of plurality is impossible to overlook; for example, the existence of transnational networks, forms of life, work and action, and even the new experience of boundarylessness of immobile TV consumers, must be denied because these phenomena blur and confuse the linguistic and group boundaries between cultures.

The national outlook is also an essentialist outlook: it separates historically interwoven cultural and political realities

In the first modernity, the either/or dominated thought and action, and hence also historical self-images and conceptions of past and future. Correspondingly, the Europe of nation-states not only drew the political frontiers in the Middle East. It also projected these frontiers onto the history, art and culture of the East. In its politics of culture and science, Europe separates Jewish and Islamic traditions from one another and thereby hardens ideological boundary-lines which have thus far thwarted a peaceful resolution of the Middle East conflict.

The literatures and arts, the cuisines and religious traditions of the Arab cultural sphere are historically so closely intertwined, often to the point of indistinguishability, that they can only be studied and described in relation to each other. Thus Islamic theology is comprised in large part of answers to questions transmitted by Judaism and Christianity to the courts and studies of Baghdad, Kufa and Cordoba. Without knowledge of these questions, the answers are unintelligible. Something similar holds for Judaism. Not only Christian Europe, but also rabbinical thought assimilated the heritage of the ancient world primarily as it was transmitted and shaped by Islamic culture. Without knowledge of this culture it is impossible to understand not only how Judaism influenced Islam but also how Islam later influenced Judaism in turn in theology, and even more so in mysticism and literature. (Kermani and Lepenies 2003)[9]

Somewhat paradoxically, the ideal of ethnic and national homogeneity can be traced back to the national empires of the first modernity, which for the first time in history violently broke the bonds between culture and territory, transcended ethnic boundaries between cultures and blended identities. As William McNeill (1985) has argued, polyethnicity is the rule in world history, national and ethnic homogeneity, by contrast, the exception. And Dan Diner writes: 'It is not that the dynastically legitimated empires comprising a plurality of nations represent an adequate analytical foil for the proposed reconstruction of Europe and its identity; but on account of their ethnic and corporative-institutional diversity they more closely approximate a European perspective on history than the subsequent constellation of a plurality of nation-states divided from each other and doggedly confirming each other in their homogeneity' (Diner 2003: 14).

The specific exclusivity of opposition: the national outlook excludes the cosmopolitan, the cosmopolitan outlook includes the national

Over the past decade, even the social sciences have opened themselves to global transformations and categories (though in different degrees in different disciplines); the 'global' has become the focus of a new, self-critical discourse. Thus it has gradually become clearer that the discursive internalization of the global has affected the very substance of social scientific categories, theories and methods and the organization of research. Some researchers try to evade the challenges of global transformation by concentrating on regional or transnational change as opposed to global change. However, the regional or transnational outlook is merely a variant of the national outlook.

Methodological nationalism theorizes and researches social, cultural and political reality in either/or categories, whereas methodological cosmopolitanism theorizes and researches the social and the political in both/and categories. The national outlook excludes the cosmopolitan outlook. The cosmopolitan outlook, by contrast, conceives the national outlook as national and reveals its constitutive failures. It follows that the cosmopolitan outlook uncovers the same national reality differently, and different, additional, realities in new ways. The cosmopolitan outlook, therefore, encompasses and reinterprets the reality of the national outlook, whereas the national outlook is blind to and obscures the realities of the cosmopolitan age.

The distinction between narrower and broader senses of methodological nationalism

A whole range of voices unite in criticizing methodological nationalism and they all contribute to the creation of a cosmopolitan methodology in the social sciences. Nevertheless, it may be helpful to distinguish between methodological nationalism in a narrower and a broader sense. In the narrow sense, the critique of methodological nationalism is directed at the core conceptual apparatus of the social sciences; in the wider sense, it highlights how difficult it is to discover a substitute or alternative conceptual apparatus. Even the concepts 'diaspora' and 'hybridization', not to mention 'denationalization' and 'transnationalization', remain in certain respects bound to the horizon of methodological nationalism, in a negative sense at any rate (Robins and Aksoy 2001). The larger question is: what is meant by the 'deterritorialization' of sovereignty? Or, more generally: what does it mean when the dualism of national and international disintegrates what is meant by 'inequality', 'justice', 'nation', 'citizen', 'state', 'security', 'border' and 'risk' in different regions of the world and of global politics?

On the one hand, the stabilizing mechanisms of the national–international order are losing their effectiveness; on the other hand, global politics does not hold out the promise of new stabilizing mechanisms beyond the national and the international. By the standards of the old order there is complete chaos: no binding decisions, no democracy, no government and no opposition. The analogical inference from the national to the unbounded postnational space leads nowhere. The result is not only a cognitive but also a global political vacuum, though the former tends to obscure the latter.

Trapped in methodological nationalism, the debate over the new transatlantic relation, for example, loses its way in sterile false alternatives: on this side of the Atlantic, in Europe (but also in South America, Africa and Asia), we desperately cling to the ruins of the old order – 'international law' which is permeated by the codes of the nation-state – as a source of reassurance when confronted with the naked will to power of the sole and unique military superpower, the USA. We repudiate and slander the cosmopolitan sense of boundarylessness and seek refuge in the ruins of methodological nationalism – the good, old international global order – to rescue what remains of sovereignty. On the other side of the Atlantic, by contrast, the USA extends the national outlook to the world as a whole.

The distinction between the international and the cosmopolitan

Even the Cold War, the emergence of the 'West' and the 'East', continues to be theorized and researched in terms of the categories of the national and the international rather than those of the global. Global and cosmopolitan relations were reduced to international relations (Shaw 2000b; Wapner and Ruiz 2000; Held and Koenig-Archibugi 2003; Archibugi, Held and Köhler 1998). The emergence of the World Trade Organization, the World Bank, the International Monetary Fund, NATO, and so forth, were interpreted as examples of institutionalized internationalism, not of an institutionalized cosmopolitanism which seeks to structure and order the globalized world beyond the national and the international. Internationalism and cosmopolitanism, however, are not just two ways of realizing the same idea. Without doubt, cosmopolitan relations presuppose, among other things, international relations; but by the same token they transform the latter by opening and redrawing boundaries, by transcending or reversing the polarity of the relations between us and them, and not least by rewriting the relation between the state, politics and the nation in cosmopolitan terms.

International and cosmopolitan cannot be equated with each other. The cosmopolitan outlook grasps the change in social and political grammar and hence, for example, the process of integration through reflexive globality. The 'either inside or outside' that underlies the distinction between national and international is transcended by a 'both inside and outside'. The cosmopolitan outlook determines multiple spatial, temporal and practical both/and realities to which the national perspective remains blind.

What, then, is the core of the critique of methodological nationalism? The fundamental criticism is that it views the nation-state as a 'self-evident point of departure' (Daniel Levy in conversation), whereas the cosmopolitan outlook retains a reference to the nation-state but situates and analyses it within a radically different horizon (see chapter 3 below). The circular arguments of methodological nationalism are false because the national outlook analyses the nation-state without questioning its own premises. It is becoming imperative to view the nation-state and international relations from the cosmopolitan perspective which sharpens our understanding not only of global interdependencies but also of how they impact on the nation-state. It is an open empirical question, which can and must be answered differently within different constellations, whether nation-states become fluid or fixed, denationalize, renationalize or transnationalize within the framework of global interdependencies, risks and crises.

3   Towards a cosmopolitan social science, or the new grammar of the social and the political

The epistemological turn, the empirical-analytical cosmopolitanism developed in this book, has a twofold thrust: first, a critique of existing methodological nationalism and, second, the development of a new methodological cosmopolitanism. A critique of the national outlook becomes concrete and scientifically credible only if it can be shown how the cosmopolitan shift in outlook modifies the grammar of the social sciences, recalibrating established research topics and casting them in a new light. I will here sketch out this substantive, conceptual and methodological transformation of core topics in the social sciences under four headings: (1) risk-cosmopolitanism: global public opinion as a side effect; (2) interference of side effects: post-international politics; (3) the invisibility of global inequality; and (4) how everyday life is becoming cosmopolitan: banal cosmopolitanism.

3.1   *Risk-cosmopolitanism: global public opinion as a side effect*

We distinguished above (pp. 18ff.) between cosmopolitanism and the cosmopolitan outlook in conjunction with the thesis that cosmopolitanization generally occurs as an unintended and coerced side effect. It is a different matter altogether whether this side effect cosmopolitanization then becomes conscious – leading to a cosmopolitan outlook – and even gives rise to a global public. The theory of world risk society (Beck 1992, 1999; Beck and Holzer 2004) presents a model of interdependence crises which makes it possible to investigate this connection between latent, coerced cosmopolitanization and the global public awareness of it fostered by scandals, both theoretically and empirically. A system of 'risk-cosmopolitanism' is developing in which an exceptional degree of cosmopolitan interdependence, itself a side effect of side effect global publics, is bringing transnational conflicts and commonalities into the everyday practices which necessitate political (state) and subpolitical (civil society) action. In its lead story on 'Living with Risk' (July 28, 2003), *Time* magazine recently traced in detail how people in developed civilization are caught up in hard-to-evaluate risks and in inescapable uncertainties produced by science. Scientists can determine ever more precisely the risks posed by genetically modified foods, mobile telephones and the everyday use of chemicals at best within a range of probabilities; but that tells us nothing about whether they are genuine risks or how a consumer can make a 'rational' choice in a particular situation. How worried should we be? Where is the boundary-line between prudent concern and crippling fear and hysteria? And who should decide? Scientists, whose results often contradict each other, who change their minds so fundamentally over longer periods that what was 'safe' to swallow today may be judged by scientists in two years' time to be a 'cancer risk'? Can we believe the politicians and the mass media, when the former declare technologies to be risk free in order to reduce unemployment, while the latter underscore the risks in order to increase circulation? *Time* reports all this in great detail. But it tells us nothing about what risk actually does, its essential feature: it creates a public by promoting public awareness of risk.

This can be seen from the major risk conflicts of the past twenty years, from the nuclear reactor disaster at Chernobyl, to the AIDS and BSE crises and the controversy over genetically modified 'Frankenstein foods', to September 11, 2001, the date of birth of the global terror risk. The law of double side effects invariably applies: self-destructive civilization produces first-degree side effects – less rather than more calculable risks and uncertainties – which in turn generate, as second-degree side effects, cross-border publics and corresponding devaluations of products, everyday practices, bureaucratic routines, market collapses, allocations of responsibility and costs, conflicts, commonalities, demands for action. Both the first- and second-degree side effects produce and accelerate cosmopolitanization through interdependence – indeed, the relationship between the two types of side effect cosmopolitanization likewise reveals how a latent, coerced cosmopolitanization can change into a coerced awareness of risk-cosmopolitanization (Beck 1999).

Hence the theory of world risk society should not be confused with a variant of the theory of the imminent decline of the West, but should be seen, rather, as a theory of ambivalence. On the one hand, there is the grim prospect opened up for the world on September 11, 2001, namely, that of an uncontrollable terror risk which insinuates itself into every aspect of life in developed societies and changes them from within. But there is a different side. It has often been asked what could unite the world, to which the standard reply is: an attack from Mars. In a sense that is what occurred on September 11: an attack from our 'internal Mars'. And, for a while at least, we actually saw the predicted closing of ranks in international and national politics against the common enemy of global terrorism. In an age in which confidence and belief in social class, nation and progress have become more or less questionable, the global perception of global risk represents perhaps the last – ambivalent – source of new commonalities and interaction networks. However paradoxical it may seem, there are also grounds for hope in the fact that world risk society marks an epoch in which coerced risk-cosmopolitanization mutates into a no less coerced emerging global public *awareness* of the ongoing process of risk-cosmopolitanization. The law of double side effects thereby also performs an enlightening function.

A shift in focus is essential to realizing the potential of this perspective. For, contrary to conventional political theory, it is not the decision itself but its unforeseeable consequences and risks that constitute the source of the public and the political (Dewey 1954). In a global public sphere sensitized to risk, the question of power is posed in particular by awareness of the fact that effects cannot be calculated. The resulting cross-border relations of responsibility for shared risks are defined negatively in two ways. On the one hand, they are directed not towards things that should exist, but towards things that should on no account exist. This is not a matter of value-based integration (as methodological nationalism postulates) but of integration through dangers and their aversion, whose binding power grows with the extent of the perceived danger. Instead of integration through national and universal values, the global character of dangers reflected in a world public entails a new dialectic of conflict and cooperation across borders. Only in this way can the necessary consensual formulas be discovered and negotiated for international initiatives and institutions, as the only alternative to decline. Of course, it remains an open question whether this will actually happen.

On the other hand, it is not so much, or anyway not exclusively, social movements or revolutionary upheavals that 'unintentionally' and 'invisibly' produce a global public, but the catastrophic intensification of global risks themselves. The more ubiquitous the threat as represented in the mass media, the greater the political power to explode borders generated by the perception of risk (Adam, Beck and van Loon 2000). Risks can be understood, accordingly, as a *negative* medium of communication; nearly everyone wants to keep quiet about them. By contrast with the positive communications media of money, truth and power, risks give rise to unwanted contexts of action beyond national and systemic boundaries. Thus this negative medium of communication *forces* people to communicate with one another in spite of themselves, and forces a public into existence where it is supposed to be prevented. It allocates duties and costs to those who decline them (often even with the backing of valid laws). In other words, risks explode self-referential systems and national and international political agendas, overturning their priorities and producing practical interconnections among mutually indifferent or hostile parties and camps.

3.2   *Interference relations among side effects: post-international politics*

A transition is taking place from a politics centred upon nation-states and international security to a non-state-centred post-international risk politics. This paradigm shift correlates with the distinction between first and second modernity. The high-modern period of classical nation-states gave rise to a structural and political logic which is only now becoming clearly distinguishable following the end of the Cold War that signalled its demise. It drew sharply defined boundaries not only between different nations and states but, more generally, between people, things and functional and practical fields, and thereby produced clear-cut ascriptions of competence and responsibility (at least at the level of expectations). Today, by contrast, the side effects of radicalized modernization reflected in a global public sphere are producing an awareness of new global dangers. Globality and the (known) incalculability of these civilizational dangers are eroding the basic differentiations and founding institutions of the first modernity: there identifiable, limited dangers, here unlimited risks and insecurities that are hard to identify; there conscious knowledge and calculability premised on state sovereignty, here (conscious) ignorance (or non-conscious ignorance) and incalculability that annuls sovereignty. There prevention follows the logic of deterrence, here the logic of interstate and post-state cooperation. However, this presages the beginning of struggles over the form and content of an institutionalized cosmopolitanism, in the sense of stable cooperation among state and non-state actors at the global and local levels, in addition to civil society groups and networks, corporations, international organizations, the UN, 'churches', etc. Of course, it is by no means the case that all boundaries and dualisms are becoming blurred. In fact, the essential point of the theory of reflexive modernization is that just the opposite is true (Beck, Bonss and Lau 2004): the removal of boundaries forces us to make choices. As boundaries are removed, the pressure to make choices and the prevalence of provisional boundary-lines increase, and a permanent condition of frontier policies and frontier conflicts prevails. All actors – governments as well as international organizations, political parties and civil society movements – have to resituate themselves within this transnational force-field: they have to redistribute burdens and costs, redefine goals, find appropriate ways and means, forge coalitions and imagine futures for a common world, which results in deep-seated resistances and conflicts. *This* is what is meant by a post-international politics not centred on nation-states (Daase, Feske and Peters 2002; Pauly and Grande 2005).

'The long-existing economic, social and technological unity of the world, the collective responsibility for preserving the conditions of life on an over-populated planet and the ever-growing military potential that protects only a few but endangers all' render the cosmopolitan outlook necessary. 'The novelty of the current situation is that global problems no longer leave us much time to create a global political order in which law is not merely a formality but a real power in the lives of peoples. If humanity does not succeed in giving a political form to its actual unity, and hence in creating organizations that make it possible to respond to priorities, then the days of the present regulatory powers are probably numbered' (Gerhardt 2003: 566). But what does that mean for the concept 'international' from which the study of 'international relations' takes its orientation (Wapner and Ruiz 2000; Held and Koenig-Archibugi 2003)?

The term 'international' must definitely not be struck from the vocabulary of politics and political theory. Relations between states remain centrally important, but they are no longer exclusive or monopolizable and, most importantly, they are changing their grammar. The coerced, unintended cosmopolitanization of international relations also follows the model of *interference among side effects* – of capital flows, flows of cultural symbols, global risks, terror attacks, migration flows, anti-globalization movements, ecological and economic crises. The units of 'international relations' – the fetish-concepts of 'state' and 'nation' – are being hollowed out because in world risk society national problems can no longer be solved on a national basis; because human rights are being turned against states, and are being 'defended' by states against other states; and because highly mobile capital forces territorially fixated states to disempower and transform themselves.

Trans-international politics, therefore, signifies a level of organized, more or less informal domestic, foreign, interstate and substate politics which mirrors all other phenomena: global economic power relations, crises and strategies, the situations of nation-states and the reactions of individual countries and groups of countries, interventions aimed at a global public, terror threats, and so on. Trans-international politics cuts across international politics. It includes international politics, but so too, conversely, international politics becomes a venue for trans-international policies. The cosmopolitan observer perspective, therefore, initiates a 'grammatical' change in the term 'international' (cf., for example, M. Shaw 2000b; Held 2003; Kaldor 2003; Linklater 1998; Wapner and Ruiz 2000). International relations theory is blind to the dynamics of globality – unless globality is restricted to spatial relations among states. In short, the cosmopolitanization of reality appears to be the adversary of international theory, for it seems to undermine the authority of the theory of the state and abolish the political monopoly of the nation-state and international relations. But precisely in this feared self-negation the international perspective misjudges the dynamics and the reality of the cosmopolitanization of international relations. What is at issue is not the undermining or abandonment, but the transformation, redefinition and complementing of forms of politics and state and of interstate relations, actors and dynamics.

3.3   The invisibility of global inequality

We are faced with the paradox that, whereas global inequalities are growing dramatically (Doyle 2000; Wade 2003), they are accorded at best only marginal attention in methodological nationalism. What should we make of this?[10]

In sociology wedded to the nation-state, the standard justification for social inequalities is in terms of the performance principle. This holds for nation-states internally, hence applies to domestic social inequalities. By contrast, the cosmopolitan outlook shows how the nation-state principle functions as a legitimation for global inequalities. The key point is that, in keeping with the introverted character of the national outlook, the nation-state principle conceals global inequalities. Since methodological nationalism focuses on inequalities within countries, it cannot systematically address, first, the question of how global inequalities are legitimated and, second, the question concerning the transnationalization of social inequalities.

The performance principle makes possible a 'positive' legitimation of intranational inequalities, whereas the nation-state principle rests on a 'negative' legitimation of global inequalities. 'Positive' legitimation means that the performance principle functions as a reciprocal and reflexive legitimation of experienced inequality. Performance (however this is operationalized) is the yardstick which makes it possible even for those directly affected to distinguish, at least in principle, between legitimate and illegitimate distributions of wealth. The nation-state principle, by contrast, must be construed as a 'negative' mode of legitimation, because it takes no account of global inequalities. Internal comparison of performance corresponds to institutionalized blindness towards external inequalities. This precludes the acceptance of those who are excluded as poor. Upon closer examination, therefore, the nation-state principle does not legitimate global inequalities. Rather, the introverted character of the national perspective renders the absence of legitimation invisible and thereby stabilizes it. What principles underlie this institutionalized invisibility of global inequalities (Stichweh 2000)?

National fragmentation

Just as in the national outlook world society disaggregates into fragmented, territorially demarcated and bound, state-organized national societies which are inwardly oriented and outwardly closed off, so too global inequalities and the resulting conflicts and dynamics fragment into national inequalities which cease to appear as global within the horizon of the national outlook and national sociologies.

In the national framework, social inequalities are situated within the inter-relation between the welfare system and the individual; the responsibility for inequality is attributed in part to individuals, in part to the state. Accordingly, justice is defined and social claims are articulated and pursued in terms of the distributive policies of the state. This mobilizes social move-ments, such as the labour and women's movements, which denounce their respective underprivileged status and demand compensatory measures from the state.

A common assumption, but one which is seldom consistently thought through and examined, is that national inequalities may be globally rather than nationally determined, that they are due to global capital flows, crises and upheavals. Only in the cosmopolitan outlook on national, as well as global and transnational, inequalities do these restrictions on thought, inquiry and research become clear and can they be overcome; only here do national welfare states cease to appear as mere guarantors of individual social security. The question then becomes how and to what extent do national welfare states shunt poverty risks onto other states and countries. The most recent textbook example of this occurred at a global conference in the summer of 2003, where, in a now rare display of transatlantic unanimity, an American–European 'coalition of the unwilling' defended Western agricultural protectionism against the demands of African and Latin American countries that they should finally open their markets and live up to the core Western principle of free trade.

Restrictive norms of equality

Inequalities are recognized as such only to the extent that social norms of equality (civil rights) have force. When the distinctions between citizens and non-citizens, foreigners and nationals, human rights and civil rights become blurred, it also becomes more difficult to separate non-national inequalities clearly from national inequalities. In other words, the experiential space of the nation-state is increasingly becoming a playground of global inequalities, contradictions and issues of justice. Realistically speaking, it is no longer pos-sible to draw political, or indeed sociological-conceptual, boundaries between the national and the international in the area of social inequalities.

Institutionalized incomparability

If global inequalities between different national spaces are to become institu-tionally invisible, they must resist comparison. Comparison of inequalities, which is a political necessity within nation-states, is not actually ruled out between states, but it is politically ineffective; that is the specific achievement of the introverted national outlook. To be sure, if international and global inequalities make the national experiential space their playground – partly in the form of legal and illegal migration and mobility, partly in the form of media representations of conflicts and lifestyles – institutionalized incomparability loses its force. In the collision of transnational conflicts in localities and in the politics of nation-states, there has to be a political-cultural and sociological reckoning with the experience of what we might call 'incomparable comparabilities'.

Already these few sketchy remarks make clear that once the stable world of national distinctions and boundaries becomes fluid, the principles of national blindness to global inequalities lose much of their validity. As a result, the interconnections between intra-national, international and transnational inequalities become politically explosive.

The cosmopolitan outlook, with its sense of boundarylessness, paints a highly ambivalent picture of reality and of the future: opportunities are boundless, but so too are the threats. The suspicion that boundless threats are choking boundless opportunities is difficult to dispel. For along with the threats goes the inability of the available concepts to grasp them and the inability of existing institutions to respond to them. Thus, as the danger grows, it becomes harder to resist the temptation to deny the danger or to normalize it into a form that fits the established categories for its prevention. In the case of the risk of terrorism this means: war against states. The Iraq War was the first war against a global risk, the risk of terror, which was fought against a state. Only in this way could the risk be (ostensibly) controlled by the state, only in this way could the state 'digest' it. Non-state terrorism is made digestible by the state by the fact that terrorism is, first, associated with rogue states which are suspected of tolerating or fostering it and can, second, be defeated through the conventional means of state-against-state warfare.

The result is a new, hidden transnational commonality based on the fact that both sides deny the novelty of the terror threat. Fighting the war on terror as a war against states is only justifiable if the difference in kind between terrorism and war is suppressed. Only if the terror threat is turned back into a threat of war can it be understood in terms of conventional concepts and controlled with the conventional means of military superiority. Only then can the most powerful nation in the world finally cease to feel insecure.

3.4   *How everyday life is becoming cosmopolitan: banal cosmopolitanism*

Consumer society is the really existing world society. Hence consumption, in which it is hard to distinguish between compulsion and decision, side effect and intended effect, is a perfect example of 'side effect cosmopolitanization'. Cosmopolitanization does not take place only in inconspicuous ways (for example, when nationally badged cars such as Volkswagens or London taxis are assembled from parts sourced from all over the world). Cosmopolitanism has itself become a commodity; the glitter of cultural difference sells well. Correspondingly, images of an in-between world, of the black body, exotic beauty, exotic music, exotic food, and so on, are globally cannibalized, staged and consumed as mass products for mass markets. 'People see black people as trendsetters, they see what we're on to and they wanna get onto the same thing, figuring it's gonna be the next big thing. They try to take things away from us every time. Slang we come up with ends up on t-shirts. We ain't making no t-shirts', writes African-American clothing designer Carl Williams, who markets his designs under the 'Karl Kani' brand name.[11] Of course, someone who listens to 'black music' and wears pictures or quotations of black people on their t-shirt does not have to identify with the culture from which the pictures or quotations are taken. But they make themselves the bearer of images and messages that cross frontiers and permeate otherwise separate experiential spaces. Black culture, styles and creativity are sold to a public that knows no borders. Once again we are confronted with a kind of 'banal cosmopolitanism'. People do not make a show of symbols of 'banal nationalism', but they do, whether willingly or unwillingly, wear the cosmopolitan badge.

Banal cosmopolitanism is intimately connected with all forms of consumption. It is exhibited not only by the vast, colourful array of meals, foodstuffs, restaurants and menus routinely found in almost any city anywhere in the world. It also pervades other spheres of everyday culture – for example, music:

Here again, an extraordinary proliferation is taking place. The news from Algeria is often appalling, but from the same country there also emanates inventive music of many kinds, disseminated by young people who express themselves in Arabic, French or Kabyle. . . . Their journey cannot fail to remind us of the older, more massive trajectory of the Africans once taken as slaves to the Americas. Today their music, whether issuing from Louisiana or from the West Indies, has spread all over the world and become part of the musical and emotional heritage of us all.

This is also part of the meaning of 'banal' cosmopolitanization: 'Never in the past have human beings had the technical means of listening at will to so many kinds of music – all those voices, whether from Cameroon, Spain, Egypt, Argentina, Brazil and Cape Verde, or from Liverpool, Memphis, Brussels and Naples. Never before have so many people been able to play, compose, and sing – and be heard' (Maalouf 2000: 108–9). (On the connection between consumption, globalization and everyday culture see, among others: Liebes and Katz 1993; Held et al. 1999; Beisheim, Zürn et al. 1999: 69–99; Gebesmair 2000; Beck, Sznaider and Winter 2003). What seems from a postmodern perspective to be 'eclecticism' or 'inauthenticity' (and from the perspective of critiques of culture as 'lack of roots' or 'lack of memory') can be understood in terms of a new reflexivity. Here elements from many different countries and cultures are continually compared, rejected, combined and remixed. Thought through to its conclusion, there arises a whole network of everyday practices and skills to deal with a high degree of interdependence and globality.

The question to what extent this inner cosmopolitanization of lifeworlds occurs only 'objectively' or also becomes institutionally 'reflexive' ultimately concerns the role of the mass media (Appadurai 1995, 1991; Aksoy and Robins 2003; Schiller 1989; Caglar 2002). The accessibility of other cultures and experiential domains, magnified by the possibility of switching between different channels and programmes, may help to create a situation in which there is a growing awareness of the everyday cosmopolitan interdependence of television viewers, though this is an empirical question (to which we will return). Mike Featherstone summarizes the argument as follows: 'the flows of information, knowledge, money, commodities, people and images have intensified to the extent that the sense of spatial distance which separated and insulated people from the need to take into account all the other people which make up what has become known as humanity has become eroded' (Featherstone 1993: 169). But the image of humanity has thereby been fundamentally altered.

Thus, insofar as global everyday existence becomes an integral part of media worlds, a kind of globalization of emotions and empathy occurs. People experience themselves as parts of a fragmented, endangered civilization and civil society characterized by the simultaneity of events and of knowledge of this simultaneity all over the world.

John Tomlinson redefines the concept of cosmopolitanism accordingly in an attempt to grasp conceptually how relations between the global and the local have been transformed (Tomlinson 1999: 194–207). The opposition between local and cosmopolitan is becoming false, he argues, because the morality of lifeworlds no longer conforms to this antithesis. He traces the rise of a form of cosmopolitanism that lends force to moral aspirations and ambiguities, both locally and across great distances. This connection between locality and cosmopolitanism forces us to examine cross-border moral conceptions and practices within specific lifeworld contexts.

Bronislaw Szerszynski and John Urry have differentiated the following cosmopolitan predispositions and practices for research purposes:

- extensive *mobility* in which people have the right to 'travel' corporeally, imaginatively and virtually and for significant numbers they also have the means to travel;
- the capacity to *consume* many places and environments en route;
- a *curiosity* about many places, peoples and cultures and at least a rudimentary ability to locate such places and cultures historically, geographically and anthropologically;
- an ability to '*map*' one's own society and its culture in terms of a historical and geographical knowledge, to have some ability to reflect upon and judge aesthetically between different natures, places and societies;

- *semiotic* skill to be able to interpret images of various others, to see what they are meant to represent, and to know when they are ironic;
- an *openness* to other peoples and cultures and a willingness/ability to appreciate some elements of the language/culture of the 'other'. (Szerszynski and Urry 2002: 470)

The authors' research points in fact to the broad dissemination – a 'seepage' – of a general cosmopolitanism. Their results show that more and more people are quite conscious of the fact that they are living in an age of global flows of money and goods and of boundless risks; that interdependencies with other human beings, places and environments are on the increase; that the boundaries of nations, cultures, and religions are blurring and intermingling; and that they are inextricably intertwined in an experiential space in which local, national and global influences interpenetrate. As an interviewee put it, cosmopolitanization 'has become more of a possibility and a reality' (Szerszynski and Urry 2002: 472).

The qualitative research data make clear how local loyalty, global openness and moral interdependence are interrelated: 'Most, if not all, of the respondents had some kind of active and compassionate commitment to an immediate community, as an actually existing way of life, as a lost world of the past, or as an ideal for the future. However, this community was not always based upon a geographical territory. People also conceived of wider, dispersed communities based not on geography but on shared interests or "affect", organised around practices and issues such as football, collecting for a hospice, scouting, work, the environment, student unions, caravanning, car racing . . .' (Szerszynski and Urry 2002: 474). Many of those questioned were only too well aware of the globalized culture in which they live and expressed their communal bonds in concepts which Scott Lash sees as proper to the second modernity and which are characterized by the simultaneity of chooseability and fixedness, of repression and memory (Lash 1999: 14).[12]

Is there such a thing as an (unequal) biographical cosmopolitanization? Is it not shown by the fact that borders are becoming ever more permeable for members of elites, whereas for the rest, the poor, these same borders are sealed? Biographical cosmopolitanization means that the contradictions of the world are unequally distributed not just out there but also at the centre of one's own life.

To put it in terms of ideal types, if a 'monogamy of place' is characteristic of the modernity of the nation-state, then internal biographical globalization represents a kind of *polygamy of place* (Beck 2000a). The symbol of a biography whose internal borders have been overcome is no longer the *'flâneur'* but e-mail. You can be reached or you can't, you don't answer or answer automatically, you send and receive (at a spatial or temporal remove) messages which the technology enables you to read and save from anywhere in the world. Such polygamous forms of life and biographies cut across rank and class, legality and illegality, mobility and migration. It is illegal immigrants who more than anyone else have to defend their cross-border polygamy of place in a continual daily struggle against the intrusions of state control and power.

4   On the necessity and difficulty of distinguishing between emancipatory and despotic cosmopolitanism

What cosmopolitanism is cannot ultimately be separated from what cosmopolitanism should be. Cosmopolitanism is no longer a dream but has become a social reality, however distorted, which has to be explored. In this book the new analytical-empirical dimension of cosmopolitanism is accorded pride of place – hence the term 'cosmopolitan outlook'. But if the normative question of what cosmopolitanism should be is put to one side for the moment, that does not mean that it could or should be ignored altogether. On the contrary, the cosmopolitan extension and conceptual reformulation of the social scientific outlook opens up new paths and perspectives on the dilemmas and the normative and political content of global cosmopolitanism (Cheah and Robbins 1998; Vertovec and Cohen 2002; Wapner and Ruiz 2000; Held and Koenig-Archibugi 2003).

The charge that has always been brought against cosmopolitanism – its idealism (or 'sentimental twaddle') – can prove to be paradoxically dangerous when translated into realpolitik. Cosmopolitan ideas have not yet had the opportunity to exhaust their utopian potential. Nationalism, by contrast, has used this 'opportunity' to produce a bloody self-contradiction, as predicted by the prophets of cosmopolitanism (who derided it as a 'Germanic farce', 'inhuman patriotism', etc.). But even the most devastating critique of nationalism will not convert anyone to cosmopolitanism. One can also be agnostic concerning nationalism and cosmopolitanism. The collapse of the Soviet Union and the Eastern bloc system again proved 'that nations are being driven to ruin, year in year out, by purely administrative means and from outside; thus it proves the invalidity of the nationality principle. Of course, this process does not make us cosmopolitans. Even though the idea of the nation no longer corresponds to anything objective and concrete, it survives doggedly as a subjective illusion' (Enzensberger 1992a: 192).

After a century such as the last in which ideologies drove humanity to the brink of complete ruin, belief in the goodness of the good simply will not do. If the cosmopolitan outlook wants to earn the honorific title 'realistic' it must open itself up to dilemmas, to dreams as well as nightmares, to good intentions as well as predictable catastrophes. In other words, an optimist of the cosmopolitan outlook can also be a pessimist of the cosmopolitan mission (Beck 2005: final chapter).

There is no direct, linear, ethical justification of the cosmopolitan project, no direct proof of its moral or functional or pragmatic superiority. There is only the 'detour' of anticipating its fundamental ambiguities and misuses. If we want to develop a cosmopolitan ethics and politics we must first ask what ideological misuses a well-meaning cosmopolitanism makes possible: *ideological self-criticism* is the criterion of validity of the new cosmopolitanism. On this criterion there is no way to avoid assessing the necessity and the radicality of the distinction between *emancipatory* and *despotic* cosmopolitanism.

4.1 Three historical moments of emancipatory cosmopolitanism

An analysis of European intellectual history enables us to distinguish at least three historical moments of emancipatory cosmopolitanism: ancient cosmopolitanism (Stoicism), the *jus cosmopolitica* of the Enlightenment (Immanuel Kant), and crimes against humanity (Karl Jaspers, Hannah Arendt) (cf. Fine and Cohen 2002).

(1)   The ancient Greek philosophy of the Stoics lays down the conceptual-logical foundation of the cosmopolitan idea with the concepts 'cosmos' and 'polis'. The cosmopolitan duality – the cosmopolis vs. membership in more or less delimited political communities – does not rest on the negation of the either/or but on the both/and principle. This means that the one refers to the other, neither is possible without the other, the one specifies and reinforces the other. It is, however, a hierarchical both/and. The cosmopolis represents (or, in modern terms, human rights represent) the 'higher' principle, by comparison with which particular communities appear secondary. The polis encompassing all humanity and the city or state polis form an inclusive duality which highlights the tension between these poles, how they make each other politically possible, place each other in question, stabilize each other, and how they can be lived individually and collectively.

(2)   The cosmopolitan enlightener Kant published a text in 1784 which, in Patrick Bahner's apt description, 'is a secret founding text of the present'. In his essay 'Idea for a Universal History with a Cosmopolitan Intent', Kant pursues two goals: first, he transforms the longing for perpetual peace cherished by followers of the Enlightenment into a quasi-evolutionary theory of world citizenship and, second, he captures it in concise juridical categories:

It is, indeed, a strange and for all appearances absurd scheme to want to write a history based on an idea of how the course of the world must go if it is to approach a certain rational goal; it seems that such an attitude can only result in a *romance*. If one may nonetheless assume that nature does not proceed without a plan and a final objective, even in the play of human freedom, this idea can still be useful; and while we are too short-sighted to penetrate to the hidden mechanism of her workings, this idea may still serve as a guiding thread for presenting an otherwise planless *aggregate* of human actions as a system, at least in the large. (Kant 1983: 38)

Kant's optimistic historical argument is realistic because it takes as its foundation the anarchy in relations between states and their tendency to become embroiled in military conflicts. Thus Kant in his essay 'Towards Perpetual Peace' begins with state law and international law and grounds a *jus cosmopolitica* beyond and between them. When the constitution in every state is republican and when the international law of free states has a federal form, then a third domain of right, the right to hospitality, can be added to them. Thus Kant's arguments are neither trans-state nor transnational but ground the legitimacy of cosmopolitan law under the presuppositions of enlightened optimism and of a world of states which is evolving towards the republican federal principle.

(3)   Kant's outline of a modern republican order with a cosmopolitan intent already takes aim at the horror of war and violence which has left a trail of blood through the centuries. At the end of the Second World War, Karl Jaspers and Hannah Arendt, with the evidence of the state-sanctioned and organized extermination of the Jews before them, were confronted with previously unimaginable examples of bestial savagery. In their subsequent discussions concerning political reconciliation and forgiveness of guilt, Jaspers and Arendt explore in an exemplary fashion in their letters (Arendt and Jaspers 1992) the associated philosophical, political and legal questions. Both take the 'breakdown in civilization' of the Holocaust as their starting point. Whereas Jaspers speaks of 'metaphysical guilt' which can be atoned by authentic repentance, Hannah Arendt emphasizes the political aspect of responsibility which has no need of 'authenticity'. Every action, she argues, becomes entangled in the irreversibility of its effects. Not only God must forgive, but human beings must forgive human beings and they must do so publicly, because only in this way can the ability to go on acting be retrieved. If that is true in general, then it is particularly true of the monstrous crime of the Holocaust. True forgiveness, as Jacques Derrida argues, consists in forgiving the unforgivable. If forgiveness only forgives the forgivable, then the idea of forgiveness will disappear. It is the historically novel category of 'crimes against humanity' that enables us to trace the dilemmas of political cosmopolitanism as an answer to the Holocaust.

These 'cosmopolitan moments' (whose argumentative richness I have abridged in a drastic fashion) exhibit three weaknesses. They remain within a normative legal horizon, which means, first, that we currently lack a sufficiently complex *political theory* of cosmopolitanism; second, issues of *empirical-analytical* cosmopolitanism do not feature in existing debates; and, third, *fundamental ambiguities* that break out with the cosmopolitanization of reality are touched on but are not systematically uncovered and explored. The latter point will be briefly sketched here before we examine it in detail in chapter 5.

4.2   The human rights regime between perpetual peace and perpetual war

The human rights regime is the key example of how the distinction between the national and the international is being superseded and the internal cosmopolitanization of national societies is being promoted, and how the grammar of the social and the political is thereby being rewritten. A consequence is the globalization of the self-obligation to respect human rights, however defined – on pain of their being implemented by others (with military force if necessary) – and the basic norms of democracy everywhere in the world. The internalization of human rights on a global scale is destabilizing despotic regimes from within and from without. The universalism of human rights produces not only a national legitimacy deficit but also a power deficit, because despotic rule can no longer refine its system of oppression behind secure sovereign borders. Equality, reciprocity and the universalism of law strip states of the attributes of exclusive power and unlimited self-determination. Dictators can be forced to account for their actions and face prosecution, which also means that ruling elites are being stripped of their inviolability and the privileges of power.

As long as a world government does not exist, human rights and the authorities who pass judgement on whether they are respected or violated produce, grant or withhold legitimacy, and thereby – this is the obverse side – expose states, countries and regions to the 'legitimate' military interventions of other states. The language of human rights changes the foundations of world politics because it pervades all levels and domains of national politics and society and opens them up to external assessment, control and intervention. From the local through the national to the global level, conflicts and their regulation are being reconceptualized. What used to be local conflicts are now being internationalized and politically globalized from within, just as are national conflicts. Human rights hollow out apparently permanent boundaries and impose new boundary-lines and selectivities which conform to the logic of power rather than the logic of law.

The key insight is that the human rights regime has a profoundly double-edged impact. It not only makes possible new forms of conflict regulation beyond borders, but it also opens the door to 'humanitarian interventions' in other countries. Like an erupting volcano, it covers the earth with a red-hot lava of military conflicts. Because human rights must overcome national resistance, the promise of pacification and stability through human rights – Kant's 'perpetual peace' – can easily flip over into depacification and destabilization though perpetual war. Only a devil's advocate who questions well-meaning cosmopolitanism as to its emancipatory function and its misuse can open the debate over the ethics and politics of cosmopolitanism.

2

The Truth of Others:
On the Cosmopolitan Treatment
of Difference – Distinctions,
Misunderstandings, Paradoxes

The cosmopolitanization of reality, as I argued in the previous chapter, is not the result of a cunning conspiracy on the part of 'global capitalists' or an 'American play for world domination', but an unforeseen social effect of actions directed to other ends performed by human beings operating within a network of global interdependence risks. This often coerced, and generally unseen and unwanted, cosmopolitanism of side effect cancels the equation of the nation-state with national society and gives rise to transnational forms of life and communication, allocations of responsibility, and internal and external representations of individual and collective identities. The nation-state is increasingly besieged and permeated by a planetary network of interdependencies, by ecological, economic and terrorist risks, which connect the separate worlds of developed and underdeveloped countries. To the extent that this historical situation is reflected in a global public sphere, a new historical reality arises, a cosmopolitan outlook in which people view themselves simultaneously as part of a threatened world and as part of their local situations and histories.

This provides the starting point for a realistic cosmopolitanism, a cosmopolitan realism. But what distinguishes the cosmopolitan outlook from a universalistic, relativistic or multicultural outlook? And what makes the cosmopolitan outlook at the beginning of the twenty-first century 'realistic', in contrast to cosmopolitan idealism? These are the questions that will be addressed in this chapter.

Simplifying somewhat, 'realistic' (in the sense of the foregoing argument) is synonymous with 'social scientific'. Realistic cosmopolitanism, abstracted from the history of philosophy, should be understood in terms of a fundamental problem of the second modernity: how do 'societies' deal with 'difference' and 'borders' under conditions of global interdependence crises? I will develop two arguments in response to this question.

First, I distinguish between different social modalities of dealing with difference – universalism, relativism, ethnicism, nationalism, cosmopolitanism, multiculturalism, etc. – which are in turn correlated with historical social formations – first modernity, second modernity, postmodernity. What thereby emerges is, among other things, that universalistic practices, for example (but also relativism, etc.), involve conflicting impulses. Universalism obliges us to respect others as equals in principle, yet for that very reason it does not involve any requirement that would inspire curiosity or respect for what makes others different. On the contrary, the particularity of others is sacrificed to an assumed universal equality which denies its own origins and interests. Universalism thereby becomes two-faced: respect and hegemony, rationality and terror. Similarly, the emphasis on context and on the relativity of standpoints springs from an impulse to acknowledge the difference of others; but when it is absolutized in thought and practice it flips over into an incommensurability of perspectives which results in pre-established ignorance.

Second, realistic cosmopolitanism – this is the conclusion – should be conceived, elaborated and practised not in an exclusive manner but in an *inclusive* relation to universalism, contextualism, nationalism, transnationalism, etc. It is this particular combination of semantic elements which the cosmopolitan outlook shares with the universalistic, relativistic and national outlooks and which by the same token distinguishes it from these other approaches.

Realistic cosmopolitanism presupposes a *universalistic minimum*. This includes substantive norms which must be upheld at all costs: that women and children should not be sold or enslaved, that people should be able to express their views about God or their government freely without being tortured or fearing for their lives – these norms are so self-evident that no violation of them could meet with cosmopolitan tolerance. We can speak of 'cosmopolitan common sense' when we have good reasons to believe that a majority of human beings would be willing to defend these minimum universalist norms wherever they have force, if called upon to do so.

On the other hand, realistic cosmopolitanism includes universal procedural norms, for they alone make it possible to regulate the treatment of difference in a cross-cultural manner. Accordingly, realistic cosmopolitanism must also confront the painful question of its own limits: should recognition of the freedom of others apply equally to despots and democrats, to anti-cosmopolitan predators as well as to those they prey upon? In other words, realistic cosmopolitans must come to terms with the idea – especially alien to cosmopolitan thought – that, in making recognition of others central to its conception of society and politics, cosmopolitanism makes enemies who can only be checked by force. Hence it must embrace the contradiction that, in order to uphold its basic principles of defending individual liberties and safeguarding difference, it may be necessary to violate them.

Cosmopolitan realism does not negate nationalism but presupposes it and transforms it into a cosmopolitan nationalism. Without the stabilizing factors that nationalism provides in dealing with difference, cosmopolitanism is in danger of losing itself in a philosophical never-never land.

1   On the social treatment of difference

1.1   *The two faces of universalism*

If we consider from a historical perspective how the Western world addresses questions of difference at the beginning of the twenty-first century, taking our orientation from such influential books as Samuel Huntington's *The Clash of Civilizations and the Remaking of World Order* (1996) and Francis Fukuyama's *The End of History* (1989), we discover to our astonishment how closely the debates at the legendary conference of Valladolid in 1550 – which concerned the extent to which the Amerindians were different from, and inferior to, Europeans – resemble contemporary debates.

Huntington's thesis is that, whereas the main lines of conflict during the Cold War were openly political and derived their urgency from imperatives of national and international security, today the lines of conflict track major cultural antagonisms in which clashes of values between civilizations feature prominently. Culture, identity and religious faith, which used to be subordinate to strategic political and military imperatives, now set the priorities on the international political agenda. We are witnessing an invasion of politics by culture. Dividing lines between civilizations are mutating into threats to international stability and global order. The democratic values of the West and the premodern values of the Islamic world are confronting and colliding with one another in ever more menacing and hostile ways, both within nation-states and between different global regions.

As for Fukuyama, his answer to the question of the future of the Western model of liberal democracy, simplifying somewhat, runs as follows: with the collapse of Soviet communism there is no longer any alternative to a liberal market economy *à la américaine*. 'Democratic capitalism' is the only true vision of modernity and, in virtue of its inner logic, it is destined to pervade and refashion the whole world. In this way, a universal civilization will arise that brings history to an end.

These two ways of dealing with difference had already confronted each other at the Valladolid conference more than four centuries ago. The Aristotelian philosopher Juan Ginés de Sepúlveda and the Dominican priest Bartolomé de Las Casas represented, respectively, the *universalism of difference* and the *universalism of sameness*. Sepúlveda argued, like the political theorist Huntington today, that human beings are characterized by a *hierarchy of values*, whereas Las Casas, like the political scientist Fukuyama, maintained that *similarity of civilizations* is the norm among human beings. Accordingly, the philosopher Sepúlveda emphasized the differences between Europeans and Amerindians. The decisive facts for him were that the latter went naked, sacrificed human victims, did not make use of horses or donkeys, and were ignorant of money and the Christian religion. He divided the human species into contemporaneous peoples at different levels of culture. For him, difference was synonymous with inferiority, from which he concluded, first, that viewing barbaric America through the lens of civilized Spain revealed that some men were the gods of others, and it followed, second, that to subjugate and exploit them was a pedagogical duty.

Similarly, Huntington conceives the current relationship between the West and its cultural other, Islamic civilization, as one of *vertical difference* involving two moments: 'others' are denied the status of sameness and equality, and consequently are accorded a subordinate and inferior status within a hierarchical ordering. From here it is but a short step to denigrating members of other cultures as 'barbarians' and treating them accordingly, whether the goal is to convert them to the true values of Christianity or democratic capitalism or to counter the threat they represent with appropriate military means. What is striking is that, whereas the sixteenth-century Aristotelian philosopher was almost bursting with self-confident superiority, Huntington's alarmist diagnosis is proclaimed with an apocalyptic undertone. We risk a new 'decline of the West' unless we join the crusade against the 'Islamic threat' in defence of Western values.

The Dominican father Las Casas eloquently defended the rights of the Amerindians who, he argued, were remarkably similar to Europeans. They fulfilled the ideals of the Christian religion, which recognizes no differences in skin colour or ethnic or racial origin. They were exceedingly friendly and modest, they respected norms of sociability, the values of family and their own traditions, and were thus better prepared than many other nations on earth to receive the word of God and bear witness to its truth. In the name of Christian universalism, this priest vehemently opposed the worldview of hierarchical differentiation. The contrary principle to the hierarchical subordination and inferiority of others affirms the dissolution of differences, whether as an anthropological fact or as the result of the progress of civilization (modernization).

How difference is treated, therefore, reveals the thoroughly Janus-faced character of universalism which is already evident in the position of the Dominican: our relations with others should not be governed by their difference but by their sameness. From the universalizing point of view, all human forms of life are situated within a single order of civilization, with the result that cultural differences are either overcome or excluded. Accordingly, the universalistic project is hegemonic: the voice of others is granted a hearing only as the voice of sameness, as self-confirmation, self-reflection and monologue. If this were translated into the terms of an African universalism, it would imply that the true white man has a black soul.

Even the United States, which is home to all ethnicities, peoples and religions, has an ambivalent relation to difference. To be an American means to live in immediate proximity with difference, which often means living with the 'Huntingtonian fear' that emphasizing ethnic differences would spell the decline of the West, that ethnic differences can never be bridged and that, unless difference is overcome through national assimilation, the chaos roiling just beneath the surface could explode at any moment. Precisely because ethnic difference is an integral part of American national consciousness, America is continually gripped by the fear that it is a nation of peoples who cannot be combined in the 'melting pot', and this leads to demands for sameness and conformism. This is what underlies the *dialectic of difference and conformity* that nationalism opposes to the threat of ethnic dissolution: the more divisive and the more unbridgeable ethnic differences appear and are publicly represented as being, the louder the calls for the conformism of a national ethos (communitarianism).[1]

From St Paul through Kant and Popper to Lyotard and Rorty, we can discern different variants of the same dialectic which involves limiting the danger of ethnic difference by stressing a universally binding humanity – in other words, by recourse to Western universalism. From this perspective, really existing ethnic diversity does not have the intrinsic value that universalism claims for itself almost as a matter of course. The obligation to respect difference is not affirmed; rather, what is affirmed is that we are all in the end equally human beings with a claim to equal rights. In cases of conflict when ethnic diversity places universal human values in question we must defend universalism against particularism.

To clarify this let us again take the example of Christian universalism with its opposition between 'Christians and heathens'. This universalism draws its power from the fact that it liberates all human beings from the constraints of skin colour, ethnic origin, gender, age, nationality and social class, and addresses them as equals before God in the existential community of Christian believers. In this way the duality denies the asymmetry that it posits: 'The contrast between all of humanity and the baptized is no longer quantifiable as were the previous categorical terms, but instead involves a duplication of the reference group. Every person should become a Christian if he wishes to escape eternal damnation' (Koselleck 1985: 175, translation amended).

In this way, imperial Christian universalism set free emancipatory impulses which can be traced back to the movements for the emancipation of slaves. Feminist movements have also appealed to St Paul. But here, too, the Janus face of universalism is evident: the blackness of blacks, the Jewishness of Jews, and the womanhood of women are for the first time stigmatized as morally inferior 'particularisms' in the boundary-negating universalism of Christianity and the Enlightenment. To reject sameness is, on this view, to exclude or efface difference. Those who affirm anything other than universalism exclude themselves, whereas the prophets of universal truth and morality always scent chaos and disorder – the divisiveness of ethnic particularisms – whenever universalism is questioned. Those who reject universalism fail to acknowledge its distinctive higher morality, and thereby expose themselves to the charge of amoral or anti-moral particularism.

In this way the particular that each individual represents becomes transfigured and suppressed in the universal. With the same move, the majority elevate their own ethnicity and proclaim their own norms as universal. In societies where whites are dominant, being white means having the privilege of not noticing that one is white. The postulate of abstract identity translates into pressure on those of different ethnicities to yield to this particular claim to equality and renounce the position of difference. In the national framework all attempts to connect universalism and particularism end in the unreasonable demand that the true black person is not black, the true Jew is not Jewish, or the true woman is the non-female woman. If blacks, Jews, Chinese, Japanese and women still call themselves black, Jewish, Chinese, Japanese or female, they lack theoretical and philosophical sanction, they are not up-to-date, they are conservative and prisoners of an 'antiquated' self-image. The self-understanding of the 'particular' is only 'ethnically correct', hence not ethnically human, when it emancipates itself from its ethnicity and submits to the official model of the non-black black, the non-Jewish Jew, and the non-female woman.

To formulate the point in the terminology of mainstream sociology: difference is a *relic* that advancing modernization ultimately reduces to irrelevance. Both Las Casas and Fukuyama conceive of the disappearance of diversity in terms of a civilizing *process* – in the one case, through conversion to Christianity and baptism, in the other, through the contagious superiority of Western values (free markets, democracy). Then as now, the imperative is to exclude alternatives. The only way forward is Christian/Western universalism. Seen in this light, the 'end of history', somewhat ironically, had already begun more than four hundred years ago.

However, it belongs to the Janus-faced character of Western universalism that it alone demands respect for principles of liberty and equality on a global scale. It is not possible to proclaim global human rights on the one hand, and to have a Muslim, African, Jewish, Christian or Asian charter of human rights on the other. Respecting others in their difference and their history means acknowledging them as members of the same humanity, not of some other, second-class humanity. Human rights invalidate the right to wall off cultures from 'external assault'. Respect for traditions that violate human rights would be tantamount to disrespect for their victims.

This creates a dilemma that is not easily resolved. Those who raise questions of global responsibility must today once again face the temptations and dangers of 'colonialism'. What used to be called colonialism is now called 'humanitarian intervention'. The problem is whether, in a world of global interdependence risks, the affairs of others can be regarded as simply their own business and their own responsibility. Or is there no other option than to interfere in the 'internal affairs of all' if we don't want to betray 'our own' values and to jeopardize 'our own' security?

This dilemma can be illustrated by the example of the Western military involvement in Africa, specifically in Liberia, which was being debated in the summer of 2003. For the people of Liberia, who for two decades had to endure war, banditry and a succession of criminal regimes, such an intervention can't come soon enough. They are even clamouring for a military intervention of the West under United States leadership to restore order. Can we resist this call without, confronted with a wave of cosmopolitan pity, appearing as cold-hearted ignoramuses who could bring themselves to invade Iraq because of oil interests but stand accused of double standards in Liberia where there is nothing more to be gained than a bloody nose? Is Hegel's verdict still valid: 'here we leave Africa, never to mention it again'? Is it still possible to assume that the 'African barbarians' who are up to all sorts of shadowy mischief 'down there' must live with the consequences of their self-generated disasters? Or does not precisely universalism in the end compel us to practise a hybrid 'human rights colonialism' in the shape of 'UN protectorates' in more and more parts of the world, first Bosnia, Kosovo and Macedonia, then Afghanistan and Iraq, and now perhaps Liberia?

1.2   The two faces of relativism

To oppose universalism is to support relativism – or so it appears to those who think in terms of either/or alternatives. Whereas universalism transcends the boundaries of cultural difference, relativism permits, constructs and imposes new boundaries. Where and how these boundaries are drawn depends on whether relativism allies itself with nationalism (national relativism), the unity of the local (local relativism) or culturalism (cultural relativism). If universalism seeks to transcend differences, relativism seeks to emphasize them. Accordingly, it emphatically rejects what universalism affirms: that it is possible to develop and gain recognition for universal norms. The validity of universal norms presupposes Nietzsche's will to power. Hence, from the relativist's perspective, universalism and hegemony are merely two sides of the same coin.

Relativism, like universalism, is Janus-faced. Universalism, as we have seen, has the drawback that it forces its standpoint on others, but the advantage that it takes the fate of others as seriously as its own. The Janus face of relativism can be understood in analogous terms. On the one hand, a dose of relativism can serve as an antidote to universalistic hubris. Relativism and contextual thinking sharpen our respect for cultural difference and can make taking the perspective of members of other cultures both attractive and necessary. However, if relativism and contextualism are absolutized, this attentiveness to others turns into its opposite: any exchange of perspectives is rejected on the grounds that it is simply impossible. The instrument we use to close ourselves off from others and to reject any outsider's perspective on 'our own' culture is the *principle of incommensurability*. If everything is relative, then the conquerors have their perspective, the conquered theirs, and the observing public still others. Between them all yawn more or less insurmountable chasms. The result is a world in which everyone is who or what they are and a disorienting relativism arises for which worldviews are so much navel-gazing.

The unintentional irony of the relativist incommensurability thesis is that it is almost indistinguishable from an essentialistic worldview. It (mis)leads us into a postmodern quasi-essentialism which agrees with straightforward essentialism that we must accept things as they are.

Relativism universalized is a polite term for non-interference. Here the perpetual (non-)peace of perpetual relativism holds sway. The desire for a quiet life is justified with the argument that the chasms between cultures are too wide to be bridged. This may be tendentious and false as regards the motivation for relativism. But the incommensurability assumption amounts to a non-intervention pact between cultures that can easily degenerate into violence in a world in which non-intervention is impossible because intervention has always been the norm.

What is more, strict relativism is historically and empirically false. On the one hand, it misunderstands or distorts the facts of interwoven histories; on the other, it is blind to the fact that drawing boundaries between cultural spaces, something presupposed and reified by relativism, is a European project and a product of the first modernity, the national modernity of the nineteenth century (McNeill 1985; Said 1978; McGrane 1989; Gilroy 2000).

Contextualist universalism, by contrast, takes the contrary fact as its point of departure, namely, that cultural intermingling is a historical reality (in fact, the historical norm) and that non-intervention is an impossibility. For this is precisely what is meant by the assertion that we are living in an era of global interdependence crises. All attempts to take refuge in a fantasy of separate worlds are grotesque and unintentionally comical. The world has mutated irreversibly into a caricature of a (non-)conversation whose participants are speaking at once with, at and past one another. We must avoid invoking false alternatives here. The opposite of the incommensurability thesis is not that intercultural dialogue is actually taking place. The counter-thesis is that there are no separate worlds. In view of the motley global 'context without connection', non-dialogue and non-intervention can seem positively idyllic.

Cosmopolitan realism supersedes the non-intervention pact predicated on the impossibility of intervention. It asserts that the dubious pleasures of incommensurability are illusory escape routes from the dangers of our involuntarily shared intercultural destiny which is the product of a self-endangering civilization. Accordingly, the only live issue is not the whether but the how of intervention and mutual interference – do we play along with it or try to resist it? We cannot remain uninvolved in the suffering on the African continent because there is no Africa 'down there' beyond the range of the West's security and responsibility. That the truth is not absolute but relative does not mean that there is no truth. It means that the truth has to be continually redefined in accordance with changing events and circumstances.

1.3   The two faces of nationalism

The ways in which nationalism strategically manages the social treatment of difference can be understood as a combination of the strategies already mentioned, namely, hierarchical difference, sameness universalism and relativism. Hierarchical difference prevails in external relations and sameness universalism in internal affairs, whereas relativism is a territorial relativism that coincides with national borders. Nationalism denies difference internally, while affirming, producing and stabilizing it externally. There is a politically effective solidarity with those like us, hence the duty to pay taxes and the entitlement to social welfare, educational opportunities and political participation; but this comes to an end at the national garden fence and may even function in such a way as to deny other nations equal rights, to stigmatize them as barbarian, and thereby itself become barbaric.

This territorially restricted historical 'compromise' between universalism, hierarchical difference and relativism is the standard way of dealing with difference in the first modernity. The Janus face of nationalism appears not only in the familiar way in which the opposition between 'us' and 'the barbarians' is used to promote national equality and integration, but also in the relation between – to use the terminology of the national outlook – the 'majority' and the 'minority'.

1.4   The two faces of ethnicism

One argument recently employed to avert the threat of global interdependence comes, interestingly enough, from the arsenal of anti-colonialism: South America for South Americans, Cuba for Cubans, Algeria for Algerians, Africa for Africans. Paradoxically, this appeal to ethnic territorial autonomy is also being taken up by Europeans to mobilize against an imminent invasion of 'the Turks' or 'the Russians', etc., with the slogan 'Europe for Europeans'.

However, the Janus-faced character of the new ethnicism is all too evident. More and more commonalities are being declared invalid. When the consciousness of freedom inculcated by modernity, which has become an integral part of personal identity, is combined with extreme poverty and discrimination, the excluded turn the argument around and close themselves off in turn. This intersection of the consciousness of freedom with systematic violations of human dignity is the historical birthplace of the 'ugly citizen', a figure not foreseen by standard genealogies of the citizen, who is always represented in political philosophy as the 'good' citizen. But in many parts of the world there is the danger that autistic ethnicism, charged with the modern consciousness of freedom, will deliberately wreck the national compromise, which at least had the merit of recognizing minority rights.

Non-violent coexistence with those who are culturally different can be legitimately demanded of everyone in a civilized society. Anyone who thinks that he has a human right to declare neighbours to be aliens and expel them on the grounds that he has suffered historical injustices cannot expect to enjoy the tolerance he denies to others by his actions. Neither violence nor systematic violations of our dignity can justify us in suddenly treating our neighbours as aliens on some pretext and using violence against them.

If a Palestinian woman blows herself up in a café filled with Israeli women and children, then we must – according to the understanding, though surely not excusing, argument one sometimes hears – also take into account that here we are dealing with 'unfortunate wretches' whose actions reflect their own history of repression; and you cannot expect people who have suffered such humiliations to grasp the fact that blowing up children is not, strictly speaking, permissible. But in this way the demarcation and exclusion that result from highlighting ethnicity set in train a dynamic of violence in which even minimum standards of civilization count for nothing.

2   What is 'realistic' about realistic cosmopolitanism? Whereas universalism, relativism and nationalism are based on the either/or principle, cosmopolitanism rests on the both/and principle

Cosmopolitanism, as we have seen, basically means the recognition of difference, both internally and externally. Cultural differences are neither arranged in a hierarchy of difference nor subsumed into a universalism, but are accepted for what they are. What this means in particular must now be shown against the background of the modes of dealing socially with difference already identified. The initial thesis is that debates concerning universalism versus relativism, sameness versus difference, and so forth, generally follow the either/or principle. Viewed from the standpoint of cosmopolitan realism, 'either universalism or relativism', 'either difference or sameness', etc., prove to be dead-end debates between false alternatives. They can be overcome by rethinking the various social strategies for dealing with difference in accordance with the both/and principle, and in the process drawing new boundaries and establishing new connections between them. Realistic cosmopolitanism should not be understood and developed in opposition to universalism, relativism, nationalism and ethnicism, but as their summation or synthesis. Contrary to how their proponents generally understand them, these social strategies for dealing with difference do not exclude, but actually mutually presuppose, correct, limit and support each other. It is impossible to imagine a practically tenable, realistic cosmopolitanism without universalism *and* relativism *and* nationalism *and* ethnicism – provided that each is understood in a specific way! What is 'realistic' about this new cosmopolitan realism follows in part from the mutual correction of these semantic elements, in part from the fact that their combination is greater than the sum of the parts. In other words, universalism does not remain universalism, contextualism, contextualism, etc.; rather, they acquire a new meaning when they are combined in cosmopolitan realism. This must now be shown, at least in outline.

2.1 Neither Huntington nor Fukuyama: cosmopolitanism means what is excluded by both positions: the affirmation of the other as both different and the same

Since cosmopolitanism recognizes difference, it must differentiate itself from universalism and its totalizing impulses, yet also look for ways to make difference universally acceptable. In itself, universalism is as ignorant as it is indispensable. Let us return to the controversy at Valladolid, in which the either/or between the universalism of difference – advocated by the Aristotelian philosopher – and the universalism of sameness – advocated by the Dominican father – found exemplary expression. Las Casas's progressiveness has often been underlined, whereas Sepúlveda's incipient racism has been widely criticized. But from a cosmopolitan perspective what both thinkers shared is no less interesting, and for two reasons. Neither of the opposed positions could allow that the Amerindians were both different and the same. Moreover, both positions presupposed a universal criterion of value that logically transformed differences into superiority and inferiority. Even the benign Christian Las Casas accepted the sameness and equality of the Amerindians only because in his eyes they were willing and able to acknowledge the universal truth of Christianity. The duality – here all human beings, there those redeemed through Christ – can only be overcome if the dichotomy between Christians and heathens is not permanent, but can be thought of and actually be made superable in time. The barbarian can be baptized and partake in the universal truth of Christianity. Or, to put it in Fukuyama's terms, non-Western civilizations can be 'modernized' and achieve the salvation of Western universalism through baptism in democracy and the market economy.

Cosmopolitanism, realistically understood, means what is excluded by both of these positions: the affirmation of the other as both different and the same. In this way the falseness of the alternative between hierarchical difference and universal equality is revealed, for both racism and apodictic universalism are thereby overcome. Cosmopolitanism means challenging the future viability of an apparently timeless racism. But that also means representing the ethnocentric universalism of the West as an anachronism that can be overcome.

2.2 Postmodern particularism

Realistic cosmopolitanism cannot remain content with demarcating itself from the totalitarian features of universalism. It also needs universalism if it is to avoid falling into the opposite trap of *postmodern particularism*. The latter refers to a strategy of tolerating difference by absolutizing it without any supporting framework of binding norms. This approach combines the principle of sameness with the relativistic principle of the incommensurability of perspectives, and hence ultimately affirms the impossibility of ordering criteria. Simplifying drastically, one could call this the postmodern project. Cosmopolitanism without universalism – this much is clear – is in danger of slipping into this kind of multicultural randomness. But how can we devise a limited, relativistic or contextual universalism that successfully squares the circle of affirming universal norms while neutralizing their imperialistic sting?

2.3 The reality test of cosmopolitanism consists in the common defence against evils

One answer to this question consists in defining cosmopolitan norms *negatively* rather than positively; a second appeals to a *procedural* universalism; and a third explores the possibilities and ambivalences of a *contextual* universalism.

The realism of realistic cosmopolitanism is perhaps best grasped if one attempts to characterize it not by what it aims at but by what it seeks to avoid at all costs, namely, fascistic conformism [*Gleichschaltung*], systematic violation of human dignity, genocide and crimes against humanity. Since cosmopolitanism respects diversity, the key political question for cosmopolitans is: Are they even capable of decision and action? What are their *actions*? What kind of connection can be made between the recognition of diversity and the compulsion to act? The answer is that the reality or practical test of cosmopolitanism is the *common defence against evils*. To what extent does this negative characteristic found a commonality reaching across borders, one which does not ask, for example, whether it is permissible to attack a sovereign member of the UN which is conducting a total war against its own minorities but simply takes the appropriate actions (as in the case of the war in Kosovo)?

The most diverse kinds of cosmopolitanism can find a place under the umbrella of this negative cosmopolitanism, assuming they all accept a second basic norm, that of procedural universalism. This holds that specific procedures and institutions are required for regulating transnational conflicts. That violent disputes can at most be pacified in this way, but never consensually resolved, highlights the ambivalences and dilemmas of the second modernity as diagnosed by realistic cosmopolitanism. Thus cosmopolitanism is another word for conflict, not for consensus. In this sense we would have to give the 'ideal speech situation' (Jürgen Habermas) a realistic twist and develop a *conflict theory* of the truth of others in a self-destructive civilization.

Negative and procedural universalism allows room for a variety of 'contextual universalisms' (Beck 2000b: 81). This signifies relations between what are generally regarded as exclusive oppositions. On a cosmopolitan construction, by contrast, they can enter into mutually confirming and correcting relations. Thus contextualism serves as an antidote to the suppression of difference propagated by universalism, and universalism as an antidote to the incommensurability of perspectives though which contextualism traps itself in the false idyll of autonomous relative worlds. Law serves as a good example for contextual universalism and the associated conflicts. Although Western in origin, human rights and their universalistic validity claim are neither alien nor irrelevant to non-Western cultures. Rather, local groups connect and affirm local and national sources of power though contextual interpretations of human rights that draw on their own cultural and political traditions and religions. New national-cosmopolitan and local-cosmopolitan identities arise out of the contextualization of universal law; indeed, such translations are examples of an *active* internal cosmopolitanization of national and local domains.

An understanding of contextual universalism may lead to a 'cosmopolitanism of humility' (Scott L. Malcomson) and responsiveness, in contrast to what might be called a pedagogical 'cosmopolitanism of impatience' more in tune with Western impulses. In the debates and activities of non-governmental organizations (NGOs), non-Western cultural relativists and Western universalists often find themselves on opposite sides. Such opposition was challenged and overcome in an exemplary manner at the 1993 human rights conference in Vienna by 'contextual universalists' in the form of an alliance between African, Latin American and Asian NGOs. Under discussion were extremely controversial issues, such as violence against women, including marital violence and incest, the extent to which respecting human rights can be a task for UN peace missions, and so forth. The synthesis of contextualism and universalism worked out by the NGO alliance for combating domestic violence was especially noteworthy because it was directed against both Western arrogance and the expectations of their own home governments. Women from the Islamic world associated the concept of universal human rights, such as the right to Western-style education, with the claim that they were first of all Muslims and wanted to continue thinking and acting as Muslims. Many women, even those who described themselves as secular, defended women who have chosen to wear headscarves and embrace a conservative theology. This both/and form of cosmopolitanism brings to light the political and cultural creative resources that contextualist variants of universalism can tap. It may even be able to prevent the new cosmopolitanism from degenerating into a 'Eurocentric, "rationalist", secular-democratic jihad' (Malcomson 1998: 237).

Malcomson reports that on one hot afternoon in Dakar he happened to be in the US embassy where a diverse group had assembled to discuss questions concerning human rights. Experts flown in for the occasion spoke about democracy and freedom of opinion and made thoroughly predictable speeches. The assembled Senegalese listened politely but, when their turn came to speak, a man in military uniform began by praising the unique character of Senegalese culture, citing polygamy as an example. But he undercut his position by chuckling continually as he spoke, showing that he did not really believe what he was saying. Everyone else, both men and women, laughed as well. The remainder of the Senegalese contributions focused on the simple question of whether every human being has a right not to die of starvation. The American experts had seen the question coming but in the end had little to say in reply except 'no'. The Senegalese continued to press the question until it was clear to all present what was going on and they erupted in laughter. The joke which everyone suddenly got was, of course, that the important issue of human rights was being discussed without even mentioning the central right not to die of starvation. From a Senegalese perspective this revealed a serious defect typical of the white ethnic group, a defect which made them feel sorry for the Western tribe. They did not attack the American experts but tried to help them with a generosity and humour that can only be described as 'cosmopolitan' (cf. Malcomson 1998: 242).

2.4   Is ethnic cosmopolitanism possible? The historicization of difference

Cosmopolitanism and ethnicity, which also appear to be mutually exclusive, can nevertheless enter into relations with one another. The resulting cosmopolitan ethnicity or ethnic cosmopolitanism is opposed to the universalist dissolution of difference; but it is also opposed to the ontological emphasis on ethnicity and it facilitates the historical and contextual recognition of difference.

As Stuart Hall has shown in some detail (Hall 1991), there has been a 'cultural self-empowerment of the marginal and the local'. Marginalized groups have rediscovered their hidden and suppressed histories. Difference is no longer universalized out of existence or viewed as an ontological given, but *historicized*. Thus cosmopolitan realism rests on a twofold negation: it negates both the universalist negation of and the essentialist insistence on ethnic difference.

2.5   Realistic cosmopolitanism presupposes nationalism, nationalism presupposes cosmopolitanism

It is ultimately a mistake to accord too much prominence to the opposition between cosmopolitanism and nationalism. For the opposite is also true:

'Cosmopolitanism also requires a certain degree of nationalism, because this is the best and most reliable mechanism for the institutional production and stabilization of *collective* difference. Where such stabilizers of difference are lacking, there is a danger that cosmopolitanism will veer off into substantive universalism' (Grande 2003: 5). Johann Gottlieb Fichte remarked that seeing cannot see itself and proposed equipping seeing with 'an eye' so that it might become reflexive. Analogously, if the national outlook is equipped with a 'cosmopolitan eye', the always threatening inversion of the national outlook into the stigmatization of others as barbarians can be averted by opening oneself externally to other nations, but also internally towards minorities.

Isn't one of the outstanding achievements of nationalism that for every problem it finds a scapegoat instead of a solution? Only a nationalism modified in a cosmopolitan direction can exploit the political potential for cooperation between states, and thereby regain the ability to solve *national* problems under conditions of interdependence. A fusion of national and international strategies is necessary to check the potential for ethnic violence created by globalization both internally and externally, but without dismissing difference as a 'premodern prejudice'.

Cosmopolitanism acquires its realism and its historical specificity, its ability to persuade and to seduce, from the way in which the different social strategies for dealing with difference interpenetrate and become so fused that their cosmopolitan impulses are reinforced and their anti-cosmopolitan impulses are weakened and held in check.[2]

2.6   *The category of 'transnationality' is the contrary of all concepts of social order, and therein lies its political, but also its analytical, provocation*

If the strategies of nationalism and cosmopolitanism in the social treatment of difference do not just contradict but also mutually complement and correct each other, then we must ask how 'transnationality' relates to the social treatment of difference. Is there a contradiction between the ordering schema nation/international and the ordering schema transnational/cosmopolitan?

As we have seen, the principle of the nation presupposes the principle of internationality. A single nation whose borders and sovereignty are not recognized by other nations is as unthinkable as a single world people or world state. Nations only exist in the plural. Internationality makes nationality possible. The field formed by the two concepts – nationality and internationality – forms an *exclusive, total* unity. The national–international exclusionary order is opposed to the conceptual order *transnational* and *cosmopolitan*. Transnationality signifies forms of life and practice that replace the national either/or with a co-national both/and. Co-national (hence non-national) forms of life, thought and practice which do not respect the boundaries between states are transnational. Among innumerable examples are the Hmong, who endeavour to forge and preserve their transnational unity across many countries in the world.

The anthropologist Louisa Schein made an ethnographic study of a 'Hmong symposium' in St Paul, Minnesota, in the USA, with the aim of analysing the scope for constituting a transnational Hmong identity in the force-field of international rivalry between the USA and China.

There are an estimated 25 million Hmong scattered across diverse countries throughout the world, and accordingly this congress was decorated with four flags on one side – USA, China, Vietnam, Canada – and five on the other – Argentina, Australia, France, Thailand and Laos. The motto of the conference was: 'In search of a shared future in questions of culture, economics and education'.

The surprising result of this study is that the expected opposition between national and transnational was not only not confirmed; rather, the USA and China are using the transnationality of this Asian diaspora culture to redefine their own nationalities. 'I want to draw attention to a pernicious zero-sum logic that portrays transnationality and the "nation-state" as mutually exclusive and as locked in competition for pragmatic primacy. Why, instead, can these debates not work towards imagining nation-state and transnational as interlocked, enmeshed, mutually constituting?' (Schein 1998: 169f.).

If we follow this line of thought further, there is room for two developments. First, we can imagine a world of *transnational nationalism* in which, if all goes well, a historicized ethnic identity may be opened up simultaneously in national, transnational and cosmopolitan ways through participation in national, political and public spaces that define themselves in exclusive terms. Second, the uncoupling of state and nation prompts the question of what constitutes 'statehood' and how the concept of the state can be opened up to global interdependence and its crises. What alternatives to the mystique of the nation-state does cosmopolitan realism reveal? And how can such concepts as the 'transnational' or 'cosmopolitan state' be developed systematically (Beck 2002a)?

That there are impulses in transnationalization that temper and overcome the sharp differentiation between us and them, and even transnationalize the sphere of state action, is shown by the Schein study. Both China and the USA gave considerable financial support to the Hmong conference. Although there were problems on both sides, Chinese officials viewed their contribution as part of a strategy of opening to the world market, whereas the USA was celebrating its own internal globalization in a double sense: on the one hand, in line with their imputed Americanization, that of consolidating its sphere of influence in global space; on the other – and here the boundaries of the concept 'America' begin to blur – the dream of the American nation is both transnationalized and 'Asianized'. A beautiful example of this is provided by the Hmong Boy Scouts.

One speaker at the symposium stressed the exotic accomplishments of these boys:

I work with a Hmong troop and an American troop. Parents of the American troop want to know what the Hmong secret is. They want to know how you raise such children, how you get them to work hard, be serious at school, listen to adults, be so polite. Hmong Scouting builds on what parents teach. The last thing I've learned about Hmong Scouting is that you must teach Hmong traditions. Many of the boys in the troop have grown up with Power Rangers, Michael Jackson, Michael Jordan, Mortal Kombat. They want to learn about Hmong traditions. We invite their fathers down to teach about music and stories. We've changed from teaching refugee kids about America to teaching American kids about Hmong tradition. (Schein 1998: 183f.)

Who is importing what here, and from whom? Moreover, bearing in mind that Latinos already represent a much larger proportion of the US population than blacks, if we speak of an Americanization of Asia, Europe and Latin America must we not also speak of an Asianization and Latin Americanization of the United States? Perhaps 'transnational Asia' and 'transnational Latin America' have already destabilized and denationalized the national-territorial self-definition of a white, Anglo-Saxon United States to its core. New categories of fusion and interdependence are taking shape, hybrid forms for which the either/or logic of the national has no name, whereas the both/and logic of the transnational and cosmopolitan is still insufficiently conceptually developed. It would be a grave error to construe the national/transnational distinction in accordance with the either/or logic. Schein's study clearly demonstrates that, although the national and transnational ordering paradigms appear contradictory, they also complement and combine with each other in a variety of ways. Behind the façade of enduring nationality, processes of transnationalization are everywhere taking place. And it is precisely the extension of power into the transnational domain that makes possible a redefinition of the national cores behind the façade of nation-state continuity. This all unfolds in a topic-specific way and includes rather than excludes the possibility that a politics of neonational closure is simultaneously declared and put into practice.

For instance, both India and Singapore are attempting to bind 'their' transnationals to their respective national projects by increasingly uncoupling citizenship from residence in the mother country. The Indian diaspora, stretching from Sydney to Silicon Valley, is involved in political and religious debates both in their countries of residence and in the Indian nation-state. The Indian government has devised the legal category of 'non-resident Indians' for these 'foreign Indians' and, in order to encourage 'foreign Indians' to invest in India, accords them special property rights, tax benefits and travel freedoms. Something similar applies in the case of Mexico, Singapore, and Malaysia, among others. Yet such practices go hand in hand with strategies of political closure and renationalization. In Singapore, for example, the financing of local

NGOs by international NGOs and other organizations is forbidden, as is foreign participation in the national mass media. The opening up of the national economy to transnational forces, including the embedding of nations in transnational networks, is accompanied by the closing off of political participation and the media within the nation-state from outside involvement. Cosmopolitan realism must develop a keen eye for this calibrated, selective transnationalization, for simultaneous inclusion and exclusion, transnationalization, denationalization and renationalization.

It is often asked to what extent deterritorialized ethnicity leads to a nationalism beyond frontiers. But the question rests on a false alternative. For transnationalization means a balancing act among political loyalties, which implies an existence involving multiple affiliations and plural nationalisms. The expansion of power associated with transnationalization makes both denationalization and renationalization possible, for the success of the positive-sum game of national-transnational opening leads to contradictions. If the state uncouples citizenship status from residence even in part, it undermines the principle of territorial sovereignty. The national framework is thereby replaced with a transnational one through which a reciprocal relation between rival states (for example, the USA and China) develops. Accordingly, a new arena of conflict arises in which the various national projects overlap and transnational identities and loyalties have to develop and assert themselves in contradictory relations between selective opening and selective closure, denationalization and renationalization (see Schiller 1989; Schiller 1997; Aksoy and Robins 2003; Riccio 2000; Salih 2000; Soysal 2002).

This by no means excludes the essential fact that transnational or cosmopolitan domains of experience undermine the 'naturalness' of ethnic absolutes, both at the national level and at the level of cultural identities. How can this be more precisely theorized? Reinhard Koselleck defends a distinction between symmetrical and asymmetrical oppositions in the field of political history and practice. With the former he associates such general oppositions as that between friend and foe, with the latter, conceptual oppositions such as those between Greek and barbarian, Christian and heathen, superhuman and subhuman. Characteristic of the latter is that the opposed concept is a contrary but an unequal one. Here we must ask how the opposed position – barbarian, heathen, subhuman – is negated in each case. The category of the transnational can be specified more precisely against this background: it eludes just these kinds of conceptual dualities. The category 'transnational' gains its disruptive power from the fact that it negates the either/or logic of all kinds of ordering concepts. Transnationals are not conceptually opposed to natives. Transnationals are natives (neighbours), though in some other respects they are not natives (whether from their own perspective or from the alien perspective of natives). Generalizing, the category of the transnational is the counter-concept to, or cuts across, all concepts of social order, and therein lies its political, and its analytic, disruptive power.

In this sense, the category of the transnational transcends the distinctions between aliens and nations, friends and foes, foreigners and natives. It concerns neither foreigners nor enemies, neither natives nor aliens, and simultaneously both natives and foreigners, both aliens and nationals. The category of the transnational points accordingly to the 'third term' which remains hidden in the distinction between nationals and aliens, between us and the others. In a word, even enemies are in a certain sense less threatening than transnationals, because enemies conform to the established 'us' and 'them' stereotypes. Because they contradict the established order, transnationals continually remind us that the world could also be different. Anyone who wants to clarify and demystify the category of the 'transnational' must in any case reject the current equation of transnationals with foreigners, and hence also the expectations of 'assimilation' and 'integration' and the denigratory evaluations they imply. Transnationality is a form of integration of what is foreign as one's own, which is both alarming *and* enticing.

By the same token, the national space is opened up to an immigration policy that is no longer tied to a conception of integration as an all-or-nothing process. Wasn't it Groucho Marx who said 'I don't want to belong to any club that will accept me as a member'? To put it ironically, a cosmopolitan immigration policy would follow the motto 'Any foreigner who wants to become like me or like us will be expelled'!

Two conclusions can be drawn from the reflections developed in this chapter. First, multiculturalism is incapable of coping with the complexity and ambivalence I have been describing. It is not surprising that the multicultural project fails – it lacks a sense of cosmopolitan realism (2.7). Second, cosmopolitanism is an age-old concept and the phenomena of (forced) mingling of boundaries are age-old phenomena. What is 'new' about cosmopolitan realism at the beginning of the twenty-first century? Its reflexivity (2.8)!

2.7   Critique of multiculturalism

Multiculturalism is a strategy for dealing with difference in society that situates respect for cultural differences, both theoretically and politically, in the national space. From this follows, on the one hand, the contradiction that national homogeneity is presupposed and at the same time theoretically and politically challenged (Hedetoft 2003: 159ff.). On the other hand, multiculturalism remains trapped in the epistemology of the national outlook, with its either/or categories and its susceptibility to essentialist definitions of identity. Briefly, multiculturalism rapturously celebrates the social accommodation of diversity, but it lacks a sense of cosmopolitan realism. It accepts the distinction between the national and the international, and consequently it is blind to the contingencies and ambivalences of ways of dealing with difference that go beyond assimilation and integration. It still resists the national and global potential for violence that results from the new experience of boundarylessness and the questions this poses: who guarantees, and how do they guarantee, that the planet will become or remain inhabitable and a place in which all, without exception, are obligated to respect minimum requirements of civilization, if necessary by force? How should we respond to the transnationalization of realms of experience and to transnational conflicts concerning the interpretation of norms of international law? What does a nationally oriented multiculturalism mean for conflicts resulting from opposing assessments of global dangers, whether of terrorism, climate change or global poverty?

Among the choicest paradoxes of multiculturalism is that it emphatically rejects the essentialism of national homogeneity when defending minority rights, yet itself easily falls into the trap of essentialism. Someone said that multiculturalism amounts to the fanciful idea of cats, mice and dogs eating from the same bowl. And in fact multiculturalism postulates an essentialist identity and rivalry among cultures, though in a very diluted form. The strategy of multiculturalism presupposes collective notions of difference and takes its orientation from more or less homogeneous groups conceived as either similar to or different, but in any case clearly demarcated, from one another and as binding for individual members. Multiculturalism is in danger of succumbing not just to the contradiction that national homogeneity should be replaced by multinational homogeneity. Multiculturalist moralism shuts its eyes to the potential for violence which has long since been shown to result from giving free rein to ethnic identities. Cosmopolitan empathy, the pity aroused by the mass media which unites the most diverse groups across borders in a negative consensus and declares, 'that must not be allowed to happen!', can itself provoke military conflicts. Well-meaning multiculturalists can easily ally themselves with cultural relativists, thereby giving a free hand to despots who invoke the right to difference.

Because multiculturalism in a sense multiplies nationalism internally, and hence affirms a contradictory national multinationalism, it is opposed to individualization. According to multiculturalism, there is no such thing as the individual. Individuals are merely epiphenomena of their cultures. Hence there is a direct line leading from the duality between Europe and its barbarian others, through imperialism, colonialism and Eurocentric universalism, to multiculturalism and 'global dialogue'. In each case individuals are conceived as members of territorial-hierarchical and ethnic-political units, which then engage in a 'dialogue' with one another 'across frontiers'. The social predetermination of the individual that marks classical sociology to this day is broken open and superseded only by cosmopolitanism. The respective claims of different identities do not determine individuals but set them free in a conflictual sense, because they are compelled to build bridges in order to survive. For which there are, no doubt, radically unequal resources.

2.8   *From cosmopolitanization to the cosmopolitan outlook: how does awareness of really existing cosmopolitanism become possible?*

'It is apparent', argues Edgar Grande,

> that cosmopolitanism must not only incorporate different substantive norms and principles; it must also integrate and balance different modalities and principles of dealing with difference. It cannot simply replace other principles of modernity; it must recognize and preserve them. Therefore I would maintain that, if cosmopolitanism is to have lasting effects, it must become reflexive and incorporate an awareness of its own conditions of possibility. Consequently, cosmopolitanism must achieve a meta integration of principles of modernity. I proposed to call this *reflexive cosmopolitanism*. Accordingly, reflexive cosmopolitanism would ultimately be the 'regulative principle' by means of which the combined action of universalist, nationalist and cosmopolitan norms must be regulated in the second modernity. Whether and under what conditions this can succeed is one of the key questions that must be posed. (Grande 2003: 5f.)

Reality is becoming cosmopolitan – this is the historical fact that this book seeks to explain and corroborate. But how does the cosmopolitanization of reality become conscious? What conditions hinder or favour a collective awareness of really existing cosmopolitanism, and how can the present book and its author constitute a moment in this process?

To discuss these questions properly, it is essential to recognize that in world history the intermingling of boundaries and cultures is the rule rather than the exception (McNeill 1985; Gruen 2002). The separate worlds and spaces maintained by territorial nationalism and ethnicism are historically false. If we trace the great migrations of peoples back far enough, it becomes evident that, exaggerating somewhat, there are no indigenous peoples. Every native began as a foreigner who drove out the previous natives, before claiming the natives' right to protect themselves against intruders as their natural right. The interpenetration of the Arab, Jewish and Christian cultures and religions was the rule already in the ancient world, so that it is hard to distinguish what, viewed retrospectively from the national era, appear to be clearly demarcated, essentialistic 'cultures' and 'religions'. The perspective must be inverted and the following questions asked: First, how is it possible that the global historical norm of the permeation and intermingling of cultures has been falsely portrayed as the exception, or has even been completely erased from our consciousness, whereas the exception to the rule – namely, the ideal of national homogeneity – has been elevated to the status of an eternal truth? Second, what conditions contributed to the *renunciation* of the eternal verities of national orthodoxy in the second half of the twentieth century? What conditions favour the growing awareness of the largely unconscious and unnoticed cosmopolitanization of reality?

The first question takes aim at the history and historiography of nationalism and the national outlook with a cosmopolitan intent (thereby breaking out of the circle of nationalism and national historiography); I cannot explore this question further here. The second question, by contrast, concerns the distinction between the first and the second modernity, and I would like to address this briefly in conclusion.

(1)   The rise of a realistic, politically effective cosmopolitanism (discernible in a whole series of key institutions such as the United Nations, the European Union, the International Court, the World Bank, NATO, the OECD, etc.) should be understood as a genuinely unintended side effect of Hitler and National Socialism – in other words, of the insane German pursuit of racial purity and all of the moral, political and psychological ravages it wreaked. Auschwitz was not an isolated event, but one of the most traumatic experiences of Western civilization. 'Never again Auschwitz!' has not only become a basic moral principle of the new Europe; the orientation to inalienable human rights also represents an essential political impulse of national and European domestic and world domestic politics (cf. Beck, Levy and Sznaider 2004; see also chapter 6 below, 'Cosmopolitan Europe'). This new orientation has discredited three key ideas in the axiomatics of the nation-state. First, any attempt to propagate and practise the ideal of *ethnic unity* within existing states conjures up memories of the Nazi horror. Second, the idea of the *assimilation* of ethnic minorities has become for ever politically suspect. It was the Jews who thought of themselves as German who were methodically slaughtered in the gas chambers. The question for all minorities is: isn't it necessary to affirm their difference and reinforce it internally and externally through transnational networks and identities? Finally, the reflexive political impact of the negative experience of the Holocaust is also shown by how it is being transformed into positive action. A *cosmopolitan common sense* is emerging that not only authorizes but demands that we break with the hallowed principle of national sovereignty. Genocide is not an internal affair of nation-states but a crime against humanity, whose deterrence or prevention is for that very reason no longer the sole responsibility of nation-states.

(2)   Another factor in the rise of cosmopolitanism in the final third of the twentieth century was the *postcolonial moment* (as highlighted by Stuart Hall, Edward Said, Paul Gilroy, Homi Bhabha, et al.). First to be discarded was the myth that the internal, unintended, coerced cosmopolitanization of Western societies and cities in the second half of the twentieth century was a historical novelty. The experience of colonized peoples was one of forced transculturation, which is never simply external but was part of the internal history of the European states and societies whose colonial and national projects developed in parallel.

Hybridity, syncretism, multidimensional temporalities, the double inscriptions of colonial and metropolitan times, the two-way cultural traffic characteristic of the contact zones of the cities of the 'colonised' long before they have become the characteristic tropes of the cities of the 'colonising', the forms of translation and transculturation which have characterized the 'colonial relation' from its earliest stages, the disavowals and in-betweenness, the here-and-theres, mark the *aporias* and re-doublings whose interstices colonial discourses have always negotiated. (Hall 1996: 251)

The discourse of postcolonialism has succeeded in disrupting our forgetfulness both politically and culturally. This is reflected in the trajectories and impacts of the most diverse transnational political movements, in which so-called marginalized minorities have developed a political and cultural self-understanding of their own. In this way they have blocked every route back to ethnically closed and centred, originary 'histories of origins'. Strictly speaking, no one can make a special claim to understand how cultural practices are constituted any longer, not even within a given locality. Neither side, neither 'us' nor 'them' in their imagined autonomy and indifference, can develop without incorporating the significant and/or excluded others in their self-understanding.

If the 'European self' is so interwoven with the 'excluded others' of the colonized world, then postcolonial discourse transforms the European self-understanding and contributes essentially to opening and expanding the national into a cosmopolitan Europe.

(3)   A transvaluation of values and words is taking place, symbolized by a veritable flood of words such as 'diaspora', 'cultural *métissage*' and 'hybridity'. These terms are shaking off their pejorative connotations and spreading like an infectious truth which announces a positive valuation of the human condition. The experiences of alienation or living in between, the loss of ontological security [*Weltvertrauen*], social isolation and existential exclusion, talk of ambivalence and ambiguity, even the reproach of 'rootlessness', have lost much of their apocalyptic meaning. The question mark has become a positively connoted form of existence, though admittedly not for the majority of settled groups, but in the dimension of collective, identity-constituting symbols.

Even the most popular of personal pronouns, the mystical and menacing 'we', has lost much of its global public appeal. Indeed, one could say that the dissolution of the national idiom is shown not least by the disenchantment of the 'we': which 'we' do we mean when we speak of the 'we'? The revaluation and inversion of the obviousness of 'we'-assertions in the national axiomatics into ever more clearly unanswerable 'we'-questions shows how fundamentally the nature of the 'we' has been problematized.

That the multiplicity of meanings and uses of a word such as 'diaspora' has literally exploded not only reveals the lack of analytic precision of the corresponding concept; it also points to the fact that this terminology contributes to transforming our understanding of 'equality' and 'solidarity'. For the concept 'diaspora' includes social ways of accommodating difference which resist either/or oppositions, and therefore do not have to suppress or conceal the cultural differences within a 'deracinated' group in order to maximize the differences between an 'essentialized' community and its others. Flirting with what counts as 'uprooted' or 'alienated' in the national either/or, the diaspora concept has fostered a cherished unease concerning the unreflectedly and thoughtlessly over-integrated concepts of culture and society. It combines a diffuse interest in safeguarding particularity with the knowledge that this will succeed only if a strategic universalism of human rights, beyond all provincial concerns, makes the planet liveable for all.

The concept 'diaspora' shows that the question 'Who am I?' is irrevocably barred from falling back on origins and essences, but that it nevertheless admits of more or less authentic answers. Seen in this light, the inflated use of the word 'diaspora' in cultural studies, and in how minorities everywhere understand themselves and their practices, reveals not only the (long suspected) analytic hollowing out of the concept but also the extent to which a quasi-collective both/and consciousness is taking shape in the self-understanding of movements, groups, individuals and publics.

3

Cosmopolitan Society and its Adversaries

The cosmopolitan outlook becomes more open and acute with the intermingling of cultures and identities. This process is accelerated by the dynamics of capital and consumption, empowered by a global market which undermines state borders, spurred on by the global public of transnational social movements, and guided and encouraged by the unlimited possibilities of communication (often synonymous with misunderstanding) in key fields such as science, law, art, fashion, music and, not least, politics. Debates over global ecological threats and technical economic global crises and their visibility for a global public have revealed the cosmopolitan significance of fear. And if we were in need of further proof that terror and war have also acquired a cosmopolitan face, it has been provided by September 11, 2001, and the war against Iraq in 2003.

Thus it is high time that we satisfied the methodological criterion stipulated by Peter Berger for sociological thought (in addition to the 'art of suspicion' and the fascination with the less 'noble' sides of society), namely, the 'motive of cosmopolitanism':

Going back to very ancient times, it was in cities that there developed an openness to the world, to other ways of thinking and acting. Whether we think of Athens or Alexandria, of medieval Paris or renaissance Florence, or of the turbulent urban centers of modern history, we can identify a certain cosmopolitan consciousness that was especially characteristic of city culture. The individual, then, who is not only urban but urbane is one who, however passionately he may be attached to his own city, roams through the whole wide world in his intellectual voyages. His mind, if not his body and emotions, is at home wherever there are other men who think. We would submit that sociological consciousness is marked by the same kind of cosmopolitanism. This is why a narrow parochialism in its focus of interest is always a danger signal for the sociological venture. (Berger 1963: 52–3)

The goal is to explode and expand the provincial national horizon of sociology through a methodological cosmopolitanism.

What does 'cosmopolitanization' mean? *Cosmopolitanization* is a nonlinear, dialectical process in which the universal and the particular, the similar and the dissimilar, the global and the local are to be conceived, not as cultural polarities, but as interconnected and reciprocally interpenetrating principles. The experience of global interdependence and global risks alter the social and political character of societies within nation-states. What is distinctive about cosmopolitanization is that it is *internal* and it is internalized *from within* national societies or local cultures. But it is also a cosmopolitanization of the self and of national consciousness, however deformed. The foundations of everyday consciousness and of identities are thereby transformed in decisive ways. Themes of global importance are becoming an integral part of the mundane experience and the 'moral lifeworlds' of human beings. In addition, they place national forms of consciousness and institutions in question and thereby lead to enormous conflicts throughout the world. The proposed account involves three theses.

First, cosmopolitanization means that reality itself, i.e., social structures, are becoming cosmopolitan. In other words, we can observe (and 'how' will concern us in this chapter) the emergence of an increasing 'cosmopolitan interdependence', that is, a second-order level of self-destructive civilization that transcends the nation-state and infiltrates our innermost thoughts and feelings, experiences and expectations.

Second, this cosmopolitanization of national societies is a long-term and ultimately an *irreversible* process. The irreversibility thesis is supported not only by the reality of global interconnectedness to which people contribute through their consumption and work, and which is best illustrated by the *global* criticism it attracts. This irreversibility and the awareness thereof are also called forth by the new dialectic of global dangers, as we will see. Global dangers place the survival of humanity in question, and thereby create global opportunities for action. This suggests the prognosis that the century of the self-endangerment of the planet will be as never before the century of the 'one world'. The realization that the tragedies of our time are all global in origin and scope creates a global horizon of experience and expectation. The imagined world of national social structures clearly demarcated from one another is being falsified by the experience of global crises of interdependence. There is a growing awareness that we are living within a global network of responsibility from which none of us can escape. In this sense, September 11, 2001, finally made publicly visible (for the first time in the past fifty years) that the peace and security of the West are no longer compatible with the existence of crisis-plagued regions in other parts of the world. But it also showed that the opponents of cosmopolitanization can claim some bloody 'successes'.

But how is this possible if cosmopolitanization is an inexorable process? The answer is provided by the third thesis. At the beginning of the twenty-first century we are confronted with a fundamental *ambivalence* and a *dialectic* whose outcome is open. The contradiction between the cosmopolitanization of reality and the categories in terms of which we understand reality that take the nation-state as the norm is emerging with increasing intensity. Perceived cosmopolitanization may very well trigger the defensive impulses of those who think in nation-state categories. The various counter-movements attempt to twist cosmopolitanization in an anti-cosmopolitan direction in an attempt to restore national priorities and categories by conferring cosmopolitan legitimacy on them. They turn the technological instruments of globalization and the concepts of cultural diversity against themselves in the service of the old ordering metaphysics of the nation-state, just as the attack of September 11, 2001, sought to promote ethnic particularity and religious fundamentalism in the postnational world.

When I speak of cosmopolitanization and anti-cosmopolitanization as two competing and contradictory movements, I understand them *both* as consequences of the progressive internal cosmopolitanization of reality. There is no necessary relation between the internal cosmopolitanization of national societies and the emergence of a cosmopolitan consciousness, subject or agent, regardless of what some cultural theorists seem to think.

The basic argument, therefore, is that the cosmopolitanization of reality is irreversible, and consciousness and politics are for that very reason fundamentally ambivalent. But the converse also holds: because consciousness and politics are fundamentally ambivalent, the cosmopolitanization of reality is advancing. For example, all 'opponents of globalization' share with their 'opponents' the global communications media (thereby enhancing their utility for promoting and organizing transnational protest movements). The globalized economy can only be regulated globally – only those who fight for regulation at the global level have the remotest chance of success. I will elucidate this interconnection and opposition between cosmopolitanization and anti-cosmopolitanization in two steps (the first in this chapter, the second in chapter 4).

1   *Methodological cosmopolitanism*: If methodological nationalism has permeated and shaped everything we do in the social sciences, how can we overcome it? We need to create an observer perspective that revives the original sociological curiosity and the sociological cognition of the concrete. This is doubtlessly easier said than done. In order to extend the rails on which standard academic sociological inquiry runs into new regions, and hence alert the 'sociological gaze' to the cosmopolitanization of reality, we have no alternative but to develop an opposed conceptual framework and generate new empirical data.

2   *Pluralization and politicization of boundary constructions*: The differentiation between a cosmopolitanization that is unstoppable and one that is hotly contested leads to the second argument (cf. chapter 4): cosmopolitanization includes the *politicization of horizons*. What forms and formations does the contradiction between national-universal categories and real cosmopolitanization assume, and how does it shape consciousness and action in the national and transnational domains? Political

cosmopolitanization, followed through to its logical conclusion, is also concerned with how to create new political forms capable of solving the problems of cosmopolitanization. This points to the fundamental difficulty that the metaphysics of the nation-state completely paralyses institutional imagination. Hence questions of political cosmopolitanism can be posed systematically only within a different frame of reference. And the institutional architecture of cosmopolitan modernity remains underdeveloped as long as cosmopolitan 'forms of intuition' have not emerged.

1   Methodological cosmopolitanism

How is it possible to tear down the structure of the traditional metaphysics of the nation-state, that is, open it up to the cosmopolitanization of reality, and completely restructure it? This is a historical rather than an academic matter. It calls for new thinkers outside the academic guilds, but also for a cosmopolitan revolution within the social scientific guild. It must inscribe on its banner the slogan 'Back to the things themselves! Away from pure theories for their own sake! Away from books!' Here the distinction between something *learned*, which is constituted in a self-referential academic manner, and the cosmopolitanization of reality, which is something *thought*, is essential. Social scientific curiosity must acquire the ability to pose *penetrating* questions which render the false certainties of the established social sciences permeable to the cosmopolitanization of reality.

When I claim that 'reality' has become cosmopolitan, it goes without saying that I do not intend this in a naïve realistic sense, but as an anti-constructivist provocation. The apparent naïvety of the word 'reality', whose mere mention in the context of the constructivist social sciences causes a scandal, is intended to indicate just how radically sociology (like the other social sciences) must open itself up thematically, methodologically and organizationally to the possibility of a cosmopolitan reality. For good reasons, sociology allows a privileged standpoint which claims to have direct access to 'reality'. Correspondingly, the relation between social reality, everyday interpretation and scientific observation must be clearly worked out, something the idea of 'methodological cosmopolitanism' attempts to do (see chapters 1, 2 and 4). Admittedly, the question of whether, when, and why a cosmopolitan outlook prevails then becomes less a matter of the adequate representation of 'reality' than one of 'definition' (Beck 1999, 2002b). It is a question of who has the requisite access and resources to define the necessity of the cosmopolitan outlook as socially binding. As we saw in chapter 1, section 3, the structural interdependence crises and risks have the capacity to inspire global public awareness.

To be sure, overcoming nationalism and replacing it with a methodological cosmopolitanism cannot be accomplished overnight. Social science is a collective enterprise involving a worldwide community of researchers. The social scientific worldview is a collective worldview and consequently can be transformed only gradually over a long period of time. It took decades before the major questions concerning modern society could even be posed. The question that methodological cosmopolitanism must *now* answer is: Where and how to begin? How can we pose the questions concerning the cosmopolitanization of reality so that it becomes possible to answer them in a systematic way?[1]

The analysis of cosmopolitanization can and must be developed in both the spatial and the temporal dimensions (Cox 1997; Jessop 1999; Jonas 1994). The former has already been worked out but the latter remains underdeveloped. Indeed, one could criticize the primacy accorded space in the discourse of globalization on the grounds that the cosmopolitanization of time, history and memory have thus far been largely bracketed out (cf. on this Levy and Sznaider 2001; Beck, Levy and Sznaider 2004). Focusing initially on the spatial dimension, how can the cosmopolitanization of society be grasped more precisely? Drawing on Mato (1997), Brenner (2000) and Smith (2001), we can reformulate our basic thesis as follows: cosmopolitanization replaces *national–national* relations with *national–global* and *global–global* relational patterns.

Notwithstanding the importance of such distinctions, we also need to recognize that these analytic divisions become spatially and temporally blurred in turn in the space of cosmopolitan experience. Who inhabits transnational space? Not only economic and scientific elites but also ordinary migrants, advocacy movements, 'Black Atlantic', European Muslims, and so forth. Old-fashioned modernists believe (whether in a positive or a negative sense) that only an all-encompassing national project, held together by language, military service and patriotism, promotes and guarantees modern social integration. Cosmopolitanization means, on the contrary, that identities and loyalties involve plural nationalities and loyalty to a plurality of nation-states.

As Natan Sznaider has shown (Sznaider 2000d), being an Israeli means reading Russian newspapers, watching Russian television, attending Russian-language theatre and listening to Russian rock music. But being Israeli equally means taking oriental Jewish identity seriously and, paradoxically, rejecting everything Western under the influence of Western multiculturalism. Finally, being Israeli also means that non-Jewish Israelis, Palestinians with Israeli passports, demand autonomy within Israel.

For inhabitants of modern nation-states who view patriotic identity as the only truly legitimate form of identity, such 'ethnic' conflicts are nothing more than primitive tribal feuds which will be dissolved in the all-encompassing state as modernization progresses. The inhabitants of cosmopolitan modernity, by contrast, are constantly engaged in overturning categories. The mixing to which this leads is not a sign of failure, the failure of integration, but of just the kind of individuality which determines identity and integration in cosmopolitan society. In this way, individuality arises through overlapping and conflict with other identities. Every individual makes a distinctive contribution to this process. National publics become spaces in which divisions can be overcome through conflicts and in which certain forms of indifference and social distance can make a positive contribution to social integration. Conflict is the driving force for integration. Cosmopolitan society arises to the extent that national societies are split and 'disintegrate'.

The tensions within national publics are buffered by the cosmopolitan outlook and simultaneously relativized by transnational identities and networks. The cosmopolitan project *contains* the national project and at the same time extends it. From the perspective of transnational domains of experience and action it becomes possible to test and combine options and shifts in perspective that are excluded by frontiers. One chooses and balances different cross-cutting identities, living in a sense in the in between of combination and its inbuilt contradictions. The cosmopolitan outlook has its home in amazement, in the expanding in between, in which seemingly eternal certainties, borders and differentiations become blurred and effaced.

The result is that the closed space of the nation-state becomes combinable in optional instrumental ways, in spite of the fact that in reality it no longer exists as such. Different groups maintain permanent contacts across state frontiers, with positive consequences not only for economic development and the promotion of science, but also for containing and restraining national divisions and conflicts through countervailing transnational loyalties and forms of life. The following question is also decisive: for whom, for which agents and institutions, do the various kinds of relations of cosmopolitanization hold true? And to what extent does the increase in trans-local, local–global, transnational and global–global patterns of relations break open or reinforce, develop or renew, the national–national pattern that still predominates in consciousness and in research?

These forms of relations essentially concern the interconnection between space and society. From this we must distinguish temporality, the historical and mnemonic dimension of cosmopolitanization. Considering the spatial dimension without reference to the temporal dimension leads us into a false *one-dimensional* real-cosmopolitanism and the reification of an ahistorical global present (Adam 1998; Cwerner 2000). The historically blind, exclusively spatial-cosmopolitan outlook exhausts itself in its concentration on the pluralization and interpenetration of identities and boundary-constructions, and in the resulting inexhaustible sources of conflict. A *deeper* real-cosmopolitanism, by contrast, alerts us to the empirical-analytical and the normative questions produced by the cosmopolitanization of society and politics, of history and memory in the temporal dimension. In what sense does the globalization of risks and crises become 'real' against the background of different contexts of historical experience, and how are they politically processed? How does globality get refracted historically in the non-simultaneity of concurrent cultural situations and self-definitions? How is social and political responsibility distributed historically – in the past, present, future? To what extent do present-day political decisions concerning technology, for example, determine the consequences and conditions of life with which future generations will have to live? The present is colonizing the future *and* the past. The polis that is extended *only* in the spatial dimension is conceived as the expansion of loyalties, identities, obligations and rights. The cosmopolitan outlook trapped in the metaphysics of the eternal, turbulent, catastrophic present remains restricted in this way (Cwerner 2000: 335). But how can the cosmopolitanization of society in the temporal dimension be conceptualized?

The experience of global risks and crises means that all over the world human beings are reflecting on a collectively divided, and simultaneously endangered, present and future which results from the crisis of cosmopolitan society when it confronts itself and the nation-state schematics of memory and history.[2] A global memory of the global past does not exist. It goes without saying that the distinction between past and future holds equally for the first and the second modernity. But whereas in methodological nationalism the future implications of a nationally divided past are in the foreground, methodological cosmopolitanism is concerned with the implications in the present of a globally shared future. What future is being realized today, and how?

Two answers to the question of how the integration of cosmopolitan society is possible over time suggest themselves: first, through the construction of presently experienced future threats resulting from the self-endangerment of civilization (cf. above chapter 1, sections 1.9 and 3.1); and, second, by imagining a transnationally shared past which takes on concrete form in the dialectic of memory and forgiveness. This calls for an inquiry into the altered understanding of the past – for example, post-heroic versus heroic – and of the future – for example, progress versus uncertainty (Levy and Sznaider 2001).

Here too we must distinguish between consciousness and practice. The global awareness of a shared collective future is an awareness to which there are currently no corresponding forms of practice. Most forms of practice, especially in politics and law (less so in science and economics), are fixated on the nation-state, and hence are oriented to the past. However, international legal adjudication and the institution of the International Court of Justice represent countervailing tendencies. The politics of the collectively shared and threatened future thus far enjoys only meagre institutional support. More important, however, is the fact that an open contradiction exists between the current consciousness of a globally shared and threatened future *without* appropriate forms of institutional practice and a backward-looking national memory *without* a globally shared collective future.

2   The three conceptions of globalization research in the social sciences

Whereas the epoch of the nation-state produced and institutionalized a monological imaginary centred on the demarcation and exclusion of others and aliens, the cosmopolitan age is founded on a *dialogical imaginary of the internalized other*. In everyday life, in politics and in all other spheres of practice, answers have to be found to the problems created by the simultaneity of competing life-paths within individual experience and by the need to compare, consider, criticize, comprehend and connect contradictory certainties. Friedrich Nietzsche spoke in this connection of the 'age of comparison'. By this he meant not just that the individual is called upon to choose between competing traditions and combine them in his own life conduct. More important for him was that the various world cultures had begun to interpenetrate. He foresaw that this process would continue until finally the ideas of all cultures would coexist in combination, comparison, contradiction and competition in all times and places.

The demonic character of the national outlook consists not least in the fact that it elevates itself to the yardstick against which reality is supposed to be measured. The cosmopolitan outlook, by contrast, breaks with the seductive insularity of national consciousness by opening itself up to the world of others, by respecting them and internalizing their point of view. In this playing with boundaries which the cosmopolitan outlook practises and perfects as a shifting of perspectives, the cosmopolitan worldview becomes an imagining of *alternative* paths within and between different cultures and modernities (see chapter 2).

A methodological cosmopolitanism not only has to solve the problem of the starting point – the unit of investigation – and the problem of comparison. It must also redefine the conceptual framework of the social sciences. When this is done with the goal of pursuing empirical research, two currently active conceptions of empirical research on globalization and cosmopolitanization can be distinguished.

2.1   Interconnectedness

This concept has been conceptually refined and operationalized, and its utility and fruitfulness have been demonstrated by the empirical data thereby accumulated, by pioneers of globalization research in the social sciences. In Great Britain these include the researchers associated with David Held, in Germany those associated with Michael Zürn (Held et al. 1999; Beisheim, Zürn et al. 1999). Thus there exist outstanding qualitative empirical studies which provide starting points for reflection on cosmopolitanization (for example, Gerhards and Rössel 1999; Gerhards 2003). The concept of 'interconnectedness' breaks with methodological nationalism by promoting the conceptual disclosure and empirical elucidation of the growing interconnectedness and interdependence of national spaces. Nevertheless it remains bound to methodological nationalism insofar as it continues to assume territorial state units and national societies as its point of departure. Yet precisely the latter are becoming increasingly interconnected and networked. Dependence theorists who highlight the dependence of the Third on the First World object that talk of '*inter*dependence' creates the false appearance that dependencies are reciprocal, which in light of growing inequality can easily degenerate into a semantic euphemism. But however well founded this criticism, it misses the key point of the new meaning of 'interdependence' in world risk society, namely, in contrast to earlier relations of exploitation, even the powerful and the wealthy who create relations of dependency are now threatened by uncontrollable risks (the environment, migration, terrorism, etc.).

2.2   The new metaphor of 'liquidity'

Neither boundaries nor relations mark the difference between one place and another. Boundaries are instead becoming blurred, though new boundaries also arise, while relations are entering into constantly shifting constellations. Thus Lash and Urry (2005) argue that social structures are dissolving into 'streams' of human beings, information, goods, and specific signs or cultural symbols. This provides the starting point for a 'sociology beyond societies' (Urry 2000), with its single-minded empirical and conceptual focus on 'mobility', so that the category of mobility supplants the hallowed concepts of 'structure' and 'community'. Appadurai (1990) argues along similar lines that the new units 'flowing' around the world are 'socioscapes' that increasingly set capital, the media, ideologies, technologies, and human beings in motion and establish new relations between them.

Since the metaphors of 'streams' and 'flows' are so compelling, we must ask whether 'streams' – or 'networks', the key concept for Manuel Castells (1997) – can be so independent of national, transnational, and political-economic structures that the social scientific gaze shifts from the latter to the former. National spaces and their institutional concretizations and manifestations remain the centres of structuring power. We must also keep in mind the ambivalent character of cosmopolitanization, in particular, the countervailing movement of anti-cosmopolitanization. Moreover, the metaphor of 'streams' does not thematize the degree to which these processes are promoted or inhibited by the agency or impotence of particular groups of actors. Talk of 'streams' brackets the extent to which these structure- and boundary-undermining 'streams' themselves define the connection to *agents*, indeed themselves define actors' possibilities of action. The stream metaphor can thereby mislead us into neglecting the analysis of relations of power.

Still others attempt to conceptualize and investigate the social beyond methodological nationalism in terms of the concept of the *transnational* (see above chapter 2, section 2.6). According to Schiller (1997), transnational studies analyse the different ways in which the bridging of boundaries by people, texts, discourses and representations is placed on a permanent footing. The transnational is often understood as the antithesis of globalism, where 'globalism' signifies globalization from above and in the interests of the managers of multinational corporations and the political elites with which they are tightly integrated. Sometimes transnationalism is restricted to cosmopolitanization from below, to the activities of migrants, social movements and groups who construct and animate cross-border networks and forms of life. So many highly stimulating and methodologically instructive studies have appeared in this area over the past decade that we can mention only a few here in a highly selective manner: Robins and Aksoy 2001; Albrow 1997; Appadurai 1995; Burawoy et al. 2000; Caglar 2001, 2002; Deltson 2000; Dürrschmidt 2000; Eade 1997; Hannerz 1992; Hiebert 2002; Liebes and Katz 1993; Kline 1995; Kyle 2000; Nederveen Pieterse 2000; Ong 1997, 1999; Pries 1997; Randeria 1999, 2001; Salih 2000; Schiller 1989; Schiller 1997; Sklair 2001; Soysal 2002; Tomlinson 1999; Trojanow 2003.

2.3 Cosmopolitanization and methodological cosmopolitanism

The cosmopolitanization approach differs fundamentally from the aforementioned approaches to the empirical investigation of globalization, in that (a) it distinguishes systematically between the perspective of social actors and that of social scientific observers; (b) it replaces the opposition between national either/or 'streams', 'networks' and 'scapes' with a both/and typology (transnational, translocal, global-local, global-national, etc.); and (c) it inquires into the congruence or lack of congruence between actor and observer perspectives, and thereby highlights discrepancies among the options open to social and political actors and institutions, on the one hand, and social scientific approaches and perspectives, on the other, and traces their implications for concepts and theories in the social sciences (e.g., of conflict and integration, domination, inequality, the state).[3]

The distinction between the actor perspective of society and politics and the observer perspective of the social sciences unfolds its disruptive potential only when the expanded options opened up by cosmopolitanization are viewed from *both* perspectives. It then becomes clear that cosmopolitanization, in both the agent and the observer perspectives, must be developed as a new *politics of perspectives* (of starting points, modes of access, standards, framings, foregrounds and backgrounds, etc.). (On the *'politics of scale'* – i.e., the negotiation of hierarchy and legitimacy among different 'scales' of social interaction – see Brenner 1999, 2000; Tsing 2000; Jonas 1994; Burawoy et al. 2000.) It follows that social science can conceptualize and thematize the relational patterns 'transnational', 'global–local', 'global–national', 'national–global' or 'global–global'

- with a *local focus* (e.g., transnational lifestyles of Turks in London; global cooperation and conflict within the World Trade Organization, the American government or NGOs; conflicts between national and communal governments over fertility policy; anti-poverty initiatives in New Delhi; the impact of the BSE risk on an agricultural community in Scotland);
- with a *national focus* (e.g., transnational forms of marriage and family in different countries; the modes and frequency of transnational communication in the USA, Russia, China, North Korea and South Africa; the nationalities and languages of schoolchildren in different countries, etc.);
- with a *transnational* (or *translocal*) *focus* (e.g., German Turks who have developed a transnational lifestyle moving between Berlin and Istanbul are being researched in both Berlin and Istanbul: this involves an exchange of perspectives which sets the nation-state framings of Turkey and Germany into systematic relations with each other – as regards values, administrative regulations, cultural stereotypes, etc., which determine, facilitate or prevent transnationalization; the transnational dynamics of risk and conflict of the BSE crisis and their cultural perception and evaluation in different European countries are being investigated in a comparative study);
- with a *global focus* (how far advanced is the internal and external cosmopolitanization of national domains of experience in particular countries, what implications does this have, and what theoretical, empirical and political conclusions can be drawn from it?).

Thus methodological cosmopolitanism is not mono- but multiperspectival. More precisely, it can and must observe and investigate the boundary-transcending and boundary-effacing multiperspectivalism of social and political agents through very different 'lenses'. A single phenomenon, transnationality, for example, can, perhaps even must, be analysed both locally and nationally and transnationally and translocally and globally.

The result is a host of methodological problems that cannot be dealt with individually here, much less solved. How can this optionality and the attendant *politics of perspectives* be made transparent and methodologically tractable? What substantive, thematic-theoretical, and what social and political consequences are associated with the various 'lenses'? And what consequences does this have in turn for the standing of the social sciences in the national, interstate and international fields (financing, public presence and legitimation, contexts of use)? How can the complexity and contingency thereby opened up in the internal and external relations of national and international sociologies be methodologically tamed? Does this imply a decline, a cultural relativization and a subjectivization of the social sciences? Or should we not rather expect just the opposite, namely, that the social sciences bring their claim to knowledge to bear thematically, methodologically, and politically beyond the state and nation in novel ways which impact on a global public? When and how will the one or the other become possible, or probable, or be excluded?

3   More on the politics of perspectives

A politics of perspectives must be applied not only to the relation between actor and observer perspectives but also to the relations among different actor perspectives. In other words, the logic of social relations and the meanings of the basic social scientific concepts (typologies and theories) founded upon them change accordingly. In what follows this will be elucidated (in outline) in connection with (1) forms and causes of *conflicts* and (2) forms and causes of *integration*.

3.1   *Forms and causes of conflicts*

Methodological cosmopolitanism must investigate the extent to which specific forms of conflict and their social scientific analysis remain tied to categories of the nation-state. And it must examine how the constellation of conflicts and the techniques of analysis of social science change when attention shifts to the incongruence between different actor perspectives, and between actor and observer perspectives. The prevailing monoperspectival logic of social conflicts is overcome when at least one of the parties to the conflict assimilates the new both/and forms. For then the national frame is no longer valid as a shared arena for settling conflicts. A new '*meta-inequality*' arises between the contending parties. One of the parties has the capacity to act transnationally, the others either really or apparently not (see chapter 1, section 3.3). Since the (legally codified) national solidarity is thereby also terminated, these national–transnational forms of conflict are an endless source of national and transnational disputes.

• *Relations between capital and the state*: Global economic actors are by no means more powerful than states; however, they liberated themselves much earlier from the straitjacket of national orthodoxy and have acquired a highly effective form of global power. Their means of coercion is not invasion but the threat of withdrawal. From the perspective of the global economy, states should be easily substitutable and completely interchangeable, stand in competition with the greatest possible number of equivalent states, and have internalized the neoliberal global market regime (Beck 2005: 122). However, since the global economy cannot operate politically, it remains dependent on states. It can compel the latter to undergo a 'self-transformation' through the global subpolitics of capital streams without a democratic mandate and in open violation of national solidarity.

- *Relations between labour and capital*: Capital is becoming transnational and global, whereas labour (and labour unions) remain national. Mobile capital can exploit the politics of perspectives to the full, but from the perspective of the nation-state it thereby exposes itself to the charge of illegitimate (il)legality. In the meantime, occupational groups that are territorially and nationally bound to their social welfare systems and to nationally organized unions become protectionist defenders of the status quo of national solidarity and law.
- *State–state relations*: The old (national–international) single-perspectivism encounters the new politics of perspectives also in relations between states. Particular states define their domain of action in transnational or global–national terms, and hence reserve the right to intervene in foreign states. Here too the 'pioneer states' that conquer the transnational and global power sphere (on the basis of human rights, capital streams and global risk prevention) meet with the resistance of states that defend the premises of the national–international order by recourse to international law tailored to nation-states. And here it also holds true that the governments and countries that declare void the solidarity founded on international law draw the suspicion of illegitimacy and illegality on their actions.
- *The relation between the state and non-governmental organizations and international organizations*: The break between the premises of national order and the transnational politics of perspectives also manifests itself in the relations between nationally and territorially bound state actors and transnationally operating NGOs and international organizations (WTO, IMF). And here too the transnational and global adventurers (Greenpeace, Amnesty International) can easily expose themselves to the suspicion of intervening in nationally constituted more-or-less-democracies without democratic legitimacy or popular mandate.
- *The relation between transnational groups and states*: The transnationality and translocality of forms of life (Chinese-Americans, British Turks, Indian Africans) run up against the incomprehension and opposition of states and societies which understand and organize themselves as nations. Here too sedentary nation-states suspect transnationality of being divisive, disloyal, subversive, rootless and criminal, whereas in fact ethnic minorities and migrants are opening up domains of transnational practice in the grey areas between illegality and illegitimacy.
- *The relation between majority and minority*: In societies dominated by national majorities, the latter lay down the cultural understanding of 'society' and 'the' state and represent the national-particular as the universal. However, this holds only for the self-understanding of a majority whose perspective becomes the standard in terms of which national and transnational minority forms of life are devalued and excluded.[4]

3.2   Forms and causes of integration

The national outlook of the social scientific observer also misconstrues problems of integration. In the tacit agreement between national–national actors and national–national observers, the breakthrough into the transnational seems 'dis-integrating' and 'fragmenting'. Correspondingly, in politics, as in science, the prejudice holds sway that transnational identities and institutions *disaggregate* national bonds. This possibility cannot be excluded. But in fact transnational identities, loyalties and forms of life can

- defuse transnational conflicts in national and transnational space;
- overcome the introvertedness of the national outlook through transnational bridge-building, interpenetration and interconnection, making 'global sense' more acute [*schärfen*] in national domains of experience, and thereby defusing [*entschärfen*] current and potential sources of conflict;
- contribute to facilitating and improving transnational and global cooperation and integration in times of global risks and crises;
- organize transnational conflicts within and between national publics, and thereby produce a transnational public self-reflexivity which is a presupposition for transnational politics.

In light of the foregoing, the following should at least be clear. When methodological cosmopolitanism supplants methodological nationalism a new view of the world arises. Within the horizon of the transnational it suddenly becomes apparent that the national cannot be clearly distinguished from the international, nor can homogeneous units be demarcated from one another in this way. National spaces are denationalized, so that the national is no longer national and the international no longer international. Thus it is clear that the concept of 'de-nationalization' proposed by Zürn (1998) and Sassen (2003) can be understood as part of the process of cosmopolitanization. As transnationalization progresses, the power-container of the nation-state is broken open both from within and from without and a new plurality of space and time, new coordinates of the social and the political, arise. To repeat, the world takes on a new form which justifies a new epoch concept, that of the second modernity with its cosmopolitan outlook.

4   Qualitative research: the global can be investigated locally – the analysis of banal cosmopolitanization

The banal nationalism of the first modernity is being subverted by a *banal cosmopolitanization* of the second modernity (see pp. 40ff.). If we take entertainment as an emblematic domain of really existing, banal cosmopolitanization, then the association between 'Americanization' and 'McDonaldization' immediately comes to mind. How badly this equation simplifies a complex reality has been shown by Tamar Liebes and Elihu Katz (1993), among others. Taking as an example the American television series *Dallas*, which was broadcast all over the world, these authors show that, depending on whether the viewers were Arab Israelis, Russian Israelis, Americans, Japanese, and so forth, you get quite different views of *Dallas*. This example can be generalized: European-American products are frequently altered to the point of unrecognizability in the course of their active assimilation within different cultural contexts (Lash and Urry 2005).

Another, less banal, example of really existing cosmopolitanism is provided by the transnationalization of law and legal pluralism. Here cosmopolitan realism means that forms of state and non-state law beyond the clear distinction between national and international are emerging and coexisting side by side on the construction site of world politics, something apparently precluded by methodological nationalism. Cosmopolitanization goes hand in hand with the fragmentation, contextualization and pluralization of law. In criminal law the nation-state has until now been able to defend its monopoly for the most part. In the meantime, in questions of patent law and in other core areas of commercial law a state–non-state public–private both/and is gaining ground. This includes a wide spectrum of actors, from NGOs, transnational concerns and private law firms, to international legal committees, the WTO, the IMF, the World Bank, etc. Thus in questions of law, too, the nation-state is far from powerless or irrelevant; but in an obscure both/and situation it has become just one powerful locus of authority among others, something more apparent in the Southern than in the Northern hemisphere. At the methodological level it follows that the banal cosmopolitanization of law can be analysed neither locally nor nationally. Rather, it must be analysed in its hybrid forms, its boundary constructions and its ambivalences and their strategic exploitation for purposes of power by governments, corporations, NGOs, etc., in multi-local and multinational perspectives and case studies (Beck 2005).

Surprisingly enough, this 'banal' cosmopolitanization can be demonstrated in an exemplary fashion by a less banal actor whose currently progressing 'cosmopolitan reform' is being followed with misgivings. I mean the military, in particular NATO. Within Europe and in relations with the USA the administration of the military has given rise to the peculiar state of affairs that the institution which was once regarded as the most revered embodiment of the nation has been denationalized to its core. Particularly troubling is the transnationalization of the arms industry, be it tanks, new fighter and transport aircraft, information systems, etc. In this way the basic premise of national autarchy has long since been tacitly annulled and inverted into its opposite. Nowadays military security and power depend on international cooperation; hence they are predicated on the self-overcoming of national military sovereignty and security, which they are nonetheless supposed to serve. Even the higher command structures have succumbed to the multicultural virus; they have become miniature cosmopolitan societies in which officers and teams from all member countries intermingle and cooperate – not unlike multinational corporations, as it happens. Large-scale military exercises have become transnational undertakings which serve as training-grounds in transnationality. And in the end we must confront the by no means banal question: What are, for example, German soldiers in Afghanistan dying for? The standard reply of the national era – for their country or for German security interests – has become an empty formula. It may temporarily mask the anomalousness of the situation by the standards of national constitutions but it cannot disguise how far removed it is from reality.

This example demonstrates once again that the nationalist doctrine of cultural homogeneity is a *historical exception* which holds only for the relatively short era of national modernity in world history (McNeill 1985). The notion that armies should be ethnically homogeneous or composed exclusively of nationals was a luxury which earlier empires and emperors could ill afford. The great global conquests from Julius Caesar to Napoleon were made possible by multinational armies. Only by attracting and enlisting new recruits from outside the borders of their own city-states could they build and secure an empire. The victories of Rome were ultimately made possible by its willingness *not* to limit citizen rights along ethnic lines but to make them available to an ever-expanding circle of possible recruits.

These examples of banal cosmopolitanization support the key conclusion that the idea that the domains and horizons of experience of national societies[5] constitute hermetic enclaves differentiated by national languages, identities and politics is becoming increasingly mythic. What counts and is celebrated as national is in essence increasingly transnational and cosmopolitan. The relation between science and the social world is thereby becoming paradoxical. Social structures and processes are becoming cosmopolitan, whereas scientific knowledge remains beholden to the axiomatics of the national. Moreover, it is to be assumed that this paradoxical relation between knowledge and reality will become more rather than less acute as economic and cultural globalization progresses. Seen in this light, the social presuppositions for the nation-state – the identity of space, people and state – no longer exist, even if the new organizational forms of the (cosmo)political are not yet clearly discernible.

For a cosmopolitan sociology there remains the problem of how to research the global. Isn't the totally global a bit too global? And would a sociology of the global necessarily cause sociology to regress to a branch of metaphysics *without* any systematic relation to the empirical falsification of its hypotheses? How, then, is an empirical sociology of the global possible?

Believe it or not, for me there is a simple answer to this question, though one which is obscured by common images and misconceptions concerning globalization and its paradoxes. The first paradox states that globalization is a matter of globalization. This is false. Globalization is also a matter of situating and localizing. It is impossible even to think about globalization without referring to specific places and locations. One of the most important presuppositions and implications of the cosmopolitanization thesis is the rediscovery and redefinition of the local. It is precisely this global–local dialectic that Roland Robertson (Robertson 1992; Robertson and Khondker 1998) has in mind when he speaks of 'glocalization' (which had given rise to a wide-ranging debate: Ong 1997, 1999; Kyle 2000; Cox 1997; Miller and Slater 2000; Miller 1995). For the social sciences this means that cosmopolitanization is not something that happens out there but in here. Thus sociology can investigate the global locally. As Saskia Sassen shows in her work (Sassen 2000, 2003), this has important implications for the analysis of cities. Cities are not bounded territorial units but points of intersection in a network of boundary-transcending processes. In addition, globalized cities cannot be situated in a simple hierarchy that subordinates them to the national, the global and the regional. The city is one of the spaces of the global with which it is *directly* connected, often circumventing the national (see also Dürrschmidt 2000; Eade 1997; Isin 2000; Espinoza 1999).

How this functions becomes clear when we examine a second misconception concerning globalization, according to which globalization is an additive rather than a substitutive aspect of national society and of the sociological imagination. In the discourse concerning globalization one frequently encounters the assumption that globalization transforms only relations between nation-states and societies but not the inner constitution of the social and the political. However, globalization signifies globalization *from within*, *internalized* globalization. Viewed from this angle, the national no longer remains national. The national must be rediscovered as the global internalized. As Saskia Sassen puts it: 'Of particular interest here is the implied correspondence of national territory with the national, and the associated implication that the national and the non-national are two mutually exclusive conditions. We are now seeing their partial unbundling.' Sassen argues that

one of the features of the current phase of globalization is that the fact a process happens within the territory of a sovereign state does not necessarily mean that it is a national process. Conversely, the national (such as firms, capital, culture) may increasingly be located outside the national territory, for instance, in a foreign country or in digital spaces. This localization of the global, or of the non-national, in national territories, and of the national outside national territories, undermined a key duality running through many of the methods and conceptual frameworks prevalent in social sciences, that the national and the non-national are mutually exclusive. (Sassen 2000: 145f.)

The methodological conclusion is that it is not necessary to investigate the global in a totally global fashion. We can develop a new, functional, historically sensitive empiricism focused on the ambivalent consequences of globalization in boundary-transcending and multi-local research networks – a continuation of the community studies of the Chicago School with a cosmopolitan intent.

What characterizes a domain of experience or horizon of expectations as 'cosmopolitan' as opposed to national? My suggestion is that cosmopolitan sensibility and competence arise from the clash of cultures within one's own life. The cosmopolitan constellation *qua* domain of experience and horizon of expectations means the *internalization* of difference, the co-presence and coexistence of rival lifestyles, contradictory certainties in the experiential space of individuals and societies. By this is meant a world in which it has become necessary to understand, reflect and criticize difference, and in this way to assert and recognize oneself and others as different and hence of equal value. The cosmopolitan outlook and sensibility opens up a space of *dialogical imagination* in everyday practice and in the relevant sciences. Cosmopolitan competence, as a fact of everyday and of scientific experience, forces us to develop the art of translation and bridge-building. This involves two things: on the one hand, situating and relativizing one's own form of life within other horizons of possibility; on the other, the capacity to see oneself from the perspective of cultural others and to give this practical effect in one's own experience through the exercise of boundary-transcending imagination.

To what extent and in what constellations this can succeed is a completely open empirical question to which, to my knowledge, no adequate answer has yet been offered. Indeed, it is important to counter promptly a cosmopolitan myth or fallacy: living between borders or in a diaspora is not an automatic guarantee of openness to the world. To repeat, cosmopolitanization and anti-cosmopolitanization are intermeshed phenomena.

At this juncture, if not before, we need to warn against the *cosmopolitan fallacy*. The basic fact that human experience is being subtly altered by the opening to cosmopolitanization should not mislead us into assuming that we are all becoming cosmopolitans. Even the most positive development conceivable – an expansion of cultural horizons and a growing sensitivity towards new, unfamiliar geographies of life and coexistence – does not necessarily foster a sense of cosmopolitan responsibility. The question of how this could be facilitated has until now scarcely been posed, let alone investigated.

But the inner cosmopolitanization of societies which are organized and conceived as nation-states also increases the likelihood of a *national fallacy*. This consists in the view that what takes place within the container of this or that nation-state can also be located, understood and explained in national terms. This 'national or territorial fallacy' holds not least for the bulk of the statistics produced by the economic or social scientific disciplines that take their orientation from the nation-state (Beck-Gernsheim 2004).

Talk of cosmopolitanization has an obvious weakness. It suggests that the local can be understood as the 'footprint' of the global. In this way a precise analysis of how the interconnection and permeation of the global and the local is produced and structured, and hence to what extent the mingling of boundaries facilitates or necessitates a politics of the local, or is even a result of the same, is precluded. Is the local perhaps something more than the 'intersection' of global streams, networks and scales, not just the 'point of application' of the global? Must not, conversely, the countenance of the local be decoded as the product of strategies pursued by concrete transnational actors in concrete situations? Who develops the perspectives that transform the local from within? In other words, social scientific interactionism, pragmatism, ethnomethodology, ethnology, etc., and their empirical-methodological know-how must be introduced into debates and research concerning cosmopolitanization. In this sense, the local or the global do not 'exist' as such but are *made*, in particular, in globalization prac- tices and projects 'that seek to redefine the connections, scales, borders, and character of particular places and particular social orders' (Gille and O'Riain 2002: 277; see also Kyle 2000; Riccio 2000; Papadakis 2000). The strategic- methodological advantage of this global ethnography of the local lies, first, in the fact that the universally presupposed hierarchy of congruence of actor perspectives and units of analysis in the observer perspective ceases to be valid and, second, in the fact that the extension, permeation and reconstruc- tion of boundaries and scales can themselves become objects of social scien- tific inquiry and reconstruction.

Examples of questions that can be pursued here in the context of develop- ing more sophisticated ethnographic methods are: To what extent are local actors capable of taking advantage of the destabilization of social-spatial hierarchies centred on the nation-state? To what extent does the destabiliza- tion of the national cosmos facilitate the production of new translocal and transnational connections? Which social actors contribute, and in the face of what forms of resistance, to the construction of 'global imaginaries' which alter the character of place, and in this way challenge the received definitions of the local, the national and the global and the boundary-lines inscribed in them?

The following questions can then be addressed somewhat more precisely (Lin 1998; Lopez 2000; Gille 2001): Who opens local doors for global actors, and how and why and against what forms of resistance? How are global eco- nomic, cultural and political enterprises rooted in a place – or not, as the case may be? Is there a process of assimilation, or does the global modify the dis- tinctive character of the local? How then can the 'permeation', the relative opening and closing, be determined and reconstructed in detail? How should the prototype of the 'migrant' – transnational corporations, non-governmental organizations, tourists and refugees – be treated? Are 'transnationals' exclu- sively or mainly 'tolerated' in the protected domains of leisure culture (colour- ful restaurants and neighbourhoods), or are they also encouraged to participate politically, to assume positions of responsibility in schools and in the police and social services? Does a public space emerge in which seemingly sharp opposi- tions between 'us and them' become blurred and a conflictual and cooperative culture of transnational openness and reconfiguration of the local arise? Could locally and nationally opposed visions of the local, which clash in conflictual ways, be conceived of and advocated? Is it possible that a city could reinvent itself as self-confidently open to the world but thereby run up against the resistance of laws and interference by regional or national governments? Is there not perhaps a more or less reflected connection between a city's (or a national society's) openness and its integration in the global economy and its prosperity? Could it even be the case that the vision of a globally and locally networked social environment with open internal and external borders represents an entry-ticket into the global public sphere, and hence also a marketing and publicity tool for individual places, which as a result could collide with the nation-state's politics of closure?

Could one in this sense even say that the extension of local politics by transnational subpolitics, in particular the cooperation with non-governmental organizations, entails an enrichment of city politics because it fosters global connections and is an effective global advertisement? Whence arises the resistance to this active cosmopolitanization of the local? Who forges the protectionistic coalitions and to what extent are they fostered by existing institutions (of law, party organizations, labour unions, etc.)? To what extent does local cosmopolitics split existing political organizations? Will resentment against foreigners produced by cosmopolitanization become an important source of votes?

All of these issues and others besides can be raised and addressed in qualitative field studies. In this way we can break the spell that confuses the question of the unit of analysis – the 'local' – with the question concerning the reality of cosmopolitanization and how it can be exhibited and investigated at the local level. The particular is not the particular but is also the global, just as the global is not the global but also the particular, the local. Hence we must distinguish the unit of analysis clearly from the translocal and transnational interconnections and permeations whose processes of production and forms of expression can be investigated at this level (but also at the national or transnational level).

5   Qualitative research: indicators of cosmopolitanization

The empirical-analytic cosmopolitan outlook can be translated into empirical research in two ways. First, as we have just shown, through qualitative research that discloses, reconstructs and investigates the active and passive cosmopolitanization of the world; second, through quantitative analyses that apply the resulting empirical indicators of cosmopolitanization. In both cases the focal unit of social scientific analysis must be determined. To heighten this point into an objection: Doesn't methodological cosmopolitanism become entangled in an open contradiction when it seeks to direct empirical research, namely, the contradiction that it chooses as its frame of reference the very national (or local) unit of analysis that it supposedly invalidates?

The answer is 'no', in the first place because the *in*congruence of the actor perspective with the observer perspective of the social sciences is the guiding methodological idea. In the local or national focus, transnational, translocal, glocal or global–national structures and pattern of relations are investigated. This means that the national focus is no longer the national focus (of methodological nationalism) since the old distinctions between national and non-national are being overcome and their both/and (in appearances, boundaries, contradictions, resistances) is being researched. The choice of a national (or local) methodological focus, therefore, necessitates conceptual self-transcendence and empirical self-correction. It is no more and no less than a starting point for empirically exploring the forms and extent of transnationalization, denationalization and renationalization within a post-national conceptual framework.

On the other hand, the national focus is just one among many that above all facilitates, in a first step, the conceptual-methodological analysis of the internal cosmopolitanization of the domains of experience and action of the nation-state beyond national borders. Further methodological steps can and must follow. To repeat, transnational interdependencies and flows must also be comprehended and researched 'transnationally' through a systematic exchange of perspectives among national framings; forms of transnationalization can only be interrogated and researched from a global perspective, and so forth. Hence the national lens is precisely not that of methodological nationalism. First, it works with a cosmopolitan conceptual scheme, second, it investigates the permeation, effacing and redefinition of boundaries and, third, it represents an initial approach that must be supplemented and completed by transnational comparative methods.

In light of these qualifications (and without any claim to completeness and systematic exposition) I will now enumerate some quantitative indicators of cosmopolitanization:

- *cultural goods, in particular, the import and export of cultural goods*: the transnationalization of publishing; developments in the import and export of periodicals, in the number and proportion of domestic vs. foreign films in cinemas, in the proportion of domestic vs. foreign productions on television, on the radio, etc.;
- *dual citizenship*: the legal basis and official practice in dealing with migrants and asylum seekers; how 'foreigners' are defined statistically, in public and in everyday life (by bureaucracies);
- *political intensities*: to what extent are different ethnic groups represented directly and indirectly in national centres of power (political parties, assemblies, administrations, labour unions)?;

- *language*: who speaks what languages and how many? (For example, a report recently did the rounds of the German media that in the small Bavarian town of Landshut more than fifteen languages are now spoken by the thirty children in a high school class.);
- *mobility*: permanent immigration, developments in immigration, in labour immigration; temporary immigration, developments in the numbers of refugees and of foreign students;
- *flows of communication*: by this is meant developments in national and international post and telecommunications, in the corresponding exchange of information over the internet, etc.;
- *travel*: developments in international air travel, in international tourism, in the number and proportion of foreign journeys;
- *levels of activity of transnational organizations and initiatives*: temporary or constant participation in actions of Greenpeace, Amnesty International, etc., participation in international signature collection campaigns, consumer boycotts, etc.;
- *criminality*: developments in international (organized) crime, in politically motivated attacks and acts of violence of foreigners or groups of foreigners;
- *transnational forms of life*: diaspora communities and their border-transcending public and private networks and decision-making mechanisms, the number and character of transnational marriages, children with multiple nationalities, etc.;
- *transnational reporting*: for example, of wars on television; to what extent this leads to a change in perspectives;
- *national identities*: what relations pertain between the number and character of national identities and citizen identity? Or is there such a thing as a 'cosmopolitan nation' and what does it mean?
- *ecological crises*: depletion of the ozone layer, changes in global climate, global fish stocks, cross-border air and water pollution; developments in attitudes towards local, national and global crises, environmental laws and legal jurisdiction, environmental markets, environmental jobs, etc.

Quantitative developments of these indicators are certainly difficult to evaluate on account of the lack of data and the immense problems presented by their comparative evaluation. Nevertheless, the first systematic analyses (Held et al. 1999; Beisheim, Zürn et al. 1999; Gerhards and Rössel 1999) have shown that cosmopolitanization can also be understood and represented empirically as a multifaceted process that varies widely according to country and the dimension of analysis. To be sure, since the 1990s at the latest, cosmopolitanization has in fact assumed a new quality as regards its scope and intensity, and this exceeds by far what could be observed at the beginning of the twentieth century. Parallel to cosmopolitanization at the micro-level of lifeworlds, forms of life and everyday social institutions (schools, districts), cosmopolitanization also occurs at the *macro*-level, and not just through dependencies in the global market but also in the network of inter- and supranational institutions.

5.1   Reflexive cosmopolitanization

It remains to be explained what a cosmopolitan society is. It is indeed easier to say what it is *not*. It certainly does not make sense to speak of a cosmopolitan society when cosmopolitanization takes place exclusively at the objective level, while being (actively) obscured by the dominant national outlook – in local administration, political parties, government, the public sphere, police, education, research, etc. It follows that we can meaningfully speak of cosmopolitanization only when it is publicly represented, commented upon, and ultimately institutionalized (e.g., through a corresponding immigration policy). This means, in turn, that the cosmopolitan outlook must encompass, criticize, extend and transform the national outlook.

It was surely Roland Robertson who made the realization and consciousness of the cosmopolitan project – what I call the cosmopolitan outlook – the index of cosmopolitanization (Robertson 1992). Likewise, Albrow distinguishes between globalization and 'globality', where 'globality' includes the everyday awareness of globalization (Albrow 1996). Armin Nassehi argues in a similar vein when he connects cosmopolitanization with the Thomas theorem and thus with the self-definition and public reflexivity of transnational forms and settings of life, not only at the apex but also at the base and the intermediate level of an emerging cosmopolitan society (Nassehi 1998).

Thus 'objective' and 'reflexive' cosmopolitanization overlap and cannot be sharply distinguished at the empirical level. Neither aspect can be properly understood apart from the other. The empirical-analytical cosmopolitan outlook reveals developments which can count as 'cosmopolitanization'. In other words, it is a relational concept in which the interconnections between cosmopolitan developments and movements, on the one hand, and the resistances and obstructions to which they give rise, on the other, can be analysed. Thus cosmopolitanization by no means signifies 'a' cosmopolitan society but rather the interrelation between de- and re-nationalization, de- and re-ethnicization, and de- and re-localization in society and politics.

A suitable way of grasping and investigating this phenomenon is offered by a *process-oriented* sociology, i.e., the systematic attempt to avoid the reduction of process to static concepts. Accordingly, we must resist the temptation to develop cosmopolitanization in terms of a phase model. If this is pursued in a unilinear fashion it is condemned to failure. For cosmopolitanization is no longer just an objective process to be described in terms of empirical categories, but a political power struggle in which groups revolt against their submission to the imperatives of national identity while others take refuge behind regional identities.

The metaphor of the 'melting pot' – the model of integration of the first modernity – is replaced by that of the 'salad bowl', an imagined world that anticipates elements of a deterritorialized conception of society, but thereby becomes entangled in a thicket of contradictions (Beck-Gernsheim 2000, 2004).

We also need to differentiate various kinds of political reactions to cosmopolitanization. In the first place, minority revolution within majority domination: in this publicly conducted conflict the national monopoly on memory collapses and multifarious, loosely connected, border-transcending strata of memory are uncovered, developed – and invented![6] This kind of critique of collective memory sharpens the perception of minorities for their histories of oppression and uncouples the latter from the equation of space, time and society characteristic of the nation-state.

5.2   Class analysis and cosmopolitanization analysis

There are certain parallels between the 'cosmopolitanization analysis' proposed here and 'class analysis' as developed (though only incompletely) by Marx. Cosmopolitanization analysis seeks to uncover the core conflict of second modernity, just as class analysis sought to uncover that of first modernity. And just as Marx distinguished between class 'in itself' and class 'for itself', one could distinguish here between cosmopolitanization 'in itself' and cosmopolitanization 'for itself'.

Cosmopolitanization 'in itself' would be the same thing as *inner* cosmopolitanization, cosmopolitanization *from within* (banal cosmopolitanization). Cosmopolitanization 'for itself', by contrast, could be made a conceptual key to unlock the doors to the new landscapes of cosmopolitan conflict and possible corresponding future institutions for regulating conflicts.

The underlying assumption here is that cosmopolitan democracy is possible. To it would correspond an architecture of transnational power and authority which responds to the transnationalization of capital and civilizational risks.

The parallels between cosmopolitanization and class analysis could be extended by a further point. Marx also assumed that differences between classes in themselves – produced by the growing interdependence of markets and the division of labour – are irreversible. Classes for themselves – the political institutions that enable 'cosmopolitan interdependence' to be brought to political awareness and be politically regulated – constitute the heart of Marxist analysis.

To be sure, the parallels also end there. In the first place, cosmopolitanization analysis has shaken off and rejected any optimism concerning history. There is no optimism, however disguised, concerning a growing awareness and politics of cosmopolitanization.

However, the following conflict may be even more decisive. The economy does not determine consciousness; the national outlook bars the space for choice and action offered by state actors in cooperation with other states, international organizations, and so forth. The point is to recognize – and use – the potential for a cosmopolitan consciousness in structural interdependencies (risk, technology, migration).

Cosmopolitan society represents the intensification of the open society, that is, the society open to the world. We must now further clarify what this means methodologically – and politically.

Part II

Concretizations, Prospects

4

The Politics of Politics: On the Dialectic of Cosmopolitanization and Anti-Cosmopolitanization

What is so exceptional about the political dimension of human existence that it has captured such enormous philosophical attention, from Plato and Aristotle to Machiavelli and Hannah Arendt, Carl Schmitt and Mao? In a word, what is the meaning of the category of the political? The dominant answer both in theory and in practice is that of methodological nationalism, namely, that we can meaningfully speak of 'politics' only if a monopoly of the decision-making powers which the sovereign political state has at its disposal belongs to society as a whole. He is sovereign who can declare a state of emergency, says Carl Schmitt. On this conception, politics and nation merge into one. Political power is exercised primarily by nations and each nation must be understood and organized as a political unit.

At the beginning of the twenty-first century, the boundaries, the basic distinctions and the basic principles on which the conflation of nation and politics rests – that is, the rule systems of power in national and international politics – have themselves been opened up to political transformation. Categorically and historically speaking, we are dealing with a 'politics of politics' or 'meta-politics' in which what seemed to constitute an indissoluble unity, politics and nation, politics and state, are being *politically* decoupled and transformed (Beck 2005; Nassehi and Schroer 2003).

In the historical context of a civilization that has become a danger to itself (on account of its own successes!), the interventions of different and, in different degrees, powerful global actors, such as global capital and NGOs (hence not just globally active hegemonic states), aim in part to demolish the system of national sovereignty and in part to transform it. In other words, the national outlook built into the category of the political is becoming historically false; it no longer understands the world because it is blind, and makes us blind, to the issues, realities, conflicts, dilemmas and fundamental ambivalences that break out with the politics of politics. Conversely, achieving a cosmopolitan observer perspective is necessary if we are to understand why the world has become a Babylonian madhouse, regardless of whether the future belongs to cosmopolitan or anti-cosmopolitan movements.

Neither Niklas Luhmann nor Jürgen Habermas, for example, provides an answer to this question. Luhmann posits a *post-political* world society but *without* giving an account of the political-cultural self-understanding of world citizens vis-à-vis national citizens (Luhmann 1975: 51–63). He construes politics in the terms of a millennial opposition and proceeds to dismiss it as outdated. The politics of the nation-state confronts a world society that is hollowing out the nation-state paradigm, and is for that very reason condemned to extinction. More precisely, Luhmann offers a *zombie theory* of the politics of the nation-state in world society – politics becomes the undead that refuses to die. It is by the same token a theory of false consciousness on a global scale. We are still playing at democracy but only in the manner of an epochal phantom pain and under the pretence of false realities. The place occupied by politics in the nation-state paradigm has become an empty placeholder which is (not) filled out by Luhmann's theory of functional differentiation projected onto a global scale.

Jürgen Habermas, by contrast, examines how politics and democracy are possible in the postnational constellation. He searches for 'possibilities of a political opening of a globally networked, highly interdependent world society without regression' (Habermas 2001), by which he ultimately means a 'European people' *qua* subject of a postnational democracy.

In both cases politics is understood on the model of the nation-state, by Luhmann as zombie or residual politics, by Habermas as *extended* national politics which has grown a historical size larger (European democracy, European nation-state, European social welfare state, and so forth). Habermas thereby ends up by entangling himself in the contradictions of a theory of the postnational nation of Europe.

The politics of politics has three characteristic features. First, it involves a 'meta-power struggle' that changes the rules of global politics (on this, see Beck 2005); second, it dismisses the view that politics is a monopoly of the state, recognizing that we must include non-state, global actors in the topics and power-strategies of the politics of politics; and, third, it is characterized by a dialectic of cosmopolitanization and anti-cosmopolitanization that cuts across the distinction between national and international, as well as intranational, oppositions. Since I have already devoted a book to the first point, in what follows I will concentrate on the latter two points.

Global actors of meta-politics

Can one in fact speak, as I have, of 'mobile capital' as a global actor directing power resources and strategies which compete with those of 'states' in 'global civil society'? Or does talk of agency in this context represent a simplifying fiction that obscures the fact that 'capital' does not and cannot exist? Who is the intended subject? Particular corporations? Social 'classes'? Managers? Shareholders? Does it refer to individual agents, collective agents or cooperative agents? Don't the practical 'strategies' of capital, state and global civil society belong, respectively, to completely different kinds of aggregations and complexes?

The answer I propose here is that the global actors of the politics of politics do not exist, but are first constituted by meta-politics *as* global actors. They must crystallize out of the politics of politics itself as its agents. In other words, questioning the politics of the nation-state, on the one hand, creates power potentials for new global actors and, on the other, propels the politics of politics. The power potentials of global actors, their resources, their status and their scope for action are not just interdependent in principle; the actors first arise through their 'moves' and counter-moves, through their practices of self-interpretation, articulation, mobilization and organization in which they acquire (or lose) their identities and agency.

The logic of meta-politics generates a specific *asymmetry of power in terms of the strategic capacity* of capital, the state and global civil society respectively. An extraordinary range of prerequisites are needed to produce political counter-power. This is just as true for the globalization of civil society as it is for the transnationalization of states. As regards capital, the very opposite is true: its particular strength lies in the fact that it does *not* have to organize itself as a single capitalist entity in order to exercise its power in relation to states. 'Capital' is a collective expression for the uncoordinated actions of individual companies, financial flows and supranational organizations (WTO, IMF, etc.) whose *outcomes* – in the sense of *politics as side effects* – put states under pressure in a more or less unseen and unintended way, and thereby expedite the unravelling of the old game of draughts known as the 'nation-state'. It is extremely heterogeneous; its immanent players and opponents are themselves threatened or affected by 'hostile takeovers' and globalization risks. But because of the phenomenon of politics as a side effect, they manage to outplay states nonetheless. 'Capital' in the singular, then, does not need to exist as a unified actor, it does not need to take its place at the table in order to bring its power to bear. The place at the global political meta-game table can be occupied by 'nobody'; and this is exactly what amplifies the power of global business actors. (Beck 2005: 15)

Cosmopolitanization and anti-cosmopolitanization

In chapter 1, I introduced the distinction between cosmopolitanism and cosmopolitanization by arguing that cosmopolitanism is located or unfolds at the philosophical level, cosmopolitanization by contrast at the level of practice. Cosmopolitanization means a 'forced' cosmopolitanism that transforms the experiential spaces of the nation-state *from within* often against their will, beyond awareness, parliamentary elections and public controversies, so to speak as a side effect of flows of migration, consumer choices, tastes in food or music or the global risks that tyrannize everyday life and transform the experiential spaces of the nation-state *from within*. This is what sparks political conflicts, specifically when cosmopolitanization (potentially) explodes taken-for-granted understandings and intuitions of national society and politics which have become second nature. Thus the conflict-laden dialectic of cosmopolitanization and anti-cosmopolitanization has the capacity to ignite awareness of cosmopolitanization.

To be sure, the latent character of cosmopolitanization also holds to a certain degree for the opposed concept of anti-cosmopolitanization. Here too the distinction between anti-cosmopolitanism, in the sense of a conscious political choice and ideology, and anti-cosmopolitanization as a side effect of business-as-usual national practices is informative. For example, union members who take to the streets to defend national labour rights against 'unpatriotic' management (who relocate production abroad to save on wages) hardly see themselves as anti-cosmopolitans; but a side effect of their actions is to reinforce anti-cosmopolitanizing processes. Just as people who enjoy exotic Indian food do not see themselves as agents of cosmopolitanization while nevertheless promoting it, so too sociologists who bracket out the global inequalities that are a given on the nation-state paradigm do not see themselves as agents of anti-cosmopolitanism. Yet the results of their research obscure both the fact that reality is cosmopolitan and that the premises of the nation-state are becoming unreal.

But what lends opposition to cosmopolitanization its superior power? The answer is that cosmopolitanization (a) occurs in a latent fashion and (b) is an analytical and political provocation to the nation-state order, developing as it does under the suspicion of *disloyal and illegal legality*.

Cosmopolitanization seems unreal because it takes place outside the field of vision of old categories. What remains national? Thought. What is no longer national? Reality! Cosmopolitanization is a compulsory re-education programme in openness to the world. And like all forced learning it can and often does meet with a stubborn insistence on 'my country right or wrong' nationalism. The national world resists the school of cosmopolitanization with all its might. It resists the instruction of cosmopolitanization, it can and must ignore it, because cosmopolitanization is such an overbearing taskmaster against which collective resistance seems justified as a general rule.

All conflicts sparked by cosmopolitanization, regardless of the level at which they are located and whether the parties are powerful or powerless, occur in the shadowy space of *illegitimate legality* or *illegal legitimacy* because they break with the nation-state order. Two things follow: first, the enormous potential of cosmopolitanization to politicize, which permeates the farthest reaches of world society and penetrates the capillaries of everyday life, goading people into public declarations and protest marches; second, it justifies the superior power of those who defend 'their rights' – the national order – against 'traitors' and 'lawbreakers'. I would like to illustrate this (in outline) with reference to (1) the average migrant: translegal, authorized, unacknowledged cosmopolitanism from below; (2) advocacy movements in global civil society: highly legitimate, precarious, mandateless cosmopolitanism from below; (3) class and power: disloyal (trans)legality.

1   The average migrant: translegal, authorized, unacknowledged
cosmopolitanism from below

When people speak of 'cosmopolitanism' they usually think of the frequent-flyer globalism of managers. But this is not the only, and certainly not the most important, embodiment of a form of life of 'flows', 'networks' and 'mobility' beyond an existence bound to the nation-state.

On the one hand, forms of life marked by mobility are spreading even in the domain of real estate. Place as the archetype of rooted existence is becoming mobilized, transnationalized, globalized – and in a certain sense even cosmopolitanized – to its very core. This paradox is expressed in the statement 'Our antennas are our roots'. The more television, mobile phones and the internet become taken-for-granted parts of the trappings of daily life, the more the private sphere becomes an illusion because it is being drawn into processes of inner globalization. Domestic information technology partially overcomes the limits of space, time, place, nearness and distance. It makes those who are absent constantly present. Interpersonal contacts are no longer exclusively tied to geographical proximity. It thereby becomes possible, as recent studies have shown, for people who live in isolation from their immediate neighbours to be wired into a dense network of transcontinental social contacts. Thus there exists something akin to an internal cosmopolitanization of real estate. What this involves largely remains to be investigated.

In addition to the global managers there is the class of transnational traders (Malcomson 1998). They don't wear ties and they don't have business-lounge tickets or credit cards and the like, only suitcases and bicycles on which they transport their wares. Few of them may read the *Financial Times* but they have the exchange rates, prices and profit margins in their heads, and they must be able to speak multiple languages and engage in cross-border trade on the boundaries of legality in order to conduct their business.

Situated somewhere alongside or below this level (it's hard to say which) is the mobility of the *average migrant* who must sell his or her labour power in the grey area of intersections, transitions and conflicts between legality and illegality (Gzesh and Espinoza 2002; Espinoza 1999; Isin 2000). If it is true that in the second modernity boundaries become blurred and blend into one another, then the average migrant is the embodiment of the blurring of boundaries between nations, states and jurisdictions and of their contradictions. In order to survive, the average migrant must become an acrobat in the manipulation of boundaries (in avoiding, exploiting, drawing, bridging boundaries, etc.) and can at any moment fall from the tightrope on which he or she is balanced. Within the national outlook, potentially criminal migrants cannot be represented as a vanguard of transnational mobility. It is equally inconceivable to represent them as experimenting with a cosmopolitan mode of existence; instead they seem obdurate because they resist assimilation.

You don't have to search for very long in major urban centres such as New York, London, Rio de Janeiro, Berlin, etc., to find transportation workers, doormen, janitors and cleaners who can successfully communicate in more languages than the graduates of the average German or French high school or American college. The counterpart of the transnationalization of capital, of which there is currently so much talk, is a highly restrictive transnationalization of cheap labour which is for the most part neither understood nor recognized for what it is, namely, the model of an experimental cosmopolitanism of the powerless in which the capacity to change perspectives, dialogical imagination and creative handling of contradictions are indispensable survival skills. Living with contradictions also means that, at best tolerated, and often criminalized, migrants are also *highly functional*, even when they seem illegitimate and illegal from the national perspective.

As Saskia Sassen has shown (Sassen 2000), there are contradictory strategies that facilitate migration from the periphery and tacitly tolerate, and even promote, the employment of migrants, ethnic minorities and women in the highly segmented labour markets of the metropole. For the extrafunctional qualifications offered by migrants combine social competences with a willingness to work for low wages in contracts without guarantees (where contracts even exist), qualifications which are highly functional in certain segments of low-skilled, part-time labour markets. This might lead to the paradoxical discovery that life under conditions of transnational anomie could become a source of social capital and transnational publicity.

But in what sense can we speak here of 'cosmopolitanization'? What basic premises of existence in nation-states are negated and reconfigured in the neither/nor and both/and of migrant existence? The cosmopolitanism of the average migrant resides in the provocation that this mode of existence is the living contradiction of the necessity of always and everywhere making a sharp distinction between 'us' and 'them', 'citizens' and 'aliens', propagated and institutionalized by the nation-state. Migrants embody all gradations of both/and: they are native foreigners or foreign nationals whose social competences are not only indispensable but also enrich cultural and public life by making it more colourful, contradictory and conflictual. Migrants are what is analytically excluded by the national either/or. Their status is at once functional, legitimate and illegal, 'authorized but not recognized' (Sassen). Their existence, their activities, their attempts to participate in public spaces contradict the understanding of civil rights of the nation-state, which they at the same time redefine. The distinction between civil rights, which only official members of the state possess, and human rights, which all persons as such possess, is suspended and reconfigured by their actions and claims. The components that thereby acquire prominence – rights of residence, labour rights, political rights, participation rights – are precipitated out and recombined.

To generalize, the peculiarities of a national-cosmopolitan society rest on extending the boundaries of ethical solidarity so as to create opportunities for both internal and external outsiders to participate. Involvement in a post-sovereign social order presupposes a certain willingness, orientation and ability, and not least a certain self-organization; for only in this way can 'natives' and 'foreigners' cooperate in the extended cosmopolitan boundaries of national spaces as equal members of a transnational civil society. As Sassen shows, the global city in particular offers a space of possibilities for this, because in it transnational and local networks and publics form both a contradictory and an uncontrollable opposition and coexistence of seemingly incompatible worlds and certainties.

One might object that questions of immigration in particular give rise to opposing nationalist movements. But that would be an unacceptable simplification which misrepresents how cosmopolitanism emerges from conflicts over immigration. For these public debates lend visibility to the problem of the nation, its borders, and the distinctions between natives and foreigners and between civil rights and human rights. In other words, it is not just the change itself (immigration, global risk) but its permanent discursive thematization which propels cosmopolitanization, invisibly and involuntarily. Thus it once again becomes clear that a moment of 'cosmopolitan integration' is inherent in anti-cosmopolitan conflicts.

2   Advocacy movements in global civil society: highly legitimate, precarious, mandateless cosmopolitanism from below

What holds for all other models of incipient more-or-less-cosmopolitanism also holds for actors in global civil society, namely, the asymmetry between national illegitimacy and transnational legitimation as a consequence of transnational possibilities of action. Accordingly, advocacy movements also constitute (il)legal, (il)legitimate hybrids that operate in both highly legitimate and highly precarious ways within the transnational power sphere. The extraordinary legitimation capital they possess cannot be compared with that on which their competitors – states, global capital – can draw. Advocacy movements are, after all, the entrepreneurs of the global commonwealth. They not only developed the categories in which global issues of climate change, poverty, human rights, women's rights, justice, etc., are formulated; they also placed them in practice on the political agenda, both at the national and the global level. States, which embodied the 'common good' in the national era, were thereby transformed into the 'egoists' of global cosmopolitanism. Moreover, the 'profit-egoism' of mobile capital, which is blind to the destruction of the environment and can draw whole peoples into the maelstrom of global financial crises (as exemplified by the Asian economic crisis), becomes recognizable as profit-egoism, and hence in need of justification, within the cosmopolitan horizon of expectations in and on which advocacy movements operate. In this way, what previously belonged to separate worlds – global legitimation and global sales opportunities – are fused. Thus, with the success of their campaigns, advocacy movements inculcate an opposition that is utterly unthinkable within the horizon of the nation-state, that between national or economic universalism, on the one hand, and cosmopolitanism, on the other. What is good for a nation or a corporation can be calamitous for everybody, and hence also for this nation and this corporation.

But what legitimates these monopolists of legitimacy? They do not have a mandate, nobody has elected them and they operate in a non-democratic manner (and, as regards their internal organization, often in an anti-democratic manner). By the same token, they often fail to recognize what hegemonic states, which have emblazoned human rights on their flags, also fail to recognize, namely, the principle of national sovereignty. They meddle in the affairs of states without regard to borders and seek to promote cosmopolitan values, e.g., the rights of individuals against the state, or to promote human rights above civil rights. If one views the right of states and governments to treat their own citizens as they wish as a basic right of sovereignty enshrined in international law, then global advocacy movements are notorious violators of international law. As such they are highly legitimate, mandateless, self-declared creators of publics and interveners in foreign jurisdictions and forms of life. They are ready and able to impose the anti-nationalist non-sovereignty principle against the opposition of states in violation of international law, and thereby create a self-fulfilling cosmopolitan horizon of expectations. What sense of 'cosmopolitanism' is operative here?

This model of cosmopolitanism is value-oriented, value-generating and information-laden. Thus it rests neither on the form of power embodied by states nor on the economic power of globalized capital to change the rules of power in the politics of politics. But like capital, and in contrast to states, non-state subpolitical actors have entered the transnational power domain. The advocacy cosmopolitanism which is here translated into practice can appeal, on the one hand, to the power of truthful information and, on the other, to the discovery and averting of civilizational dangers which threaten life in both its physical and moral dimensions. But therein also lies the precariousness and limits of advocatory legitimating power: it is destroyed by misinformation and remains dependent on the more or less voluntary cooperation of states and economic enterprises for the active aversion of harm.

Moreover, there is no shared vocabulary of conflicts, only a Babylonian confusion of many languages of conflict – ecological, feminist, religious, ethnic, nationalist, and those of human rights or labour unions. In other words, a cosmopolitan language of conflict does not exist; or, better, the boundaries between cosmopolitanism, multiculturalism and pluralism are becoming blurred because the absolutized both/and is ultimately limiting the scope for choice. The cosmopolitanism being put to the test here is located in global space (by contrast with migrant and minority cosmopolitanism). It acquires sharp contours in competition with the self-serving universalizing strategies of states and capital. This advocatory model of cosmopolitanism may indeed – like migrant cosmopolitanism – spring from powerlessness and develop at a snail's pace. But this global public cosmopolitanism nevertheless produces the global controversies in which the violation of human rights, violence against others, or the destruction of nature are uncovered and transformed into global public scandals.

This is at the same time a historically contextualized, biographically rooted cosmopolitanism of compassion and memory. Whether it is the record of the suffering of the tortured or the recollected histories of genocides and expulsions, the conscience of the world is constantly awakened beyond all borders. The memory of past crimes which continue to have effects in the present is kept alive, and hence the memory of standards in terms of which the difference between illegitimate violence (genocide) and legitimate violence (ending genocide), which is crucial for cosmopolitanism, can be translated into practice.

However, the fundamental question of this NGO cosmopolitanism does not follow from the dynamics of the competition and conflict with its external adversaries, 'state' and 'capital'. The real challenge lies in the internal competition among the various global factions of non-Western cultural relativists and Western universalism (see above chapter 2, sections 1.1 and 1.2).

3   Class and power: disloyal (trans)legality

The activities of enterprises and corporations in the context of the new transnational production paradigm are prima facie rational or functional from an economic point of view and, to the extent that they are not prohibited, legal. However, by the standards of the national consensus, they are often disloyal and illegitimate. Major corporations such as Siemens and BMW now generate two-thirds of their revenue abroad, which is good for jobs abroad but bad for jobs at home, good for profits but bad for the domestic tax base.

Clearly methodological nationalism presupposes not only a specific interrelation between production, social classes, political power and territoriality, but also particular standards of solidarity and legitimacy which can be undermined by 'rational' and 'functional' economic actions. The 'third-wave technologies' – communications and information technology, etc. – undermine the historical territoriality of industrial production, and thereby also the forms of culture associated with 'patriotic-national' modes of production and economics.

Here too we encounter a kind of involuntary cosmopolitanization. Economic decisions, specifically those of local or national firms, are being influenced by global opportunities and global competition. Enterprises of all sizes *have to* confront cross-border influences and must begin thinking and acting across borders if they want to protect their interests. Even if they remain committed nationalists they are forced to become side effect cosmopolitans in practice by promoting the cosmopolitanization of production, competition, turnover, etc. Since markets (and not just firms) have become transnational, the congruence between loyalty and the nation, which lent opposition between labour and capital a national stamp and held it together in spite of conflicts, is crumbling. The result is a new incongruence between the perspectives and the loyalty expectations of labour and capital.

This breach between first and second modernity also changes the horizon in which familiar concepts in the social sciences, such as class are power, are understood. 'Class' or 'social stratum' are still situated *within* the national paradigm and are organized and investigated *within* this paradigm. For a variety of reasons, this approach is becoming increasingly unreal, not least because at all levels of national institutions and political and corporative organizations new kind of conflicts are arising between active globalizers, who operate both nationally and transnationally, and those who take an opposing national stance and restrict themselves to the national domain. Thus the denational and transnational 'class struggle' is a power struggle with at least a twofold frame of reference. The globalizers, not unlike migrants and NGOs, play with the borders and horizons of the nation-state, whereas their adversaries act and defend their rights within the legal forms in which national certainties have crystallized.

One need only consider for a moment what would have happened if Marx had been right when he argued that workers know no nation, whereas capital is bound to the nation. In that case a transnational workers' movement pursuing a politics of actual or potential transnational strike-mobility would have hounded territorial capital, which would ultimately have had to appeal to 'its' state for help in securing the preconditions of economic rationality by protecting it from harassment by a globalized workers' movement! But in reality an asymmetry arises between the national and non-national, territorialized and deterritorialized 'classes' which is alien to the class concept of methodological nationalism.

Could it be that globalized capital represents a model of 'economic cosmopolitanism'? Here the distinction between globalism and cosmopolitanism becomes important. Abandoning the national paradigm under the banner of the economy is by no means synonymous with a global cosmopolitanism of the common good as articulated by the advocatory civil society movements. However, we cannot exclude the possibility that national 'non-solidarity' neoliberalism (globalism) could take a cosmopolitan turn. This could happen if solidarity with fellow nationals or fellow citizens were replaced by solidarity with strangers in the context of a global distribution of labour and wealth. We can distinguish three possible scenarios:

1   *Global migration*: The migrations of the future will be marked by two conflicting age pyramids. The aging societies of Western states are confronting

young societies in many countries on the periphery and semi-periphery. This generates, first, immigration pressure from outside and, second, internal pressure to admit immigrants; in one way or another, migration will become the key political theme and a matter of survival for a Europe open to the world. Since the scope for action by states is collapsing, transnational enterprises can assume the role of cosmopolitan mediators and balancers.

2 *Labour migration*: It is not people who are emigrating, but jobs. Jobs are being exported (together with the attendant training opportunities) to places where the poor are hungry or starving, to the overpopulated regions of the world. This scenario also shows how the distinction between globalism and economic cosmopolitanism could develop, even in the teeth of national resistances!

3 *Transnational job sharing between rich and poor countries*: New ways of sharing labour and wealth across borders – without migration – are emerging. Thus, through the annihilation of distance made possible by modes of production based on information technology, a cosmopolitan distribution of labour and wealth could arise in the long run in which low-skilled jobs are exported from rich to poor countries; concomitantly, jobs requiring higher qualifications would be sourced in countries with low population densities but highly skilled workforces.

For the national outlook the first of these scenarios is a nightmare. However, the 'necessities' of national politics are delusory and self-destructive, for only a Germany or a Europe that is open to the world can reverse the rapid aging of its population and the loss of economic creativity and the resulting fiscal and public penury. Assuming that a division of labour that includes the distribution of life chances can give rise to corresponding cosmopolitan publics and communities, would this entail a lessening of the pressure of immigration? Does economic cosmopolitanism provide a model for defusing global migratory pressures because it would put an end to the need to look for work on a different continent? Or, rather, is not the opposite the case, that the need to migrate defuses the impulses that foster the cosmopolitan opening of society?

4 Anti-cosmopolitanism and its contradictions

The thesis of this book may be summarized as follows: *cosmopolitanization means the disappearance of the closed society for good.* But this is not felt as a liberation by the majority of people, who instead see their world in decline. People who have succeeded with great difficulty in orienting themselves in the labyrinths of a closed society based on sharp oppositions between us and them, inside and outside, national and international, are now suddenly faced with the contradictions of a tolerant form of society and a liberty they can neither comprehend nor live with, which reduces them to strangers in their own land. Reality has conspired against its own concepts. What kind of a world is it that no longer responds to the consolations and imperatives of 'nation', 'people', 'class', 'us or them'? The main problem is not merely that people can no longer understand the world or orient themselves in it, but that that they must defend taken-for-granted prerogatives and privileges that are now suddenly placed in question. Doesn't cosmopolitanization mean selling out the country, delivering it into the hands of foreigners, who already pull the strings anyway?

To put the same point differently, the nation is leaving the container. But what does that mean for the symbolic and integrative unity of the hybrid which replaces it? The problem is not boundarylessness, but that boundaries are no longer being drawn solely along national lines. But the human need for closure, identity and integration does not thereby simply disappear. We cannot remain content with presenting billions of confused people with an alternative between an exaggerated insistence on their identity and complete loss of identity, that is, between fundamentalism and loss of tradition.

That nationalism made independence possible is especially true of post-colonial countries. It enabled them to adapt to the West while simultaneously resisting its expansion, its insatiable greed and, all too often, its contempt. Is all this invalidated by cosmopolitanization? Is history being reversed? Is cosmopolitanization merely a euphemism for colonization?

The concept of the foreign is gaining an overwhelming power, not least because we are facing challenges and ambivalences which transform us into foreigners. Hatred of foreigners is being inflamed by the existential anxiety of nationalisms and nationalists; xenophobes have themselves become foreigners. They have become superfluous and absurd. People feel disoriented in the tolerant society, discomfited and alienated by a freedom that is too capacious. Doesn't cosmopolitanism mean writing a blank cheque which can never be cashed in? Even in our own back yard things have gone off the rails. Now we are expected not just to send care packets to all corners of the world but also soldiers, doctors and social workers to smoke out terrorist cells, fight AIDS and banish the wide-eyed accusatory, stares of starving children on the evening news. The boundaries between cosmopolitanism and anti-cosmopolitanism no longer run primarily between nations, ethnic groups and religions, but between tolerance and intolerance, the ability to tolerate and affirm contradictions and the impulse to suppress and demonize them, between toleration and hysteria, curiosity and fanaticism. In what follows I will develop these ideas in the form of six theses.

4.1 Cosmopolitanization begets its own resistance

How should we respond to the irreversible openness of a society which is thereby challenged in its very foundations and self-understanding? Cosmopolitanization is putting this question on the agenda everywhere, thereby triggering lasting and frightening conceptual seismic shifts. We generally speak of political revolutions, and in the past tense. That ultimately an even more momentous creeping revolution in deep-seated concepts of the political is silently taking place unnoticed is completely beyond our comprehension. Anti-cosmopolitanism gains its power both because cosmopolitanization is difficult to recognize and reverse, *and* because this transformation of the world imposes itself as a transgression, a violation of law in the twilight zone between (il)legality and (il)legitimacy. For instance, should we lend credence to the renowned national jurists and theorists of human rights who, at a time when state and nation are becoming uncoupled, decry the 'murder' of their nation-state legal logic and want to put reality in the dock? Or should we not rather issue the star jurists with a warrant for intentional misunderstanding of reality, a warrant which we cannot execute because they have already locked themselves in the impregnable prison of their own assumptions?

Cosmopolitanization itself promotes resistance to cosmopolitanization. Wherever we look we find false concepts, false coordinates, latent processes, denial of reality – who knows anything about cosmopolitanization? The old global order no longer functions or no longer exists (it is said). Life at the edge of chaos – this probably still reflects a Western perspective. The good news and the bad news are the same: distance has been cancelled. The chaos at the other side of the world also affects the centres of affluence. And over it all hovers the 'liberating' message that a new world order is nowhere in sight. In light of this, do we need an explanation for anti-cosmopolitanism?

Even the *word* cosmopolitanism, not just the reality, is a source of contradictions and resistance. It is the totalized victim-word of the Nazis, and not just the Nazis – victimization become word and deed – we should never forget this! 'Can the Holocaust produce values?' Imre Kertész asks. 'In my opinion, the decades-long process in the course of which the Holocaust was first repressed and then documented has only just arrived at this question with which it is struggling. The Holocaust is a value because it has led to incalculable knowledge through incalculable suffering, and hence represents an incalculable moral reserve' (Kertész 2003: 8).

On account of its peculiar history, the word cosmopolitanism also connotes incalculable suffering, incalculable knowledge and hence an incalculable moral reserve. In Europe at present there is no longer a legitimating language for hatred and persecution, for destruction and bureaucratically administered genocide, only a practice which inspires outrage as soon as it finds expression. This at any rate is the hope implicit in the word cosmopolitanism.

This choice of words is an experiment – and an open question. Anyone who finds this meaningless, nominalistic, a form of language fetishism devoid of any sense of scientific conceptual rigour, has not grasped that actions grow out of *language*, one way or another, and that the total negativity of the Holocaust may well have a formative effect on history.

4.2 *Everyone else may be able to shut their eyes to the cosmopolitanization of reality, but not social scientists*

Cosmopolitanization is irreversible, yet anti-cosmopolitanization is gaining acceptance. How should we understand this? The sole task of sociologists is to understand and interpret reality, which at present means the cosmopolitanization of reality. If they fail in this they are not doing their job. The zombie science of the national outlook is becoming an unreal 'national-social' science.

Resistance to globalization and cosmopolitanization at the beginning of the twenty-first century is something new. Anti-cosmopolitanism arose as the negation of the modern, globalized world, yet it is an original product of the dark underside of the cosmopolitanization of reality. Anti-cosmopolitanism 'swims' in the 'flows' and 'scapes' of 'liquid modernity', like global capital or the networks of the advocates of civil society. We need to make conceptual, empirical and political sense of these media and expressions of a macabre postnational anti-cosmopolitanism. A social science that fails to confront this task renders itself superfluous.

It is simply not true that group egoism and xenophobia are anthropological constants which are prior to all justification. Their alleged universal validity is a construct of the national outlook. In fact, the opposite is the case: large-scale migrations, the slave trade, abductions, forced displacement and exile, and more or less voluntary emigrations and transplantations are the rule; even the most recent European history proves this. And now a great new migration, the migration and mingling of peoples through communications media, is under way. Anyone who concludes from his mere being here that he has rights as a 'native' that include the right to exclude foreigners must, if taken literally, claim that he and his like have always been here, a thesis that can now be easily refuted. Hence a coherent national historiography and national sociology presuppose a highly developed capacity to overlook the fact that their assumptions concerning the supposed indispensability of borders and belonging are a historical exception.

4.3 *The prophets of anti-cosmopolitanism are forced to operate on the terrain of cosmopolitanization – this is what makes them so dangerous*

As the word already signals, the concept of 'anti-cosmopolitanism' is conceived in opposition to cosmopolitanism. This negation would not be very surprising if the contradiction were conceived as the return of the old, the premodern, and not as the product of the second modernity, as its *total bastardization*. Thus in the concept 'anti-cosmopolitanism' the word 'cosmopolitanism' is also intended adjectivally, that is, as cosmopolitan anti-cosmopolitanism. This means that, for example, the Islamic terrorism of al-Qaeda first became possible as a result of the inner cosmopolitanization of societies and knew how to turn this – organizationally, militarily and ideologically – very skilfully against itself (Beck 1997: chapter 4).

In contrast to nation-state terrorism (of which the ETA in Spain and the IRA in Ireland are examples), the activities of al-Qaeda are transnationally oriented and organized. This terrorist network can strike anywhere in the world because it exploits the inaccessibility and the power and adaptability of transnational networks. This is not to say that al-Qaeda's strategic goals are essentially global. It conflates anti-cosmopolitanism, anti-Americanism and anti-modernism and directs them against the Arab world, in particular, Saudi Arabia, and exaggerates them in the struggle against US-American mega-power. Its target is expressly the inner cosmopolitanization and Americanization of the Arab world, both locally and transnationally. Both its means and its ends are local *and* transnational.

This is shown in an exemplary fashion by the attack on the twin towers in New York, which was staged simultaneously as a local catastrophe and as a global media event. The message that the sole superpower at the zenith of its military superiority is vulnerable to its very core was directed both to the Americans and to the Arab resistance.

That al-Qaeda is a phenomenon of the second modernity is shown by many factors, not just the fact that its members are networked by satellites, laptops and websites. Its mode of organization is in addition a type of transnational communication and action network, for which we use the term 'multinational' in the economic sphere and the term 'NGO' in the sphere of civil society. Moreover, al-Qaeda is well aware of the chronic vulnerability of civil society, which it turns against civil society militarily with ruthless amorality, as demonstrated by its transformation of passenger jets into missiles. Al-Qaeda is 'the first multinational terrorist organization, capable of functioning from Latin America to Japan and on all the continents in between. Unlike the terrorists of the 1970s and 1980s, al-Qaeda is not guided by territorial jurisdiction – its theatre of support, as well as its operations, is global. Instead of resisting globalization, its forces are being harnessed by contemporary Islamist groups, constantly looking for new bases and new targets worldwide' (Gunaratna 2002: 11). However, the fact that al-Qaeda terrorism is a phenomenon of the second modernity is shown above all by the fact that underlying its actions is a kind of 'militant patchwork ideology' in which Islamic and European elements – borrowings from Nietzsche and Bolshevism – are synthesized with radical Islamic traditions. 'As elaborated by Azzam, al-Qaeda's ideology is a highly syncretic construction.' One of its spiritual fathers, 'Azzam took from Qutb the idea of a revolutionary vanguard – a notion whose affiliations are more with Bolshevik ideology than with any Islamic source. His attack on rationalism contains echoes of Nietzsche. Modern Western influences are fused with Islamic themes' (Gray 2003: 79).

4.4   Europe is the source of the Enlightenment and the counter-Enlightenment; modern anti-cosmopolitanism is part of the European tradition

The situation of Europe is special in spite of everything. Nowhere in the world are transnationalization and cosmopolitanization so far advanced. We must speak in terms of an 'institutionalized cosmopolitanism' as exhibited in the EU, for example, by the European Council, European law (the European Court), the single currency of the 'Euro' (which has replaced the sacrosanct national currencies), European frontiers (which have taken precedence over national frontiers, the symbols of sovereignty), and so forth.

On the other hand, on account of its globally relatively high standard of living, the obstacles to a European-cosmopolitan common sense are greater than elsewhere, at least at times of economic depression and high unemployment. Cosmopolitan realism teaches us that economic factors essentially condition the swings between tolerance and intolerance, between the cosmopolitan and the national outlooks. Foreigners are felt to be less foreign the more secure is the apparent guarantee of complete employment and economic prosperity; and they become more foreign with the increase in fear of unemployment and the erosion of welfare. Conflicts resulting from mass migration became acute only when unemployment became chronic in the receiving countries. At times of full employment, which are probably gone for good, millions of labour migrants were solicited by the USA, France and Germany, among others. In contrast to America, where new arrivals cannot expect to be supported by a social net, new arrivals in many European states have a claim to at least a minimum of social insurance in the form of unemployment benefits, health insurance and social welfare. What was intended as a protection turns into a factor of exclusion once it is endangered. Here too it holds that 'nationals' once again become 'foreigners' when the scarce resource of social welfare is threatened.

How (economically) irrational this 'alienization of nationals' is can be shown by two reflections. First, new arrivals are not only beneficiaries of social welfare systems but also contributors, and hence an important precondition if the aging process of society is not to lead to the total collapse of the social security system. Second, the more we demarcate and wall ourselves off against 'foreigners', the less we will ultimately have to defend and distribute. We rob ourselves of the opportunity created by the cosmopolitan outlook, namely, to promote the solution to apparently national problems (an aging society, sinking economic prosperity) through transnational opening and cooperation (immigration policy).

To be sure, the specificity of the European situation also results from the fact that Europe was from the beginning the source both of the Enlightenment *and* of the counter-Enlightenment. Modern anti-cosmopolitanism belongs to the European tradition which is reinventing and reorganizing itself under the influence of progressing cosmopolitanization. Isaiah Berlin proposed three cardinal ideas for understanding this modern anti-cosmopolitanism through a critical reading of Gottfried Herder (Berlin 1976): populism, expressionism and pluralism (cf. Holmes 2000).[1]

Essentialistic populism

In the spirit of the universalism of diversity (see above, pp. 50ff.), I will here proceed from the assumption that (a) there are essentialistic distinctions between 'the' Germans, 'the' Italians, 'the' Welsh, 'the' Kossovars, 'the' Serbs, and so forth (though the apparently original and indissoluble group bonds are hard to define); and (b) the members are ultimately held together by their belief in the overriding value of their belonging to this culture. Inclusion pre-supposes, indeed (according to the legend) 'logically' presupposes, exclusion. Hence essentialistic populism is one side, the other being the exclusion of, and contempt for, foreigners and exiles, and also of majorities and other minor-ities by which one feels 'oppressed' or 'threatened'.

More and more groups insist on their 'cultural identity' (however this is understood), appealing, on the one hand, to 'pure' ethnicity and, on the other, to postmodernity. In Europe, in particular, we can discern a kind of postmodern romanticism in the way ethnic ideas and ideologies are treated. It has its source in the 'identity politics' pursued by many minorities in the USA, including blacks, women, homosexuals and Hispanics. The end of Marxism, which reduced the individual to a subjective factor in conditions of production and social class, is followed by a new collectivism whose aim is to reduce the individual to his or her existence as a member of a minority culture.

The 'postmodernity' of this identity-construction consists in a symbiosis of relativism and fundamentalism. It is assumed that only members of the minority know the 'truth' concerning this group, and as a result are aware of the oppression it has suffered. Only group members, because of their origins, have access to what 'really' constitutes the cultural and political identity of the group. In this way postmodern relativism, according to which the spe-cific history of oppression is only accessible to those who have suffered it, becomes fused with a fundamentalism from which militant representatives derive their separatist demands.

Interestingly, these symbioses of relativism and fundamentalism can attack the nation-state while simultaneously claiming democratic rights and enter-ing into alliances with the European Union. Thus Pakistani fundamentalists in Great Britain have formed a 'Muslim' parliament on the grounds that the Islamic population of the country constitutes a separate political entity. In northern Italy, the Movimento Friuli campaigns for a 'Friulian nation', which it regards as part of the European Union but at the same time as inde-pendent of any state (Holmes 2000: 21f.). This involves a perverse concat-enation of ideas: apartheid and human rights – apartheid as a human right.

Talk of 'identity' and 'autonomy' ends in the principle of ghettoization: people want to be both against the state and for Europe.

Expressionism

The reinvention of tribalism in the second modernity does not have to remain bound to a naïve essentialism. It can also use 'expressivity' in all spheres of life (from food to art) to define, demarcate, reaffirm and celebrate the 'we' in its various modes of expression:

> expressionism claims that all the works of men are above all voices speaking, are not objects detached from their makers, are part of a living process of communication between persons and not independently existing entities. This is connected with the further notions that every form of human self-expression is in some sense artistic, and that self-expression is part of the essence of human beings as such; which in turn entail such distinctions as those between integral and divided, or committed and uncommitted (that is, unfulfilled), lives. (Berlin 1976: 153)

With this expressionistic turn in the 'we' and essentialism, a variety of affiliations become possible, in particular with the diverse forms of the 'invention of culture', from regional cuisine to religion. Two seemingly mutually exclusive ideologies are thereby connected with each other, the ideology of individualism – 'Your life is an artwork, reinvent yourself!' – and the ideology of collective identity, which reinvents itself and demarcates itself from others in light of the fluid boundaries in the self-confirming circles of creativity.

Pluralism

Here we also encounter a modern anti-cosmopolitan conception of diversity which defines boundaries anew. It draws on a 'cultural relativism' that appeals to respect for difference while simultaneously affirming the postmodern incommensurability of perspectives among group memberships, understood essentialistically (see above chapter 2, section 1.2). Although speaking the language of recognition of difference, it thereby brings about the anti-cosmopolitan exclusion of others through a reciprocal non-intervention pact in the internal affairs of others. At the extreme this goes along with a rejection of all forms of universalism. Overarching obligations, solidarities, legal constructs, etc., must appear as 'untrue' to this essentialistic (anti-)pluralism and must be denigrated and resisted as 'unreal', as 'false idealism' and 'humanist delusion'.

The perverse character of this anti-cosmopolitan understanding of the 'recognition' of difference resides in the fact that the principle of tolerance is twisted into its opposite, namely, an aggressive intolerance of others. The principle of incommensurability makes it possible to draw sharp new boundaries in a world of imprecise divisions only because it repudiates and destroys any form of transnational reality and understanding.

4.5 Anti-cosmopolitanism suffers from a clinical loss of reality: cosmopolitanization does not disappear simply because we refuse to acknowledge its existence

Al-Qaeda terrorists, skinheads, right-wing populists and neonationalists form the self-appointed militant vanguard of anti-cosmopolitanism. In reality, however, this anti-cosmopolitanism permeates all possible political camps, organizations and parties, and leads to the amalgamation of an anti-modern and an anti-cosmopolitan modernity. Modernization processes are at once intensified – technological and economic competition in global markets – and reversed. The result is the coexistence of the reintroduction of the death penalty, obligatory school prayer and the prohibition of abortion with the mythologization of 'high-tech', genetic technology and the hypertrophy of military technology.

All kinds of organizations – labour unions and the old left, not to mention conservative political parties and churches – try to insulate themselves against the gravitational pull of cosmopolitanization, grasping at whatever ideas are in the air, in particular, the new anti-cosmopolitan appeals to 'populism', 'expressivity' and 'plurality'.

In many regions, including European regions, 'amalgamation' is a euphemism. Thus in the case of many Eastern European populations, the spirit of renewal did not spread once they had achieved political freedom; instead the spectre of the bad past, of resentment and of the reopening of age-old ethnic wounds returned to haunt many places in the form of real or possible genocides. Self-pity over historical traumas and frustrations is cultivated under the guise of 'national consciousness', and behind the façade of democracy the language of ethnic hatred and anti-Semitism is spoken. (Imre Kertész reports that, following Nazi and Stalinist anti-Semitisms, he had to get used to a new, democratic anti-Semitism.)

There is no mistaking that this anti-cosmopolitanism, whether understated or vociferous, right- or left-wing, union- or church-driven, strictly speaking acts in an anti-national fashion because it is tantamount to a clinical loss of reality and hence betrays the interests of the nation in a global age. The economic, cultural and political challenges and contradictions of globalization cannot be conjured out of existence because we do not like reality and refuse to accept it – on the motto 'Globalization? I'm against it!' The falling of leaves in autumn can't be prevented by looking the other way, and certainly not by insisting that you hate winter.

This means that even the most radical anti-cosmopolitanism can re-erect the old boundaries only in theory, not in reality. The global risks of finance markets, the environment and terrorism are indifferent to the boundaries so dear to ethnic populism and pluralism. The tense relationship between minorities and majorities is not dissolved, but instead enflamed, by ethnic exclusion. The practice of 'incommensurability', as a politics of 'ethnic separation', has to justify itself before a global public in light of the threats of humanitarian intervention and the withdrawal of investment. Under conditions of cosmopolitanization, the boundary between human rights and civil rights has everywhere become fluid, and the resulting questions of who does and who does not belong can no longer be answered by appealing to a 'natural, essentialistic pre-given reality'.

4.6   Anti-cosmopolitanization movements propel cosmopolitanization

Opponents of globalization must globalize their protest if they are to have any hope of success. And because they organize their protest actions at summits in transnational ways, the police must also organize their countermeasures transnationally. National police forces have to overcome their national inhibitions and denationalize themselves if they want to accomplish their national task concerning transnational anti-globalization movements. The result is a spiral of side effects which propels cosmopolitanization ever further. Transnational protests call forth transnational police, a corresponding system of transnational information exchange, transnational legal institutions, and so on.

However, it is not just its side effects, but also its goals, which make the anti-globalization movement into the motor of cosmopolitanization. Clearly there exists a peculiar compulsion to be able to justify and practise opposition to globalization in terms of the goals of a different globalization, namely, the good, true globalization. Its adherents oppose pure economic globalization ('globalism') but in the same breath advocate the universalization of human rights, workers' rights, women's rights, and so forth. Those who pass for 'opponents of globalization' turn out to be also 'proponents of globalization' when we examine their motives more closely. The same is true, by the way, of other global actors, such as states and global capital. They operate in coalitions and anti-coalitions which propel political globalization, contradictions notwithstanding. The result is the peculiar phenomenon that people generally complain about cosmopolitanization and often even actively oppose it, yet it is continually propelled by the confusion of opposing, agreeing and jumbled voices, in part as a side effect, in part through the confluence of complementary aims. Something similar even holds for the invasion of Iraq in early 2003 by the USA, in opposition to the overwhelming consensus of world opinion (dismissed as 'military delinquents'). Precisely the fact that it incited world opinion against it proves once again that unilateral military action can set in train the opposite of what was intended, namely, the rallying of a relentlessly questioning global public.

Cosmopolitanism is not a recipe for global integration or global consensus. Anyone who makes the expectation that the Americans, Europeans, Arabs, Israelis, Latin Americans, Africans, and so forth will at some point unite in consensus the index of the success or failure of cosmopolitanism is mistaken. Even firmly established ideological fronts are being continually shaken. The democratic mission of the Bush administration is a continuation of an original project of the liberal left, although with paradoxical military means. What holds cosmopolitanism together lies less in what the various interrelated countries and cultures stand for individually than in what they at all costs vote and struggle *against*, namely, the systematic violation of human dignity and the new plagues of genocide and terrorist violence.

5   The cosmopolitanization of international relations

We investigated first the cosmopolitanization of society (chapter 3) and then, in this chapter, the cosmopolitanization of politics; now the same argument must be extended (at least in outline) to the domain of international relations. Here we have an excellent demonstration that the transition from the national to the cosmopolitan outlook is demanded by experience. By the same token, it makes clear the extent to which the significance of current developments remains beyond the purview of the national outlook, in particular, the completely new significance acquired by the relation between international law and human rights, starting with the war in Kosovo, if not before, continuing with the campaigns against Afghanistan and Iraq, and culminating (at least at the time of writing) with the intervention of the EU in the Congo.

In the field of international relations, in particular in the realist school in political theory, if we follow the logic of the national outlook the 'interconnectedness' of an ever more complex global society remains subordinate to the order of independent sovereign states established by the Peace of Westphalia of 1648. This implies that the magnitude of the problems that states must henceforth solve cooperatively, the authority acquired by supranational organizations, the emergence of transnational regimes and rule-governed procedures for legitimating decisions, the economization, even the ecologization, of foreign policy and the resulting blurring of the classical boundaries separating it from domestic policy – all of this has zero impact on the principle of non-intervention in the 'internal affairs' of foreign states in international law. And now the war in Kosovo and the Iraq War (as previously the activities of advocacy movements or global capital – see above, chapter 4, sections 2 and 3) force upon us the alternative between legality and legitimacy which disrupts the global order of international law.

5.1   *The question of legitimacy*

The war in Kosovo teaches us that defending human rights on foreign territory with military force, or what is called 'humanitarian intervention', can take place without the mandate of the UN Security Council in violation of international law, and yet be propelled by Western governments with high-sounding moral claims ('Never again Auschwitz'). Here an opposition between legality and legitimacy breaks out which goes beyond even the worst nightmares of a theorist of the nation-state such as Max Weber.

Sociologically speaking, we here encounter the hybrid of an illegal legitimate war. How is it possible that the use of military force beyond one's own borders could appear 'legitimate' even though it violates international law? We can throw light on this problem by reflecting on the contrary claim that a merely legal action which conforms to the letter of valid law can be condemned as immoral and irresponsible, especially when seen in light of the state-administered barbarity unleashed on Europe by fascist Germany. This drifting apart of legality and legitimacy itself inspires fear. What kind of an impasse has the world come to in which highly militarized powers launch themselves against underdog states in order to save the world from ruin with the slogan 'Never again Auschwitz!' or 'Never again September 11'? What can be of such moment – not in a moral but in a social scientific sense – that legality is outweighed by 'legitimacy'? One possible response is that a war which was illegal when it was declared is justified *post facto* by the relevant authorities, in the case of the war in Kosovo, by the UN Security Council and the German Federal Constitutional Court.

But this criterion of *post hoc* legitimation of illegal actions only makes the dilemma more acute. This criterion is of no use when we are faced with a decision. Indeed, overwhelmingly powerful, well-meaning state agents could treat an anticipated *post facto* permission as a carte blanche. Wouldn't that simply boil down to the claim that power produces legality?

These kinds of questions also arise, of course, in the case where legality and legitimacy diverge most extremely from one another, namely, the Iraq War. As is well known, the Bush administration had no end of aims it wanted to pursue with the Iraq War, among others, the elimination of weapons of mass destruction, the overthrow of Saddam Hussein, regime change and the democratization of Iraq – and ultimately of the Arab world. Let us examine the last goal. Who decides whether the domino theory of the democratization of the Arab world has failed? Does the road to peace in the Middle East, including the almost inconceivable defusing of the underlying Israeli–Palestinian conflict, lead through regime change in Baghdad? Who is authorized to make this historical decision? A subsequent democratically elected government of Iraq? Or the Arab 'brother states' whose rule would be threatened by even a minimal democratization of Iraq? Or the victorious USA? Or the Europeans standing on the sidelines? Or the UN Security Council which, viewed in the light of day, is a collection of mainly non-democratic states who at home trample on the very same human rights they pride themselves on defending in the spotlight of global publicity? This shows that in the transition to the second modernity fundamental outrages are committed that outstrip all familiar theoretical frameworks, all traditional hopes for the future, and most especially all classical political means.

In the case of the war in Kosovo,[2] in the global conflict between state sovereignty and the defence of human rights, Western regimes have decided, under the leadership of the United States, to rate genocide against Kossovars higher than the procedural rules of international law enshrined in the UN Charter. This is based on a double criticism of the legal system that states agreed among themselves and institutionalized in the UN. International law contains rules for the international use of force and makes a distinction between what is allowed and what is prohibited. But it does this in a completely inadequate manner because it does not examine whether the state powers *themselves* have a right to exist or, more precisely, whether they satisfy the requirements of the Human Rights Charter. With this the always tense relation between national sovereignty and human rights takes a profoundly fateful turn. In the transition from a nation-state to a cosmopolitan global order, a far-reaching shift in the relations of priority between international law and human rights takes place. The principle 'international law trumps human rights', which holds in the first modernity dominated by the nation-state, is superseded by the principle 'human rights trump international law', which governs global relations in the second modernity and whose implications have not yet been followed through. We don't know which is more dangerous, the eclipse of the world of sovereign subjects of international law who have long since lost their innocence, or the murky complex of supranational institutions and organizations which operate globally but remain dependent on the good will of powerful states and alliances, or the self-authorization of a hegemonic power which 'defends' human rights in foreign territories under the banner of 'military humanism'. However one assesses and evaluates this highly ambivalent state of affairs, the confusion between the old regime of international law that underlies the national outlook and the new regime of human rights which first reveals itself to the cosmopolitan outlook enables us to give a precise specification of the epochal difference between the first and second modernity as if through a magnifying glass.

The principle that international law trumps human rights rests on the principles of collectivity, territoriality and borders. Both in its conception and its origins, international law was intended to promote peace. It regulates relations between states, that is, collective subjects, not between individuals. This is how Hugo Grotius understood it, and this is also how it is understood in the articles of the UN Charter and the OSCE Final Act. Hence, the high-sounding formula in which 'the advent of a world in which human beings shall enjoy . . . freedom from fear and want' is declared to be 'the highest aspiration of mankind' , as proclaimed in the preamble to the 1948 Universal Declaration of Human Rights, could not lead to actions against the will of concerned states for reasons rooted in international law. Not for the first time the question arises whether the UN has the capacity to reinvent itself in light of these developments and experiences.

The principle that human rights trump international law, by contrast, refers to interstate relations under the cosmopolitan paradigm of second modernity. The category-forming principles of the first modernity – collectivity, territoriality, borders – are superseded by a system of coordinates in which individualization and globalization are directly interconnected and provide the conceptual framework for new definitions of state, law, politics and the individual. The bearers of human rights are individuals (not collective subjects such as 'people' and 'state'); hence human rights are essentially *individual* rights. But they must be understood at the same time in a globalized sense, since they are unthinkable apart from a universalistic claim to validity that grants these rights to all individuals, without regard to social status, class, gender, nationality or religion.

If new norms and conceptions of law emerge in relations between states according to which human rights no longer count among the 'affairs' which 'by their very nature belong to the inner competence of a state', then this is a more revolutionary development than would be a new interpretation of the relevant second article of the UN Charter. For it implies that one is not merely permitted to intervene, one is obliged to intervene. This would amount to a paradigm shift from national societies to cosmopolitan society. For international law is now addressed directly to individuals over the heads of states and it posits a legally binding cosmopolitan society of individuals.

If national sovereignty is weakened, then traditional international law loses its classical subjects. The national outlook thereby loses its empirical base and the social science founded upon it is working with the wrong categories. Among other things,[3] the cosmopolitan outlook of the second modernity creates the prospect that international law conceived in accordance with the national outlook will develop into the constitution of a world domestic politics, if only in the distant future. Individual human rights are indistinguishable from domestic political legal claims. They do not post border guards between individuals, as did the old international law, but instead dismiss them. Accordingly, Jürgen Habermas calls for a cosmopolitan law to ensure that support for persecuted individuals and peoples does not remain purely a moral matter:

For the establishment of a cosmopolitan order would not mean that violations of human rights would be judged and combated *immediately* in accordance with moral standards; instead, they would be prosecuted like criminal acts within national legal systems. A thorough juridification of international relations is not possible without established procedures for resolving conflicts. The institutionalization of these legal procedures will itself protect the judicial processing of human rights violations against a moral de-differentiation of law and prevent an *unmediated* moral stigmatization of 'enemies'.

Achieving such a cosmopolitan condition does not require a world state that enjoys a monopoly on the means of violence or a global government. The minimum requirements, however, are a functioning Security Council, the binding jurisdiction of an international criminal court and the complementing of the General Assembly of government representatives by a 'second chamber' made up of representatives of world citizens. Since these reforms of the United Nations are still a long way off, insisting on the difference between juridification and moralization remains a correct, but double-edged response. For as long as human rights are comparatively weakly institutionalized at the global level, the boundary between law and morality can easily become blurred, as we see in the present case. With a deadlocked Security Council, NATO can only appeal to the moral validity of international law – to norms for which no effective, internationally recognized institutions of application and enforcement exist. (Habermas 2006: 26–7)

But how do the states of the West respond to the criticism that it is essentially their interpretation of human rights which NATO has inscribed on its banner and seeks to legitimate by military means, in violation of standing international law? The individualistic character of human rights is criticized above all by African, Asian and Chinese scientists, intellectuals and politicians, on three grounds: (1) an emphasis on duties in contrast to the priority accorded rights, which would imply (2) upholding a communitarian hierarchy of human rights, and thereby (3) an affirmation of the priority of the common good and of communal values over a primarily negative and individualistic human rights regime. What would happen if some day a military alliance from another region, let us say Asia, were to conduct a human rights policy with military force which rests on a communitarian conception of human rights?

To be sure, this leads to an unholy confusion. The two images of world society clash, the one beholden to the national outlook, the other to the cosmopolitan outlook – on the one hand, world society viewed as a patchwork of nation-states (hence the sum of the sovereign nation-states) and, on the other, an at once individualized and globalized world society as a cosmopolitan human rights regime. But an equally important consideration is that in both cases we are also dealing with a global *power* regime. Hence the principle that human rights trump international law must be understood not only as an order of values but also as a power regime. For anyone who seeks to validate this principle presupposes, first, the end of the Cold War, hence of the bipolar global order, and, second, the military and political hegemony of the USA.

5.2   The neonationalism of the international

The issue of legitimation is a tough one. It continues to smoulder even after a military victory, as the war in Iraq demonstrates. Like no other event, this hybrid illegal-legitimate war both alarmed and individualized world opinion. It was as though each individual was confronted with the existential choice between war and peace and either was drawn into a maelstrom of moral and political dilemmas or appealed to the available positions to take a clear stance for or against.

But the controversy over legality leaves the question of legitimacy open even after a military victory has been declared; indeed, it continually reignites the question. American and British unilateralism was justified, among other things, on the grounds that the present danger, that the Iraqi dictator Hussein had weapons of mass destruction that could be quickly activated, had to be averted. The collapse of this legitimation showed that the presumption of illegality makes the question of legitimacy explosive even after the war is officially over, both nationally and internationally, both in 'domestic' and in 'foreign' politics (given that these partial global publics cannot be easily sealed off from each other). In other words, the absence of a global, or at least a Western, legal and procedural consensus on the Iraq War transforms illegal legitimacy into an open-ended issue in which 'defeats' (daily US press reports of American soldiers killed in skirmishes) and 'successes' (the painfully slow progress in democratization) intensify the explosiveness of the question of the legitimacy of the war, even in the electorally sensitive fault lines of domestic politics. Here too it again becomes clear how US military unilateralism set in train an unintended and unwelcome cosmopolitanism of side effects.

The world is struggling to develop new rules for global domestic politics. The founding principle of the United Nations was the inviolability of the sovereignty of nation-states. But in the one world whose continued existence is threatened by transnational terrorism, climate change, global poverty and unbounded military violence, this principle no longer guarantees peace, and hence the internal and external security of states and societies. It protects neither citizens against tyrannical violations of their rights nor the world against terrorist violence.

The ambivalences in the transition to the second modernity which breaks with the international legal order should lead us to 'expect' contradictory positions on the Iraq War from a sociological perspective. When a whole global order becomes suspect, the unanswerable questions and undecidable decisions are foisted onto individuals. The result is the inner anguish over the Iraq War experienced by individuals in modern, highly individualized and expressive societies.

For this reason a decisive issue is how the relation between law and power in international relations is and should be regulated in the short and the long term. In order to counteract global dangers, international law, instead of being thrown on the rubbish-heap of the Cold War, must be strengthened and made sensitive to the challenges of a world that is in the process of becoming cosmopolitan. With and following the Iraq War, a historical 'moment of decision' has arisen which announced itself with the fall of the Berlin Wall and the end of the Cold War and has been imminent since the terrorist attacks of

September 11, 2001. Decisions over the reforms to be undertaken in the coming years will shape global political geography for decades. We are experiencing a decisive moment in which nations have a choice between a cosmopolitan regime which interprets the values of modernity in such a way that the new threats can be effectively countered, and the return to a Hobbesian war of all against all in which military might replaces global law.

In autumn 2002 the USA announced a new 'national' security policy which amounts to the handbook of an American global domestic politics, the Pax Americana, to which both friends and foes are expected to conform from now on. If the *Communist Manifesto* documented a revolution from below in the nineteenth century, the national-cosmopolitan manifesto of global America at the beginning of the twenty-first century is little short of a government revolution from above. This future-oriented document, which amazingly equates domestic with global security as though this were obvious, can be read as the Magna Carta of an *American* anti-cosmopolitan cosmopolitanism.

The alternative between isolationism and multilateralism, which marked the extremes between which US foreign policy previously swung, is rejected. The spur was the shock effect of September 11. For reasons of domestic security, the USA *has to* establish itself as a global ordering power. Pre-emptive defence against the terrorist threat is imperative. American national cosmopolitanism means that American democracy can prove itself to be a universal democracy only if in the long run it spreads to all parts of the globe.

Cosmopolitan America has an elective affinity with Amnesty International (this is also clear from the text of the global-national security strategy): American mega-power throws its weight behind the global realization of human rights and democracy. Of course, this American cosmopolitanism is an abridged form of cosmopolitanism. By recognition of others it does not mean the recognition of their *difference* but of their *sameness*. The absolutistic variant of American universalism ultimately boils down to the assumption that the only true Muslim is an American Muslim. If Muslim, Africans, Arabs, Chinese and women behave in an un-American, or even an anti-American, fashion, the conclusion is that they lack authorization, they are trapped in 'anti-American prejudices', they are latent 'racists', and are in any case held prisoner by an 'out-dated' self-image.

The same pattern of an abridged (anti-)cosmopolitanism is shown by the way the US government 'solves' the problem of the overlapping and interwoven sovereignties of the second modernity. It outlines and acts on an image of the world in which one nation possesses a super-sovereignty (guess which one), whereas all other nations are granted only conditional sovereignty. The problem of the collapsing boundary between the national and the international is resolved in favour of an 'American nationalism of the international'. The anti-cosmopolitan moment resides in the fact that the US government sets itself *above* all borders in an absolutistic manner, while demanding that all other countries and governments respect them, by force if necessary. But it thereby endangers not only the legitimacy but also the effectiveness of its interventions. For example, because the USA categorically refuses to submit to the disarmament norms whose global observance it itself supports (militarily), it destroys the contractual architecture which is ultimately the only reliable guarantor of the security of American citizens. Moreover, the contradiction between committing oneself to the cause of global democracy, if necessary militarily, while paying scant regard to democratic consultation and cooperation with its allies cannot be kept off the domestic political agenda indefinitely. For this hegemonic unilateralism conflicts with America's self-image as an anti-colonial nation.

Two options: war or contract

The fight against state-supported terrorism, together with the dangers of chemical, biological and atomic weapons, can follow one of two interdependent courses, the *war option* and the *contractual option*, that is, the containment and legal restriction of explosive conflicts that endanger international stability, and hence also the security of affluent Western states.

The seemingly incompatible positions of America and Europe, viewed more closely, are actually complementary in that they reflect critically on each other. Specifically, the European option 'Make law, not war' can be inverted into a social-romantic self-delusion if the military and security components are ignored. Precisely these deficiencies were revealed by the war in the Balkans, which showed that Europeans are helpless even in the face of violent conflicts in their own back yard.

Overcoming its history of bloody wars can easily mislead Europe into the fallacious conclusion that only a pacifist political economy can lead to reconciliation and peace. Thus military conflicts unhinge the European Union, which was founded as an economic, not a military, power. There is a straightforward reason for this non-existence of Europe: there is no European offensive military force, at least not for the moment, though perhaps one will soon emerge. But even with such a military component the European Union will never be able to protect itself, let alone others, against the danger posed by terrorists bent on mass slaughter.

Europeans like to cherish illusions concerning the fact that, without the military hegemony of the USA, they would have a rude awakening from the social romanticism of their politics of reconciliation. The superior power of the USA also has a cause internal to Europe, namely, its collective renunciation of the means of violence. Only when this deficiency is recognized and rectified will a European Union foreign policy worthy of the name become possible. It will require an answer to the critical question of the authority of common institutions. A European foreign policy will become possible only when the individual state capitals recognize that transferring competencies to Brussels does not weaken but rather strengthens them, because it increases the global influence of EU states.

That global dangers can found transnational commonalities provides a necessary impetus in this direction. Environmental and peace activists draw their strength from this fact in particular, and are now finding to their annoyance that the claim to solve global problems is being colonized by the US military. The Pentagon has discovered the legitimating power of global problems and is attempting to exploit it. An autonomous source of global political legitimation has arisen with, and in, world risk society. Global actors – states as well as advocacy movements, and also corporations – can draw on it to avert, and even counteract, self-generated threats to humanity. With the insane images emanating from New York on September 11, 2001, the most powerful military and economic nation in the world saw itself abruptly empowered by the majority of humanity, as though by acclamation, to avert such dangers. The USA, the global military power, discovers in the terrorist risk the source of a global security populism.

5.3 Military humanism, or the paradox of the threat of war

The worldwide conflict over what the global order following the Iraq War should look like will have to reconcile two principles in a novel way. The idea of the national will have to be extended and reformulated into that of cosmopolitan democracy. This is ultimately the only way to alleviate the dilemmas of illegal-legitimate wars. The cosmopolitan global order too will not be able to dispense with the means of violence. If cosmopolitan law cannot be enforced, then there is no law. Of course, there is also no law where the use of post-sovereign force is undertaken by nations alone without regard to the expectations of legitimacy of a global public. Here we encounter the problem of squaring the circle of how to coordinate law, force and peace at a time of global dangers.

The despot Saddam Hussein, who led the UN weapons inspectors by the nose for years, underwent a Pauline conversion *before* the American invasion and opened the doors previously barred to the inspectors. Why? The overwhelming military power of the USA, legitimated by the fact that it represented global law, left Saddam Hussein no alternative.

Here an alternative to war or the status quo emerges which has not previously been systematically thought through, namely, a politics of military threats to bring about global change peacefully. This alternative resides in the dangerous distinction between war and the threat of war, and the no less daring dialectic involved in a refinement of the threat of war that excludes the possibility of both toppling a despotic regime *and* avoiding war. One might consider this as a kind of 'military enlightenment': only the unconditional threat of a multinational military force without rival can render the actual use of military force superfluous – this is the central paradox. Anyone who wants to make the world a better place and to avoid war must speak, and act on, a language of violent global change that comes across as completely dishonest.

The recipe is, on the one hand, to reserve the option of military pressure and, on the other, to extend the scope of the UN agreement to cover serious violations of human rights. Then it would no longer be just a matter of weapons inspections; Amnesty International would have to be granted access to prisons in order to thematize issues of legitimacy both internally and externally which are anathema to despotic regimes. Internally such regimes would be unmasked as despotic, and externally the threat of military intervention would acquire legitimacy in the eyes of a global public.

The contradictions of this 'militaristic enlightenment' are manifest. Kant's rational idea of a 'peaceful, though not yet friendly, thoroughgoing community of all peoples on earth who can enter into effective relations with one another' is rendered suspect by the revival of the medieval doctrine of 'just war'. Only a rhetoric and a strategy of military force that does not let itself be deflected from the threat of coercion even by provisional successes can bring about peaceful regime change. Any flexibility, any readiness to compromise, any hesitation prevents dictators from recognizing that they have no alternative.

The more inexorable military power is, the more futile is any attempt by a dictator, tyrant or despot to resist disarmament by military means, and hence the more probable that disarmament will succeed with just the *threat* of force, and thus by peaceful means. To be sure, the so-called peaceful means are synonymous from the start with incessant preparations for war. Indeed, their possible 'peacefulness' rests on the credibility of the threat of force. Only afterwards, when it is already too late, could they prove to be 'peaceful means'. Hence the paradox: the military conquest of a country tyrannized by a despot can be prevented insofar as military conquest is as certain to follow as night follows day. The hope that the moment war begins is also the moment it ends can, of course, prove to be a dangerous illusion. This highly questionable 'military humanism' presupposes not only absolutely superior power, the absolute politics of threats, and the despot's recognition of the utter futility of any resistance. It also requires international cooperation, collaboration and the possibility in principle of arriving at a contractual legal agreement. (It may also be tactically expedient to leave the principal evil-doers and their henchmen the escape hatch of exile or amnesty.)

The success of this politics of threats depends, first, on the weakness of the dictators against whom it is directed. It is not an option against North Korea, for example, which has atomic weapons, or against China. Second, its success depends crucially on the global political isolation of the despots in question. Hence a skilful accompanying diplomacy is required to avert any possibility of the despotic regime forging defensive coalitions. Third, the thumb-screw tactic of threatening military force is more likely to succeed if the despotic regime is already rotten from within, and hence finds itself in at least a potentially revolutionary situation. For when the power of a despotic regime is hanging by the thread of the despairing apathy of a suffering population, at the decisive moment weapons can easily change hands and sides. Thus the neighbouring states that are able to influence the despotic regime must be won over to the politics of threats. In this way, the internal elites may be emboldened to declare their opposition to the dictator at the decisive moment. It is absolutely clear that a unilateral implementation of such a policy of threats is condemned to failure, if only for the reason that it sabotages itself by parading the internal doubts and divisions of the West before a global public, and thereby loses its cutting edge and efficacy in the eyes of the despots. Only a multilateralism based on the cooperative power of states and law, hence also on a cosmopolitan diplomacy, is capable of intensifying and directing the pressure, so that the chances of success outweigh the risks. Also the temporal dimension of politics, the gradation of (feigned) impatience and (diminishing) patience, requires careful consideration and coordination.

The contrary position of mere pacifists (Europeans) has two shortcomings: it protects the tyrants and torpedoes the peaceful democratization of the world through the politics of military threats. European protectionism, which sanctifies the sovereignty of the nation-state, is morally and politically problematic. It washes its hands in public in an almost obsessive way and stubbornly ignores the burden of guilt it incurs.

The Iraq War teaches us two lessons. First, we are experiencing the paradoxes of a politics of military threats as a means of promoting global peace; for it is making clear how difficult it is to win the peace after the war has been won if the latter is branded with illegal (il)legitimacy. Second, the division of labour in global politics, according to which the Americans play the free-shooting sheriff in the poker game of war while the Europeans play the peace-loving judge, does not work. If, by contrast, warlike America were to realize that even the most overwhelming military power is futile when it opposes global law, and, conversely, peace-loving Europe were also to become a military power, then the Atlantic alliance could be revived.

5

War is Peace: On Postnational War

In George Orwell's novel *1984* the Big Brother regime employs the three slogans '"WAR IS PEACE", "FREEDOM IS SLAVERY" and "IGNO-RANCE IS STRENGTH"' (Orwell 1983: 4). These mottos of the all-powerful party are 'picked out on [the] white face' of the Ministry of Truth 'in elegant lettering' (ibid.); they epitomize 'doublethink' as the basis of all action, the schizophrenic way of thinking in which words such as 'peace' or 'democracy' can have two mutually exclusive meanings. Orwell was profoundly disturbed by the manipulative fantasies of domination opened up by doublethink; by the same token, he seems to have been fascinated by the idea that established oppositions could be overcome by doublethink – that is, applied to second modernity, the creation of categories and institutions of a postnational, cosmopolitan order. Doublethink acquires its truly alarming menace only in light of the latter possibilities, namely, the danger of the boundless manipulation of human existence through insight into the need for new categories for a world without boundaries.

The topic of this chapter is the ambivalence of a kind of 'meta-doublethink'. Doublethink has acquired a whole new dimension in virtue of the fact that it is unfolding within a global framework and space. On the one hand, the extent to which 'Oceania' has now been institutionalized and has permeated the self-understanding of politics and everyday life is alarming. Who is any longer bothered by the fact that in the West 'ministries of defence' conduct wars or that 'ministries of justice' see systematically undermining human rights as their primary task? Or that the American government spreads the values of democracy with fire and the sword, yet categorically rejects any form of consultation with other countries and governments? On the other hand, the menace of global doublethink grows out of the insight that cosmopolitan society requires new institutions to regulate and secure coexistence in the context of an interdependent and self-destructive civilization. Hence it is necessary to revise the foundations of international law that allow free play to the doublethink of 'War is Peace' and 'Dictatorship is Democracy'.

Already in 1948 Orwell realized that fascism had not in fact disappeared, despite its defeat in the Second World War. This insight finds literary expression in the sharp-witted description of the Big Brother regime as 'post-racist'. Racial discrimination has also been eliminated from the Big Brother empire which is beyond war and peace. Jews, blacks and Latin Americans of pure Indian descent are found among the highest ranks of the Party. *Fascism is Democracy* – may humanity be spared this piece of doublethink. Rather than excluding it from our future scenarios, a new Orwell might help to realize this by depicting this version of second modernity as a dystopian hell.

This brings us to the question to be addressed in this chapter: to what extent does cosmopolitan responsibility, a responsibility which does *not* end at national borders, conjure up new forms of war?

This book introduces a distinction between political and analytic cosmopolitanism, that is, between philosophical cosmopolitanism and the cosmopolitan outlook, in order to separate clearly the question of why reality has become cosmopolitan from the question of whether the store of ideas of normative cosmopolitanism can provide *political* answers to a self-destructive civilization (see introduction and part I). I hope to have shown that the concept of empirical-analytic cosmopolitanism is fruitful, viable and capable of development and that it fosters productive debates. Normative-political cosmopolitanism, by contrast, must confront from the beginning the uncomfortable paradox that the successful institutionalization of the cosmopolitan outlook, which is supposed to promote global peace, calls forth just the opposite, namely, the legitimation and legalization of war. Hence a self-critical cosmopolitanism must come to grips with the perverse supposition that the legal regime which is supposed to lead to the recognition and protection of the rights of others contributes to making war 'just' and more probable by conferring on it the blessing of the law.

This negative 'justification' of a normative and politically oriented cosmopolitanism through the apparent detour of self-criticism and critique of ideology (cf. Beck 2005: final chapter) will be set forth here in five steps. First, two models of global order – 'Pax Americana' and 'global cosmopolitanism' – will be contrasted; second, the distinction between national war between states and postnational war will be sharpened; then two key characteristics of postnational war – the ambiguity of a 'human rights war' and the ambiguity of 'wars against terrorism' – will be explored, respectively, in a third and fourth step; and, finally, in a fifth step the implications of the national, international and cosmopolitan perspectives for models of a new global order will be subjected to a comparative examination.

1   Pax Americana or global cosmopolis, global hegemony or global law

The hope that the end to wars between states would also mark the end of war as such and the dawn of an age of peace has proven to be an illusion. The monster of war has not been defeated, it has merely changed its countenance.

'New wars' (Kaldor 1998; Münkler 2002) were and are being conducted, adding new outrages to the old, which have not for that reason become any less. Whereas wars between states in the past ended with the victory of one side, wars of the new type know no temporal or spatial boundaries. Here too the law of reflexive modernity holds (Beck, Bonss and Lau 2001; Beck and Lau 2004), according to which the apparently fixed anthropological dualities – war and peace, civil society and military, friend and foe, military and police – are becoming blurred. This blurring of distinctions means that 'postnational war' (Beck 2000b) has become unpredictable. Whereas the classical wars of the first modernity rested on the state's monopoly of the means of violence, now war has become boundless, first, because of the demonopolization and privatization of organized violence (by terrorists and warlords) and, second, because of the globality of dangers and of sensitivity to issues of human rights, and hence because states collaborate in preventing or stopping violations of human rights. We are here faced with a grim variant of the sorcerer's apprentice paradox: the means which are supposed to promote freedom justify new forms of war.

Two competing models of global security policy in an era of civilizational dangers present themselves. One model of global order marches under the banner of *Pax Americana*; the alternative model may be called *global cosmopolis*, by which is meant a federal planetary system of states which is not ruled by a 'solar' world state but is composed of regional and continental alliances of states (Europe, Latin America, Asia, Africa, North America) as 'points of crystallization' which both enable and counterbalance the centralization of power.

It should be noted from the outset that, in spite of all oppositions, we must not overlook or underestimate certain generally hidden commonalities: *both* models of global order are variations on the principle of global responsibility; accordingly, they advocate overcoming the old international legal order of sovereign nation-states both in word and in deed with the goal of promoting 'humanitarian intervention'.

The distinction between Pax Americana and global cosmopolis resides in two mutually exclusive models of order: whereas the former is governed by the principle of hierarchy concerning relations between states, in the latter the principle of equality and cooperation prevails. The Pax Americana system operates on the assumption that there are deep-seated differences between states – on the one side, 'us', the community of Western states, representing peace and democracy, on the other, failed states, dictatorships and 'rogue states' suspected of fostering terrorism. Given this global state of affairs, the postulate that all states are equal is merely unrealistic wishful thinking to the American way of viewing things. America is *qualitatively different*, militarily and morally superior to the rest of the world, an 'exceptional' world power. The distinction which emerges here between American 'realism' and European 'idealism' plays a key role in the self-understanding of Americans, both in politics and in political science (Kagan 2003).

The principle of cooperation underlying global cosmopolis, by contrast, states that America may be the most powerful nation on earth, but this is merely a quantitative difference. The United States is in principle 'equal', at most a *primus inter pares*. The model of civil society, in which the idea of equality reigns, is thereby turned outwards and globalized into the idea of 'cosmopolitan civil society'. The equality that Tocqueville declared to be the birthright of all Americans is projected onto relations between countries and states.

Exaggerating somewhat, Pax Americana amounts to replacing the United Nations by the United States (at least in the middle term). The US president George W. Bush declares that the USA is the hope of the world. In a world which is no longer divided by the opposition between communism and capitalism, but is becoming increasingly interdependent and increasingly dangerous, the threats to peace have become diffuse and unsurveyable. To combat them it is necessary, in particular, to concentrate world military power and direct it against the new dangers. One premise is that a new era began with the collapse of the Soviet Union, because the global atomic threat no longer exists. This gives the USA the unique historical opportunity to create an international system of freedom and fairness based on American values of freedom and democracy. For the only power capable of imposing and safeguarding this new global order is the global hegemon, the USA (Speck and Sznaider 2003). If it is to play this role within a radically unequal world of states, it must liberate itself from old and new fetters. Among the latter are the principle of non-intervention in the internal affairs of sovereign states, and all international agreements and institutions which legally constrain the global hegemon and require it to consult with other states. The uniqueness of its task justifies the USA, first, in refusing to sign and support key international agreements, including the treaty on the non-proliferation of chemical and biological weapons of mass destruction; second, in downgrading the Security Council, which should be restricted to its original function of a global Mother Teresa; and, third, as the 'exceptional' global power, in claiming veto power in the International Court of Justice, notwithstanding that it is a logical extension of American post-Second World War cosmopolitanism. Gulliver's self-liberation from the fetters of international treaties and institutions is celebrated as the steadfastness necessary to make the world a better place or, in Wilsonian terms, to make the world safe for democracy.

This hegemonic role involves defending two principles which are highly controversial across the world: first, the principle of *prevention of potential rivals* and, second, the principle of *preventive war*. If the only hope for the world in the long run is the Pax Americana, this implies that the USA can never permit the emergence of a rival to its overwhelming power. Accordingly, the 'National Security Strategy of the United States of America' states that the military power of the USA must be so great that it inhibits potential rivals even from attempting to challenge it. At the same time, it is argued, it is necessary to engage in preventive military interventions, given the diffuse character of the terrorist threat. Thus the new resoluteness of the US administration is demonstrated by the fact that it claims the right to violate the prohibition on preventive wars, a fundamental rule devised by the international legal system to limit armed conflicts. Its validity can be traced back to the League of Nations and the Kellogg–Briand Pact;[1] it underlies the Charter of the United Nations, and has been repeatedly confirmed by the UN General Assembly. This prohibition renders the power of 'preventive self-defence' claimed by the USA illegal.

Such a militarized definition of the global situation also implies that the role of actors, that is, states and international organizations such as NATO and the European Union, must be renegotiated and restructured. The territorial self-understanding of NATO, the restriction of its operations to attacks on European states, must be suspended in order to counter the growing dangers resulting from international anarchy, the chaos of collapsing states and the privatization of the means of violence. The NATO states must be re-equipped and made 'fit' for the struggle against the global turbulences fuelled by economic disparities between centre and periphery, North and South, and by the outbreaks of violence and terrorism sparked by the confluence of poverty, religious intolerance, racial hatred and anti-Americanism, and by ethnic states and civil wars.

As noted, the alternative model of global order, *global cosmopolis*, rests on the contrasting principle of equality of states and accordingly emphasizes the importance of global (civil) law, even against the global hegemon. The global cosmopolis should be realized step by step through a corresponding reform of international law and international organization, in particular, the United Nations, in accordance with the principles of a cosmopolitan regime which rests on recognition of the difference of others, and in particular on recognition of multiple modernities. A global law would have to be formulated accordingly which envisages both contractually regulated possibilities for consultation of continental alliances and their obligation to act in concert. This would include, for example, something akin to a veto-free UN which could function as a global parliament equipped with a standing army for peacekeeping purposes and capable of imposing disarmament worldwide.

The conflicting principles of the vertical and the horizontal are in fact reflected in the conflicts between Pax Americana and global cosmopolis: American global unilateralism on the one side, multilateralism on the other; dismantling versus expansion of global law; weakening versus strengthening of the United Nations, etc. The mutual recriminations are thereby pre-programmed. Those who want a stronger UN – let us call them Europeans – fail to show the necessary resoluteness; they are not ready to face the remorseless facts of a world balanced on the edge of the abyss. In the eyes of others, the hegemonic USA is in danger of becoming a 'war criminal' which betrays its own values – democracy and freedom – both internally and externally.

What so complicates the relations between the two models of global order and makes them an inexhaustible (and baleful) source of transnational misunderstandings is, in the first place, the weaknesses of both models: 'civil society' disappears in the Pax Americana, politics, by contrast, in global cosmopolis. The one side wants to make 'politics' the underlying principle of a new global order, the other the 'society of equals'. Europe as the advocate of global cosmopolitanism stands as the (unwilling?) defender of a status quo that is scarcely worth preserving. The US government, by contrast, makes unilateral distinctions between friend and foe and is unmasked as a 'global revolutionary' who promises and defends the globalization of democracy with military means.

On the other hand, the question arises whether the two models are in fact mutually exclusive. That a ruthless either/or prevails between these visions of a new world order can surely be excluded. Also how far the conflicts extend and where the commonalities begin certainly depends on how rigidly or pragmatically the positions are defended. As regards the situation of Iran in summer 2003, for example, Europe could win the United States over to 'a common, realistic Iran policy that even some members of the Bush regime could actively support, a policy that takes account of Iranian realities in order to change them' (Navid Kermani). Generally speaking, the commonalities of the two models of global order depend on how 'realistic' the Europeans and how 'idealistic' the Americans are willing to become. Moreover, conflicts are not a crime but, on the contrary, necessary preconditions of a global liberalism and an open cosmopolitan society.

This is all the more true because a new heterogeneous 'global class' (Sklair 2001) (composed of European and non-European governments, the military and the US administration, and also of global NGO actors, transnational experts of international organizations, etc.) is busy ordering the self-destructive planet. In everyday (world-)politics different factions of the 'global class' are competing over how to accomplish for global society what elites previously accomplished for the nation, namely, creating a well-ordered society. The prospect of this taking place without alternatives and without opposition would be a nightmare.

2   On postnational war

The postnational forms of war of the second modernity do not mean that classical war between states has been abolished. Rather, new, *additional* postnational wars are occurring alongside the 'old' wars between states. One cannot even preclude that postnational wars will culminate in national wars, and hence even in new kinds of world wars. For the purposes of historical classification, however, we need to distinguish clearly between old and new wars, between wars between states and postnational 'military interventions' for humanitarian purposes or as prevention against terrorist attacks.

The classical right to go to war lays down the distinctions between war and peace, enemy and criminal, soldier and civilian, and thereby defines the category of war between states of the national first modernity. As Carl Schmitt (1963) emphasizes, this also shows respect for the enemy who is acknowledged as such: the enemy is an enemy, not a criminal. On this definition, war is a matter between states, conducted and brought to a conclusion by state-organized armies. The common criticism was that formalized, regulated war is a special kind of atrocity, because the regulated butchery of enemy soldiers is no better or more noble for the fact that it follows specific rules. Despite its brutality and organized inhumanity, war between states 'civilized' by the laws of war at least rests on mutual respect for the guiding differences; consequently, the options for unconstrained brutality afforded by modernity are at least tentatively restricted. War has a beginning and an end, and there are limits to what is permitted; there are political aims and peace negotiations that put an end to war. The lid to Pandora's box is kept ajar, but it cannot be thrown wide open at will.[2]

What, by contrast, characterizes postnational war? The blurring and dissolution of the basic distinctions which are constitutive for wars between nation-states. The either/or is replaced by a both/and – both war and peace, both police and military, both crime and war, both civilian and soldier. Two phenomena, in particular, highlight this border-transgressing and border-effacing character of postnational 'war': first, the defence of human rights on foreign soil and, second, the attempt to minimize the global terrorist risk by military means and control it with the resources of the state.

How should we categorize the Kosovo 'conflict' in which NATO (without a UN mandate but with the consent of a majority of European peoples and governments) flew bombing raids to prevent a genocide in the former Yugoslavia? Was it a 'war' in the sense of war between states? A 'peace war' supposed to halt a crime against humanity, and hence promote peace, in a civil war zone? Was it a 'police war' with NATO playing the global policeman restoring public order? Was it an 'anti-war' to end a total war being waged by a state against a portion of its own citizens, whom it was supposed to protect, behind the bulwark of sovereignty claiming the right to non-interference by other states? In fact, postnational war is born of this implosion of the classical distinctions.

What made the NATO attack on Yugoslavia so confusingly (il)legitimate could easily lead to the normalization of a new kind of war. This war is postnational, and hence no longer conforms to Clausewitzean precepts, because it is neither conducted in the national interest – 'the continuation of politics with other means' – nor can it be understood in terms of the old rivalries of more or less hostile nation-states. Rather, cosmopolitan responsibility makes postnational war possible by *annulling* the restriction on the responsibility of states to their national territories and their lack of responsibility beyond national frontiers. Human rights must be guaranteed and enforced beyond the boundaries of sovereign nation-states, as well as *within* individual states and possibly *against* their resistance. The unlimited sovereignty of sovereign states, which made classical war between states possible, makes the enforcement of human rights impossible. Only if the principle of state sovereignty is restricted can the validity of human rights be assured against violations of civil rights by governments. States are no longer the sole legal subjects of cosmopolitan law but also *individuals* whose rights must be protected by superstate authorities against 'sovereign' states. The resulting 'post-wars', postnational both-wars-and-not-wars, break with the national state-against-state warfare of the first modernity.

The logic of the nation-state is not, of course, automatically suspended. Thus on 26 June 2003, the German Federal Constitutional Court in Karlsruhe rejected a suit brought by four siblings whose parents were shot by SS soldiers in June 1944 in Distomo in Greece. The SS shot a total of 218 men, women and children there in June 1944 as reprisals for attacks by partisans. The siblings' suit was rejected on the grounds that, according to the international law valid at the time, only states but not private persons can claim reparations for war crimes. The Federal Constitutional Court judged the case in accordance with international legal jurisprudence valid in 1944.[3] This judgement prompts the question of where acts of war end and the torture of civilians begins, a crucial distinction that can be easily effaced in view of the danger emanating from transnational terrorist networks.

The national outlook or, to put it in terms of political science, neorealism, fails because it cannot comprehend the new logic of power in global society. Anyone who believes that the global policeman NATO or the USA is merely pretending to play the role of global policeman while really pursuing ur-American economic and geopolitical power interests in the powder keg of the Balkans or the Arab world not only misunderstands the situation but also overlooks the extent to which the politics of human rights (like the imposition of 'free markets') has become the civil religion, the faith of the United States itself. In addition, the one thing does not exclude the other. The defence of human rights on foreign soil can peacefully coexist with geostrategic, economic and hegemonic interests. A new kind of postnational politics of *military humanism* is emerging.

Postnational war must also be distinguished from other causes of war with which we are simultaneously confronted. Mary Kaldor (1998) and, following her, Erhard Eppler (2002), Herfried Münkler (2002) and many others, have analysed the privatization of violence in this connection. This can be viewed as a radicalized neoliberalization of the state, in particular, of the state monopoly on the means of violence. Where states in the European sense never developed or have collapsed, force has never been monopolized by the state and has never been privatized. Such pre- or post-state wars are not fuelled, for instance, by age-old ethnic rivalries, as is often supposed, but by a 'civil-war market' in which the prices and profits for buying and using privatized force are determined or negotiated (Collier 2003).

Hence, what is here called 'postnational war' and is analysed in terms of the transition 'From Monopoly of Violence to Market for Violence' (to use the title of Eppler 2002) involves quite different kinds of crises in the state's organization and use of violence. The 'market for violence' thesis essentially applies to parts of the world in which state structures either do not yet or no longer exist, not to advanced Western states. Where (for whatever reason) organizing state power does not exist (or no longer exists) the guiding idea of state formation can serve as a model for what has to happen if the condition of freely fluctuating power, and the resulting danger of war, is to be overcome. Here it is the recipe of first modernity that promises to provide help. In the case of postnational wars, by contrast, it is the *triumphs* of advanced states and of cosmopolitan empathy and the human rights regime that unleash 'world-police wars'.

This also holds for the 'war' against terrorism. Terrorist violence is indeed an extreme form of the privatization of violence. But it conforms neither to the profit principle nor to the market principle; it serves neither to enrich the terrorists personally nor to satisfy their private rancour, regardless of how much the latter constitutes the attackers' motive and the driving force for their acts. There is a categorical difference between the national terrorism of the first modernity and the transnational global terrorism of the second modernity – even though this difference often becomes blurred in concrete cases. Islam as such is not terroristic, nor is transnational terrorism necessarily restricted to radical Islam. Perhaps radical Islam, as advocated by the Egyptian thinker Sayvid Outh and put into practice by the al-Qaeda network, is only the source, and this plague will infect other world religions and global regions.

At the centre of the radical Islamic critique of the West as presented by Outh is the notion that modern Western society is infected with a spiritual emptiness. Ironically, this overlooks the fact that the USA, which it regards as the epitome of the diabolic West, is one of the most religious societies in the world. By the same token, this critique of the West draws on Western ideas, in particular on European anarchism. Thus – although we cannot go into the details here (see Gray 2003) – it is by no means a revolt of tradition against modernity, but a modern *anti-modernity*, both in its ideas and in its choice of instruments of terror. The recipe for success and the novel connection between the weapons of terror and radical Islam and transnationality (in contrast to the terrorism of the IRA, for example) are fuelled by the conscious connection between modernity and anti-modernity – just think of how the attack on the World Trade Center transformed the mass media into the global stage on which the terror was played out.

National terrorism, by contrast, whether nationally or ethnically motivated, aims at founding a national or ethnic state of one's own (this is its definition of success). The terror elites of today are the potential heads of government and ministers of tomorrow. This all-or-nothing game, this career path from illegality to legality, from control of terrorist violence to control over the state monopoly of the means of violence, is part of the old, national terrorist motivation and ideology.

All of this applies only with qualifications to transnational terrorism of the al-Qaeda variety. The active units and their 'handlers' are motivated neither by territory nor by the state, and they are not fighting for their own state. This is what makes them so inscrutable.

What has shocked humanity since September 11, 2001, is a diffuse *political* terrorism directed against the foundations of modern society and the modern state, symbolized by the USA and the cathedral of the global economy, the World Trade Center. This form of terrorism – in contrast to the market for violence that arises in a failed state – can no longer be eradicated by constructing a state. Rather, the guiding idea of the state as the guarantor of security is being effectively put in question.

The terrorist attacks derive their significance from their specific characteristics, on the one hand, and from the characteristics of hegemonic state power against which they are directed, on the other. The American President George W. Bush was literally rendered speechless by the horrific images in the mass media of the two civilian aircraft which, transformed into human missiles, caused the twin towers of the World Trade Center to go up in flames. Was it a crime? A second Pearl Harbor? Who was the relevant authority, the police, the US military, NATO? Unlike Pearl Harbor, no military base had been attacked. And it was *not* an attack by one state on another. Those who carried it out did not wear uniforms, the identity of the instigators is unclear, they have no address. Only when the word 'war' fell from the lips of the President – 'A war has been declared on America' – did the terrorist attack become *political* terrorism and then *global* terrorism, even though America continues to pursue this 'enemy' not as an enemy (in the sense of the laws of war) but as a *criminal against humanity*, devoid of rights. It may be that at first the talk of 'war' against terror was still meant in a metaphorical sense (like the 'war against poverty' or against 'drugs'). Yet the more the 'war' against terror narrowed into a military war, a war between states, the more the inscrutable terror was elevated in world politics to the status of global terrorism.

Nevertheless, the means of control deployed by the global hegemon, in spite of its unique military superiority, are failing in the face of this terrorist threat. The power of the state rests both internally and externally on the logic of deterrence, which ultimately plays on the threat and the fear of death. But these kinds of terrorists cannot be deterred: how can you threaten suicide bombers with death? The deployment of the instruments of power at the disposal of states presupposes either control over or conquest of a territory. These terrorists, however, do not control a territory, and unlike the state they are not tied to a particular territory – they are stateless, present everywhere and nowhere – a bad starting point for military deterrence and intervention.

One answer to the problem of postnational wars is to treat them like classical wars between states and assume that the warring parties, though not states, represent quasi-states. This makes it possible, first, to take advantage of one's military superiority and, second, to bring about a negotiated settlement 'from above'. Examples of this approach are the Dayton Accord (through which Bosnia-Herzegovina was 'pacified') and the Oslo Agreement (which was supposed to bring about peace between the Israelis and the Palestinians). The alternative is to ignore ethnic slaughter within 'sovereign states', to turn a blind eye, erect walls and take refuge in the protectionist fictions of a national global order. To be a mere spectator, however, is scarcely possible because streams of refugees, transnational criminality, diaspora groups in one's own country and, not least, transnational terrorism did away with these fantasy borders long ago.

3   War is peace: human rights wars

Human rights represent a European source of conflicts. And yet compelling reasons to object to or resist the moral and political influence of the human rights regime are difficult to imagine. The appeal to humanity and its rights carries a claim whose force is impossible to escape. Who would want to deny that he or she is a human being? And is it not more urgent than ever to protect elementary human rights across the globe against egregious violations?

More than 3 billion human beings – approximately half of the world's population – not only do not enjoy any protection of their rights, they do not even have a claim to protection. As a consequence, all manner of violations are routine occurrences, including torture, genocide, ethnic cleansing, mass executions, complete disappearances, trade in people, slavery, illegal imprisonment, illegal treatment of refugees, asylum seekers and migrants, murder of the handicapped, theft and trade in organs, prostitution and, not least, mass mortality as a result of the vicious cycle of poverty, hunger and illness. All analyses confirm that violations of basic rights are increasing. Even the number of states in which human rights violations are a routine occurrence, rather than diminishing, is on the increase.

A new exchange logic, involving turning a blind eye to human rights violations, is even beginning to take hold. The danger of terrorism *suppresses* the alertness of political allies to human rights violations. Under the spell of the terrorist threat, a lawless space has opened up which permits what was until recently forbidden, a double carte blanche in interstate relations. Each state can combat its domestic enemies as 'terrorists' with the blessing of the international community, *and* the human rights violations of allies are treated with discretion and thereby facilitated.

What makes the human rights regime so powerful? What are its unwanted, but at the same time revolutionary, 'side effects'?

3.1 The human rights regime becomes a counter-concept that affirms the divided world in its diversity and creates new hope for possibilities of action

Faith in the secular religion of human rights makes no distinction between Germans and French, *citoyen* and *bourgeois*, Christian and Muslim, circumcised and uncircumcised, men and women, people of colour and those whose skin is white. All positions involving the negation of individuals – of ethnicity, caste, class, religion and gender – are transcended in the equality of the basic rights of all human beings. Human rights represent the dream of a new, more humane global order: all peoples, states, religions, ethnic groups living united under human rights raised to the status of law. It is ultimately a matter of an age-old principle which can be traced back to the philosophy of the Stoics and which had already become policy, or at least a political ideology, during the Roman Empire.

Understood in this way, the normatively oriented cosmopolitan outlook modulates all dualisms that have divided and separated human beings physically, spatially, temporally, spiritually or ideologically. The difference between the ontologically other and the other recognized in human rights is surmounted. The result is a reflexive human being who can appreciate the diversity of human forms of existence because he is assured of his human rights. The stoic model of cosmopolitanism propounds the two-persons doctrine of human being and citizen. In this way the discourse of human rights permeates the whole world. Oppositions and differences are assimilated, even symmetrically affirmed. But we should keep in mind that human rights also have a moral-totalitarian aspect. There is ultimately no pardon, no compromise – either one violates them or one does not.

The implication – or, more cautiously, the intention – is that it is no longer the power of one state, or a plurality of states, but rather law that determines what constitutes peace. Ultimately, belligerent global politics would be replaced by global law; just as within the framework of the nation-state the combination of the monopoly on the means of violence and the rule of law was able to rein in, though not to eliminate, civil wars, so too could human and cosmopolitan rights rein in interstate global civil wars. However, this could also lead to an increase in military conflicts.

3.2 The logic of law and treaties is fundamentally two-faced in world domestic politics: it civilizes states while simultaneously liberating them from the national constraints on power and violence

The human rights regime inaugurates a new duality, namely, the distinction between groups and regions in which human rights are respected and those in which they are not, whether not yet or no longer. This difference between worlds gives rise to permanent tensions between centre and periphery, North and South, Christian and Muslim countries, democracies and dictatorships. The opposition between human rights and human groups relates to spaces, and hence can be reterritorialized in the form of calls on states to transform themselves from national to cosmopolitan states, that is, to see their primary task, internally, in protecting and fostering human rights and the wealth of cultural diversity and, externally, in contributing to guaranteeing human rights in other countries. The measure of this inner cosmopolitanization of the world of states is the extent to which the opposing concepts of the first modernity are de-essentialized. Thus nationalists become the neonationalists who cut themselves off from or defend themselves against the de-essentializing demands of human rights.

Even the opponents of human rights are bound into a human rights order. The prosecution of states and groups who trample human rights under foot is just, but not the prosecution of groups and states who enforce human rights against others. An asymmetry of conflicts arises: not the rejection of human rights but only their unconditional recognition and realization legitimates states in intervening in other states.

Depending on the situation, the new asymmetry permits 'human rights crusades': human rights are secularizing the Last Judgement in the shape of the ever-present possibility of 'humanitarian interventions'. The anticipation of the global validity of human rights is inaugurating something which for the present is still regarded as precluded. In this way an external obligation is becoming the global self-obligation to respect human rights and the basic rules of democracy. Internalized evaluative standards potentially and actually destabilize despotic regimes from within, but also from without. But ultimately no state any longer possesses a monopoly on the use of *legitimate* violence because the legitimacy and legality of the use of violence is becoming subject to the condition that human rights are respected as the highest good.

3.3   Human rights empower the powerless within states and expose powerless states to the military aggression of powerful states

Max Weber restricted the legitimacy of political action strictly to the domestic sphere. The human rights regime eradicates the boundary between the internal and the external and questions the legitimacy of state action both internally and in external relations between states. A purely internal, national legitimation is ultimately excluded and a new both/and is inaugurated: state action first acquires its legitimacy from both internal (national) and external (interstate) approval, where different criteria apply in external and in internal relations, with human rights increasingly playing a complementary role in relations between states.

The human rights regime gives rise to a geography of human rights which founds a new geography of power, once again both within and between states.

Within states it empowers powerless groups and persecuted individuals and minorities; in relations between states it empowers powerful states to intervene beyond the territorial sovereign order. But even given this new hierarchy of morally and militarily highly armed crusader-states and underdog-states, it is difficult to escape the moral gravitational pull of the human rights regime. For resistance to it awakens the suspicion that the old privileges are being defended in order to persecute one's own population, which is often enough the case. 'We remain extremely sensitive to any undermining of our sovereignty, not only because sovereignty is our last defence against the rules of an unequal world, but because we are not taking part in the decision-making processes of the Security Council nor in overseeing their implementation', declares Algerian President Bouteflika, and points to the important questions that remain unanswered: 'When does aid end and interference begin? Where is the dividing line between humanitarian, political and economic intervention? Are only weak and weakened states candidates for intervention or does the principle hold for all without exception?' (quoted from Crossette 1999).

In fact, the concept of 'humanitarian intervention' is situated in a grey zone. The guiding concepts of transnational, cosmopolitan accountability – 'aid', 'defending human rights', 'containing conflicts', 'preventing genocide and state violence against minorities', etc. – open up the possibility of effectively and legitimately pursuing one's own national or hegemonic aims under the pretext of a cosmopolitan mission. What is worse, the countries affected by such interventions are politically demoralized.

The crux is twofold. On the one hand, the principle of sovereignty loses the unconditional validity that it enjoyed as a matter of course in the first modernity. On the other hand, the assertion of the boundlessness of the new accountability amounts to robbing states selectively of their sovereignty and, by the same token, it means that weak and poor states – if they accept the universal validity of human rights – give the rich and powerful states carte blanche for 'legitimate intervention'. Cosmopolitan accountability, therefore, does not imply a general abolition of sovereignty but its *redistribution*. The cultural, legal and moral transcending of boundaries favours the emergence of a cosmopolitan monopoly of the West on morality, law and violence. In fact, the key question of the second modernity is the one posed by President Bouteflika: In view of the new boundlessness of accountability, how can the boundaries between aid and interference, accountability and disempowerment, be redrawn, justified and internationally guaranteed?

To be sure, each of these decisions faces a dilemma: both intervention and non-intervention produce resistance and delegitimation. This fundamental ambiguity becomes all the more acute the further the realization of the human rights regime progresses. Failing to intervene can invite the charge of ignorance, double standards and selectivity. Conversely, the enforcement of cosmopolitan law in the face of resistance (not just within the country affected but also in the international community) triggers a standard avalanche of accusations of imperialism and feeds the suspicion of fomenting the 'clash of civilizations'.

In this situation the key contradiction continually reappears: whereas international law forbids interventions in foreign countries, human rights command them. The new cosmopolitanism is balanced on a knife-edge. The aim of juridifying international relations, and thereby overcoming the martial atavism of the first modernity, is threatened, on the one hand, by indifference or ignorance and, on the other, by the self-authorization of the major military powers to conduct good and hence perpetual wars.

3.4   The economy of war-for-peace, or why the world has not yet been consumed by a military conflagration

The political double standard of an interventionistic human rights policy is evident: interventions are expensive and risky propositions for the countries and governments that want to or are supposed to carry them out. Hence, the imposition of human rights will always remain a selective matter in a world in which the guarantee of human rights is internalized and institutionalized as a hope but which is simultaneously characterized by persistent human rights violations that cry out for remedy.

To be sure, there is also a theoretical double standard. This becomes apparent when authors who deny the existence of postnational wars present the ever-widening gap between the duty to intervene and non-intervention as proof of the (relative) irrelevance of the phenomenon. Certainly the 'economy of war' (Münkler) precludes an omni-interventionism. And whether interventions actually occur depends on how much the human rights regime shapes the foreign policy of the states involved. Let us assume for the sake of argument the best-case scenario in which the costs of humanitarian war-for-peace hinder or prevent de facto interventions. Let us assume further the classical legal position that the prohibition on violence (Article 2, Number 4, of the UN Charter) which excludes humanitarian interventions has priority over the practice of the Security Council in the 1990s that contradicts this position. Even this in no way alters the fact that, first, the globalized human rights regime today already confronts militarily weak states that egregiously violate human rights in particular with the permanent *possibility* of intervention. Second, the human rights regime has profoundly transformed the foreign policy of powerful states, especially the USA, but also Europe, and power relations at the global level. Thus the *Report of the Commission on Global Governance* issued by the United Nations underscores that supranational organizations should not only regulate economic globalization but also enforce the new ethics of global democracy and human rights. Many may regard this as meaningless verbiage. But even before the Bush administration, the Clinton administration had declared that it wanted to integrate closely foreign policy and human rights policy. In the words of the Secretary of State of the Clinton administration, Madeleine Albright:

Support for human rights is not just some kind of international social work. It is vital to our security and well-being, for governments that disregard the rights of their own citizens are not likely to respect the rights of anyone else. In this century, virtually every major act of international aggression has been perpetuated by a regime that repressed political rights. Such regimes are also more likely to spark unrest by persecuting minorities, sheltering terrorists, running drugs or secretly building weapons of mass destruction. (Albright 1998)

This in no way diminishes the importance of the question of the economy of war-for-peace: how long will the superpower be willing to bear the risks and costs of a war? Or, conversely, whence the pressure to intervene, in spite of the costs and risks? Why did the 'humanitarian use of violence' occur in Somalia, in Kosovo and in the Congo, while no less brutal excesses of violence, for example in Sudan, in East Timor, in Angola, in Liberia or in Rwanda, did not lead to interventions?

The factors that trigger interventions have been investigated and have inspired a range of hypotheses:

- *Asymmetries of power*: The weaker the 'rogue state' the more likely it is to be attacked. The imposition of the human rights regime presupposes and intensifies asymmetries of military power among states. Here, too, it holds that the weak get trodden upon. Consequently, to reverse the argument, the preservation or maximization of the geopolitical asymmetry is the precondition for powerful states maintaining their superiority, and thus their appetite for 'post-heroic victories'. This precondition was fulfilled in the case of the Kosovo War, the war in Afghanistan and the Iraq War.
- *The synthesis of idealism and realism*: An intervention that rests *exclusively* on moral arguments is as idealistic as it is improbable. The probability of intervention grows where human rights idealism is connected with the realism of expanding the scope for action of the state. Globally acting nation-states are hardly so meek and pious in their commitment to human rights that they do not expect some 'pay-off' for their cosmopolitan mission in support of human rights and against the terrorist threat, in other words, some national benefit (in the form of oil, geostrategic advantages, etc.). This means that human rights policy is a prime illustration of the fact that, and the way in which, idealism and realism complement, reinforce and merge with one another.
- *The principle of egoistic altruism*: What awakens the vigilance and readiness to assume the risks and costs of an intervention in globally engaged states? The alarm bells sound when violations of human rights dominate the evening news and threaten to unleash waves of refugees (Zangl 2003).

Ethnic violence is a contagious virus. The readiness to intervene grows proportionately with the risk of civil war for neighbouring states and for the neighbours of neighbouring states. In other words, in an interdependent world, an unrestrained civil war can easily develop into an uncontrollable risk of civil war for all. If states collapse, the boundaries to organized criminality and terrorism are erased. Sooner or later local crises become global problems because of their consequences for the global economy, in the shape of waves of refugees, threatened terrorist attacks, not to mention alarmism in the mass media.

- *Change in perspective*: The cosmopolitan outlook poses the question of the perspectives of those whose countries are intervened in. In other words, the legitimacy question presupposes a change in perspective. The view of the interveners and the view of those affected by the intervention must gain validity independently of each other: How can the opinion of those affected by the intervention win the attention of a global public? Who represents them – the government, the opposition, civic associations, exiles? Who is viewed as trustworthy? Who decides who is to be viewed as trustworthy? At what point are they asked for their opinion? Before? When the goals of the intervention are being determined? Afterwards? How can procedures be developed to regulate this in a 'cosmopolitan' fashion?

- *Circular globalization*: Economic globalization weakens weak states, it contributes to their collapse and hence to civil wars, the privatization of violence and organized criminality, and it promotes terrorism. Corresponding to this is a limited readiness to intervene militarily. The discrepancy between the increasing breakdown of order and the possibilities for a global ordering politics is growing ever greater. *Both* the occasions and the costs of intervention are increasing, so that the probability of the twenty-first century being plagued by war nor the probability of a peaceful global order being established by military interventions is decreasing.

4   War is peace: war against terror

The war against terror is also a war-for-peace. The 'war' against terror has no declared beginning and no declared end. The separation between war and peace is cancelled both in space and in time. The goals of transnationally operating terrorists are non-negotiable. Conversely, violations of the human rights of terrorists (torture, indefinite imprisonment without trial, etc.) are often not viewed as illegal. There are no valid demarcations between criminal, enemy and terrorist. The label 'terrorism' empowers and justifies states to free themselves from the constraints of the laws of war, which are in any case weak and pliable.

Transnationally organized suicidal terrorist networks set in train a regressive spiral. Their contempt for moral constraints, the utter inhumanity of their attacks, can easily provoke an abandonment of legal constraints and civilized constraints on the use of force by the state.

4.1   The war in Afghanistan and the Iraq War were unprecedented because they were the first wars in human history against a culturally generated risk

One of the key questions of the second modernity is: What justifies the *legitimacy* of force in an era of new threats? With the advent of transnational terrorism, the danger of war, insofar as it does not take the form of open attacks, has lost its visibility; it has become anonymous and derives its effectiveness in large part from its anonymity. If the danger of war of the first modernity took the 'immediate', tangible and perceptible form of military uniforms, troop deployments, and the physical reality of weaponry and its destructive force, this no longer holds for terrorism. Hence the globalized terrorist threat clashes with the defining characteristics of war in international law, namely, 'immediacy' and 'presence', which reflect the reality of the interstate wars of the first modernity. Hence the reactions of almost all actors – the Security Council, governments, publics, civic movements, journalists – are based on an ineffectual international law which is historically blind to the new dangers. 'In view of the privatization of international force, the application of international law becomes problematic because it is still tailored to spatially and temporally circumscribed conflicts between state actors' (Zanetti 2002).[4] Thus the key question of the second modernity is more precisely: What grounds the legitimacy of force in an era of new threats if legality is not tailored to these threats? A comparison between the war in Kosovo and the Iraq War provides a suitable context for addressing this question.

Why was the violation of legitimacy in the war in Kosovo regarded as 'legitimate' by the majority of Western states and their populations, whereas the violation of international law in the case of the Iraq War split Western governments and populations and plunged NATO and the European Union into an existential crisis? The Western consensus in the Kosovo War (which is nonetheless still subject to criticism) also clearly rested on the fact that Europe was witnessing genocidal atrocities within Europe. As a consequence, the Europeans found themselves in the dilemma of having to violate either international law or human rights, and hence either way of incurring guilt as measured by the European tradition.

Neither factor holds in the case of the Iraq War. Here the USA and Europe are divided by stark contrasts in their respective perceptions of the threat. The shocking images of September 11, 2001, branded global terror onto the American worldview. The wars in Afghanistan and Iraq are the first wars waged against a global risk. It is the new threat to humanity represented by nuclear terrorism that, in the eyes of the Americans, marks the fundamental difference between the security situation before and after September 11, 2001, whereas the Europeans view this new threat to humanity more as an expression of American hysteria. As the Americans see it, in the world before September 11, doing what France, Germany, Russia, China, etc., demanded would have sufficed, namely, disarming Saddam Hussein step by step. In the world after September 11, by contrast, this is foolish and irresponsible, because even a 1 per cent probability that 'evil' dictators like Saddam Hussein (or failed states) could supply suicide attackers with chemical, biological or nuclear weapons is unacceptable and provides compelling reasons to intervene militarily. From this perspective, what is threatened is a stateless, even socially atomized nuclear age in which the very existence of humanity is endangered by suicide attackers who will stop at nothing. For the Americans, the present danger is the horror of terrorism, for the Europeans, the horror of war. Indeed, banishing the horror of terror with the horror of war is inconceivable without conjuring up the apocalyptic vision of perpetual war.

In the transatlantic disputes one parallel nevertheless stands out. Just as the opponents of nuclear power regard even a 1 per cent danger of a nuclear disaster as utterly irresponsible, and consequently reject the peaceful use of nuclear energy in principle, many Americans regard even a 1 per cent probability of terrorists using weapons of mass destruction as utterly irresponsible and consequently invade Iraq (with a clear conscience).

Just as nuclear protesters appeal to a 'higher necessity' to justify breaking the law (for example, to block the transportation of nuclear waste), the US government appeals to the 'higher necessity' of protecting humanity from the threat of atomic, biological and chemical weapons terrorism to circumvent the Security Council and international law. Of course, the differences are striking. In the case of the anti-nuclear power movement, the idea of prevention leads to the peaceful abandonment of nuclear power. In the case of the terrorist threat, by contrast, the same idea of prevention leads to military invasions in foreign countries. Nevertheless, both anti-danger movements have one thing in common: in the eyes of Greenpeace and of the Bush administration the aversion of the threat to humanity justifies the violation of international and national law.

Who can liberate us from these starry-eyed American visions of saving the world? The suspicion of terrorism gives the most powerful nation in the world carte blanche to construct ever-changing representations of the enemy and to defend its 'internal security' virtually anywhere on foreign territory with military force.

The Americans do not live on Mars and the Europeans on Venus, as Robert Kagan (2003) maintains. But they do inhabit different worlds. The absolute certainty of many Americans that the threat posed by atomic, biological and chemical weapons is 'real' is matched by the unshakeable conviction of many Europeans that humanity is endangered, that climate change is imminent, that genetically manipulated foods are dangerous, and so forth. Research in the social sciences has shown that dangers acquire reality because they exist 'in the eye of the beholder'. Perception and reality are hard to separate in the case of danger. More pointedly, threats do not have 'objective' existence independently of how they are culturally perceived and evaluated. The 'objectivity' of a threat derives essentially from belief in it.

In the case of nuclear threats no less than the threat of nuclear terror, this 'objectivity' must 'manifest' itself in global public discourse and must be branded in the minds and hearts of people through global information and symbols. Someone who believes in a specific danger lives in a different world from someone who does not share this belief. At any rate, the divisive factor in the Western alliance, which threatens to scupper NATO and is transforming the European Union to its foundations, is also rooted in the denial or, respectively, the recognition of dangers that appear to some to be life-threatening, but to others crazy, pathological, anti-scientific, and the like.

4.2   Terrorism unfolds its political power in the interaction between catastrophe and danger

Terrorism operates with a distinction between *danger* and *catastrophe*. Without the demonstrative brutality of a catastrophe, the danger remains merely more or less probable. For example, just a couple of weeks before the terrorist attacks in New York and Washington an expert commission had predicted them and presented President Bush with a detailed account of their likely consequences. This warning was dismissed as 'too hypothetical', in other words, as completely lacking in credibility. *After* the national and global shock, however, the effects of the terrorist danger – in other words, the perceived danger of anticipated, but not yet committed, terrorist acts – are suddenly omnipresent. The catastrophe has fixed spatial, temporal and social coordinates, it has a clear beginning and a clear end. None of this holds for dangers. Their effects do not have fixed spatial, temporal and social boundaries. The danger extends as far as the believed threat, which, in turn, depends essentially on how the mass media transmit and stage the danger.

A crucial insight connected with the distinction between catastrophe and danger is that it is not just catastrophes that have an impact – that is, the human drama, the scale of the physical destruction expressed in the numbers of dead and injured, the level of the insurance costs, and so forth; dangers also have a global impact that is capable of transforming the world (as the consequences of September 11 demonstrate). Thus it is only in the interaction between catastrophe and danger that transnational terrorism develops its political force. Clearly the terrorists are not in a position to destroy or conquer America. Yet it is the perception of risk and its consequences that decide how the campaign against terror will be waged.

In this way, terrorists incite and kindle the fantasy of a threat to civilization. That is their recipe for success. They fashion the instrument with which they really or virtually poison reality from the potential for danger that is latently or directly omnipresent in developed civilization, or is soon to be so. The knowledge and the resources required for the production and use of the old, conventional weapons of mass destruction – atomic and chemical warheads – can be localized, and thereby controlled and monopolized by the state. Hence the practical possibility of their independent production by non-state terrorist networks can be ruled out. But this does not hold for the impending technological advances in nanotechnology and gene technology and their combination. As pioneers of these leading-edge technologies have recently publicly warned, it is possible that practitioners and users could produce functionally equivalent 'bombs' and plague-like infectious viruses and put them into circulation, or at least threaten to do so. This would have the effect of neutralizing the state's monopoly on war and of individualizing it. Those who are willing to use their own lives as a weapon to advance their goals can declare war on states.

Hannah Arendt made a distinction between violence and power and argued that power does not grow out of violence, but rather that the use of violence presupposes power, that is, agreement or consensus. This insight acquires renewed significance in the present context. The superior practical capacity of states does not rest on violence but on power; but their power ultimately rests on the fact that the threat of death is a proven means of deterring potential offenders from their crimes. Only when superior military force is combined with the fear of death can state violence be transformed into state power. The readiness to deploy one's own life as a weapon blunts the state's instruments of violence vis-à-vis the terrorist, in spite of its incommensurable superiority, and empowers the terrorists. This dialectic of empowerment and disempowerment is intensified by the fact that the terrorists are not targeting the state's superior military power but the general vulnerability of an ultimately indefensible civil society. The destruction of the original faith in the security of the invisible spreads fear and panic. Civil society in all its glory and freedom becomes the hostage of terror.

4.3   The new master–slave dialectic of state and terror: on the political construction of the danger of terror

Anyone who wants to understand and investigate terrorism within the framework of sociology and political science must connect two questions. First, what are the preconditions and cultural background that produce suicidal terrorism? And, second, against what background is the deadly terror weapon perceived as a 'danger to humanity'? Here I will concentrate primarily on the second question, which concerns the *social and political construction* of the danger of terror.

In answering it, it makes sense to make a further distinction, first, between *terror attacks* and *terrorism* and, second, between *terrorism* and *the state*. Terror attacks are related to catastrophes, terrorism to dangers. Terrorism and the state are interrelated; more precisely, the power of terrorism is ultimately determined by the power of the state against which it is directed. Granted, the acts and networks of terror alone have transformed terrorism into a global phenomenon – the ruthlessness of the terrorists, not the new social category of suicidal terrorists operating with Western means, nor their hatred and religious fundamentalism. However, the increase in power from terror to terrorism to global terrorism is essentially conditioned by the global mega-power of the state against which it is directed. I would like to illustrate this thesis by a simple thought experiment.

Imagine that, instead of the World Trade Center and the Pentagon, the Eiffel Tower, the Brandenburg Gate, the British Houses of Parliament and the Kremlin had been blown up by hijacked passenger jets turned into human missiles. Would the 'war against terrorism' have been declared in that case? Would NATO have declared it to be an attack against the whole alliance? Would the USA and its allies have marched into Afghanistan to capture bin Laden? Would it have come to a second Iraq War to cut off the terrorists' access to weapons of mass destruction? The answer to the these questions is necessarily speculative. But everything points to a negative. If one accepts this negative answer, the obvious inference is that the terror would not have been promoted to terrorism and to global terrorism, but would have remained a European problem. It is highly questionable, one could speculate further, whether in that case responsibility for the terror attacks would have been systematically attributed to states. But making this causal attribution amounts to promoting terror to the status of global terrorism. There are many indications that the depoliticizing ascription of responsibility to individuals which defined the political construction of terror throughout the world before September 11, 2001, would have been retained in the European context. As a European problem, the terrorism would presumably have been interpreted in the European tradition of terror and its attendant nihilism, and have met with a political response.

Is it not the attack on the global hegemon and the fact that the USA, the military superpower, is shaken to its core that have promoted the terrorists to a kind of irregular counter-hegemon? Earlier historical attacks, in particular acts of terror in Europe, in Russia and in Israel, lacked this cultural, military and political resonance.

However, there is a fundamental difference between the Hegelian master–slave dialectic and the dialectic of state and terrorism. The master–slave dialectic, followed through to its conclusion, leads to the overthrow, the inversion, of the relations of domination: the slave becomes the master. By contrast, the state–terrorism dialectic unfolds as a mutual *empowerment through disempowerment*. Each challenges the existence of the other and they thereby reciprocally magnify their dreams of power.

This can be shown first from the point of view of the state. Here the distinction between the enemy and the representation of the enemy is of fundamental importance. The impalpability of terrorism necessitates and facilitates the construction of representations of the enemy that are no longer constrained by the physical tangibility of enemies of the state. The fusion of the concepts 'enemy' and 'terrorism' has opened up new strategic options. Terrorist enemies are at once civil and military, state and non-state, territorial and non-territorial always-and-everywhere-enemies; both internal and external enemies are, in a word, open to interpretation. With their help the classical enemy images of interstate wars can be made at once more flexible and more radical. Just as firms produce goods translocally, states can engage in the military production of ever-changing representations of the enemy independent of place and state. Not the declaration of war by an enemy state, but the self-authorized declaration of war by the 'threatened' state determines who the (next) enemy is and who must be prepared for military interventions. Thus the flexibilization of the concept of the enemy and its radicalization into that of the terrorist enemy enables powerful states

- first, to deploy military power anywhere for the purposes of self-defence; the reciprocal definition of adversaries as enemies is replaced by a unilateral definition;
- second, to engage in transposed 'wars of self-defence' against states without having been attacked by them;
- third, to institutionalize a state of emergency internally and externally;
- fourth, to delegitimize not only international relations but also the constitutional state, both at home and abroad.

In this sense, suicidal terrorists set in train a dialectic of impotence and omnipotence. Their acts represent the power of the powerless, but also, conversely, show the omnipotent its limits. Even the greatest military power in the world, which can hold all the states in the world in check with its absolute superiority, is in a certain sense impotent in the face of possible attacks by suicidal terrorists.

It is not only the catastrophic act but the *danger* as transmitted by the mass media that heightens terror into terrorism. Belief in the danger of terror is transformed into an economic danger. The costs incurred by a drop in consumer confidence can outstrip by far the costs actually caused by terror attacks. That terrorism knows no borders means that possible acts of terror are (potentially) directed against everybody, and everybody becomes a potential or actual witness to the horror. Terror sheds the limits of a local or national act and becomes terrorism, as regards both the victims and the spectators. Granted, television viewers are not victims, they do not have to identify with the victims, and hence it is possible to subject the expanded threat of terror to new constraints (for example, by renationalizing the victims – aren't the

Americans or Israelis themselves to blame?). But setting restrictions on the boundless suspicion of terrorism presupposes that our own national space, which defines our horizon of experience and expectation, does not become the target of terror attacks.

One could even say that the generation of a sense of unlimited vulnerability is in the hands of the terrorists. The latter have not exhausted their potential power with their choice of a state and civil society to victimize. Their recipe for success is not the physical destruction of specific infrastructure or military resources alone but the universalization of dread, which sets in train a self-propelled self-destruction of the economy, self-restriction of freedom and self-imprisonment of civil society. Just as the USA claims to be policeman, judge and executioner all rolled into one, it must also be made into the self-defeater of its own values and liberties. The goal is to perfect a kind of 'judo politics' on a global scale with the instruments of terror.

4.4   The danger of terror and its consequences: the demolition of social structures

Fifteen suicidal terrorists armed with carpet knives sufficed to compel the global hegemon to see itself as a victim. Here, as I said, we must distinguish clearly between terror and terrorism, catastrophe and danger, local acts and the global effects of the perception of limitless dangers: branches of the economy suffer or collapse (airlines, tourism, the stock market, insurance), countries and governments are suspected of supporting terrorism, and thereby become targets of possible military interventions ('axis of evil'). International law is aging. Alliances are crumbling and new ones must be forged. Original civil societies are mutating into cultures of fear in which the boundary between justified fear and paranoia is no longer easy to draw. In sum, what destroys social structures and reconfigures them is not the physical destruction but the political explosiveness of the attacks which have been promoted to global terrorism.

Terrorism has weakened the foundations of international politics. The alliances of the future, so it is said, grow out of the pressing questions of tomorrow, not out of the blocs and institutions of yesterday. Has NATO outlived its usefulness? Will the alliance have to assume the role of global policeman in order to renew itself? National and global security policy are both expanding and merging. The German Bundeswehr, for example, is being retooled from its role of 'defending the country' prescribed by the Basic Law and is being reoriented for global deployment in cooperative engagements against terrorism or for the continuation of global social work with military means. In other words, the threat of terrorism is rewriting the global geography of power.

5   Utopian perplexity: the new global order in the conflict of perspectives

The distinction I introduced in this chapter between conventional war between states, which rests at least in principle on clear demarcations between war and peace, police and military, military and civil society, and the new type of post-national war, which cancels these demarcations and creates an Orwellian both/and – war is peace – involves an uncomfortable truth: the concepts of an emancipatory and a political cosmopolitanism are interwoven with the concept of a *despotic* cosmopolitanism. In the horror of the twentieth century, nationalism unmasked the monster into which the national modernity can transform human beings. Is this also supposed to hold in modified form for the era of the second modernity, which has to rein in and civilize the moral and political catastrophic potential of nationalism with the recognition of difference? Is it even perhaps precisely cosmopolitan responsibility, that is, concern reaching across national boundaries, which globalizes the Orwellian dystopia of a manipulative 'war-peace'?

What does the formula of a 'time of transition' between the first and the second modernity mean for the future of nations? The hope that a cosmopolitan global idyll would emerge from the demise of the bipolar global order and that nations would lead a peaceful coexistence under the umbrella of international law has been shattered. Not lawful peace, but open, boundless, molecular violence is the signature of the emerging second modernity at the dawn of the third millennium. Terror, the war against terror and human rights wars have taken the place of the Cold War. We are now caught in a double bind: if you are against humanitarian interventions, then you are for ethnic cleansing and crimes against humanity; but if you are against ethnic cleansing and crimes against humanity, then you must support the new 'war-peace' of 'military humanism'.

Is there an alternative path to the horror of war among nation-states and the looming horror of postnational war which is gradually dawning on us? What is the alternative to a Pax Americana? A global cosmopolis? What would it look like and how can we ensure that the new order of a global cosmopolis would not bring about the normalization of war with other means? Are we threatened with a permanent war for permanent peace? The key question is: What would a global order that would eradicate the sources of violence, while in a *realistic* way excluding the imperial, despotic instrumentalization of cosmopolitan values and legal principles, have to look like?

The thesis of this section is that the standpoint from which we judge these questions – whether (1) the national outlook and (2) the global-national outlook or, alternatively, (3) the cosmopolitan outlook – is crucial. The first two standpoints are defended by the self-conscious advocates of realpolitik, first from a national and second from a global perspective. The third represents the opposed position of the self-critical cosmopolitan. What is obscured and what illuminated by the spotlight thrown by each of these three positions, and how? What short-term and long-term possibilities of criticism do they open up? How is the tension between human rights and security, global and national power and violence, balanced in each case? What future prospects does each of them open up for a new order of global values for the single, divided world?

5.1 The national outlook and the preventive irrelevance of the new world order

The national outlook grows out of and defends the ideas and concepts of the first modernity. It perceives and assesses the dilemmas that have been catapulted onto the global political agenda by human rights interventionism and the dangers of global terrorism with unshaken faith in the 'conceptual necessity' of the axioms of national society and politics. We can distinguish two variants, a globalized US-American variant (of which more later) and a European variant. The position that dominates European discourse rests on an inability or unwillingness to distinguish between change and meta-change (Beck, Bonss and Lau 2001). All upheavals, catastrophes and breakdowns that occurred in the course of the second half of the twentieth century can, on this view, be effortlessly subsumed under the axiomatics of the national and the international. The same is true of the character of the interdependences and dangers confronting politics at the beginning of the twenty-first century. Everything is changing constantly and radically, yet ultimately remains as it is and was.

This expectation of *invariant change* can be heightened into the principle of the 'before-after-invariance' of historical events, according to which the geopolitical situation will remain the same after historical event X as it was before. For 'event X' you can substitute September 11, 2001, or the collapse of the Warsaw Pact. For methodological nationalism before-after-difference shrinks to an extensionless point. The logic of the differentiation between national and international, together with all the premises of the state and politics, democracy and we-community, are immune to historical meta-change (understood as change in the premises of change). And this immunity represents the consensus across a broad spectrum of theories, debates and empirical research programmes in sociology and political theory which presuppose the axiomatics of the national outlook and hence exclude the possibility of meta-change *analytically* (see chapter 1).

The intellectual and political sense of superiority afforded by this position is obvious. When faced with the 'ferments of the zeitgeist', its adherents can rehearse the argument of the return of the same with the cool intellectual confidence fostered by a sophisticated paradigm that is ready for all eventualities. Perhaps even more important, however, is how it successfully exploits the axiomatics of the nation-state to normalize potentially theoretically disruptive historical intrusions and upheavals, and thereby dismisses the moral and political dilemmas thrown up by the controversies over the new global order. Since in the end there neither is nor can be anything new under the sun, the interconnection between foreign policy, human rights policy and military policy is declared to be unreal. The global terrorism that is shaking the foundation of national–international global politics does not really exist, so we have only to confront the ideology that it does. Whereas the picture of more or less imperial national interests remains constant, the ideologies that frame it are relatively easily interchangeable. The diagnoses concerning the past, present and future of methodological nationalism and internationalism 'relieve' political actors and empirical and theoretical political scientists from having to deal with the dilemmas concerning power, morality and politics of the second modernity. The defence of the analytically oriented national outlook is thus a preventive measure against the unanswerable questions which are otherwise relentlessly posed – 'unanswerable' for the simple reason that the nation-state paradigm logically excludes these questions.

The national outlook argues, accordingly, from two premises. First, really existing international law lays down the standards in accordance with which the legality and legitimacy of international actions and organizations can and must be judged. Second, the struggle over the new world order, hence (a) the global imposition of the human rights regime and (b) the campaign against global terrorism, is a kind of ideological parsley sprig with which the major powers, in particular the mega-power, the USA, 'garnish' their national-imperial, geostrategic strategies. For the worldwide conflicts over violations of human rights, humanitarian interventions and the war against terror there is a simple, slick three-letter answer: oil. Thus the 'critique' of the national outlook consists in dismissing out of hand the 'ideological balderdash' vented in the uproar over human rights and the terror threat with the superior air of the critique of ideology, thereby underlining the 'naked brutality' of what has always motivated the world at heart and will continue to do so in the future. What is meant is the expansion of imperial power that in one way or another exploits the national calculation to the full. By contrast, the idea that the USA might actually want to defend human rights, or even humanity as such, against the threat of nuclear terror is dismissed as abject naïvety. Anyone who believes this succumbs to the warmongering propaganda of the Bush administration and makes himself its willing accomplice.

The conclusion is obvious. On the logic of the national outlook, the USA becomes a 'war criminal' (because it violates international law) or an 'empire' (because it forces its values on other states and cultures against their will) (Speck and Sznaider 2003). By contrast, the diagnosis that the predetermined divisions and differentiations between war and peace, internal and external, us and the others, are becoming blurred is twisted into a US imperialist strategy of the global state of emergency. 'The United States is now using the state of emergency not just as an instrument of domestic policy but also, and above all, to legitimize its foreign policy. In this respect one could say that the United States government is trying to impose a permanent state of emergency on the whole planet, while presenting it as the mandatory response to a kind of global civil war between the state and terrorism' (Agamben 2003). Thus the premise of methodological nationalism, projected outwards, is offered as a justification of this thesis.

The critique offered by methodological nationalism is *nostalgic*, just as the future it conjures up is stuck in the past. The good old times of nation-state sovereignty are supposed to be defended against the violent intrusion of reality. Simply put, the national outlook no longer understands the world. Since reality has long since outstripped textbook knowledge, whatever resists the status quo categories is morally reviled. The world is false, not the concepts we use to describe it.

5.2 The new world order in the national-global outlook: Americanism versus internationalism

We need to distinguish between two oppositional variants of the national-global outlook: first, *global Americanism*, in which a particular model, the American way of life, is universalized; and, second, *internationalism*, in which the achievements of domestic politics – e.g., the state monopoly on violence, democracy, the constitutional state and the welfare state – are universalized on the model of a world domestic politics. Both variants of the national outlook writ large can be distinguished, in turn, from the cosmopolitan outlook (which we will discuss in the following section). Whereas both global Americanism and internationalism presuppose the axiomatics of the national–international and make the corresponding premises the basis of their arguments (and research), the cosmopolitan outlook, as we have seen, annuls this national–international axiomatics.

Viewed from the perspective of the realpolitik of *global Americanism* or the *Pax Americana* (see above), there is no alternative to the global imposition of American modernity with its unity of capitalism and democracy. Accordingly, particular national interests are fused with global interests in the American vision. On this view, any rational person must recognize that it is in his enlightened self-interest to become an American (if he is not already one), regardless of his skin colour, his religious community or where he was born. Because America represents the world spirit and defends its cause with military means, and hence is a 'unique' world power capable of protecting the freedom of all, its role as the new hegemon must be accepted by everyone. The USA is the effective UN, and hence has no need of the latter. This presupposes that preventive intervention must be accepted as well as the determination to promote the cause of democracy and capitalism throughout the world, if necessary without, or in opposition to, international law and the Security Council.

By contrast with the European perspective, the American perspective accommodates selective meta-change and selective reforms. If, for example, the establishment of free-trade zones in the Middle East were to succeed in promoting prosperity and democracy, that would be an important step towards peace and stability in that region. However, anything beyond that, such as the dream of putting states on an equal legal footing, a global law, and above all the hope for a supranational monopoly on the means of violence, is obsolete on this model. The national–international article of faith is that there is only one route to modernity, the American route. Even to entertain the possibility of alternative, and hence multiple modernities, is heretical. Resistance to the American logic of history is not only futile but also morally wrong.

Completely different, by contrast, is the perspective of the *internationalists*, which differs from the cosmopolitan perspective only by degrees (as will be explained in the following section). The logic of this perspective could be characterized as the *domestic political analogy*: inter-national politics is understood on the model of intra-national politics. Thus the question it asks is: How can we construct a counterpart to the nation-state's monopoly on the means of violence at the global level? Doesn't this necessarily lead to the disempowerment and disarmament of nation-states, just as in the nineteenth century the disarming of local militias was the precondition of the nation-state's monopoly on the means of violence? Similar questions can be posed concerning all essential aspects of the axiomatics of the nation-state. Won't democracy on a global scale become a possibility only when a 'world parliament' has been created, regardless of the principles on which it is constructed?

Conceiving of world politics on the analogy of domestic politics can have thoroughly ambivalent motives. One can show how the projection of various institutions onto a global scale can open up new global possibilities for political thought and action, for example, the elevation of the state to a world state, of national to global law, of national to international organizations and communities, of the national constitution to cosmopolitan law, and so forth. However, the pictures of the future projected in this way can just as easily serve as foils for driving all attempts to break out of the national conceptual cage to absurdity.

The new world order understood in accordance with the maxims of internationalism does not replace but extends the nation-state order. In other words, methodological nationalism contains two compartments, one responsible for national, the other for international order. The relation between the two is understood on the architectural model of 'foundation' and 'superstructure', where priority is clearly accorded the nation-state foundation. This reciprocal relation of self-inclusive priority is shown by two features.

1   The political architecture (both practical and theoretical) of the super-structure, that is, of the global-national conceptions of order, is the national order *writ large*. Accordingly, a global democracy, for example, is only possible if there exists some kind of 'global nation'.

2   The legitimacy of the superstructure of the global order is a *borrowed* legitimacy which rests exclusively on the legitimacy of the foundational order of the nation-state. Hence the legitimacy of the global order and its actors and organizations remains tied to the nation-state's monopoly on legitimacy. Thus the international order is like an extra floor built onto an existing structure. One floor is added to another, and another may even be added. They are all ultimately constructed on the same political architec-ture; they all contain the same building blocks of the national axiomatics. But this international Tower of Babel presupposes national legitimacy and national interests. The international superstructure does not alter, but is merely an extension of, the national foundation. It follows that, should the national powers think it opportune, the international superstructure can be done away with, razed to the ground, without the national foundation being destroyed.

In this way Hobbesian contract theory can be applied to relations between states. The anarchy that reigns at the international level and makes war between states possible can be overcome if one applies the principles govern-ing state-formation to the formation of the world state. States must enter a contract which lays down rules for resolving conflicts peacefully (in accord-ance with a procedural universalism to which all parties give their consent). However, this international legal order presupposes that the nation-state's monopoly on law and the means of violence is relativized or annulled in favour of a cosmopolitan monopoly on law and the means of violence. The states that uphold this global order must be or become 'republics', to employ Immanuel Kant's concept. Hence they must be as far as possible democratically legitimate states which view themselves as obligated by their constitutions to guarantee the freedom and rights of their citizens. The answer to the question of whether the international Leviathan would necessarily be despotic because of its massive concentration of power is that this centralization of power and law must be complemented and legitimated by a corresponding international democracy. The latter should be oriented in turn to guaranteeing human rights beyond the borders of individual states and to downplaying the claims of the latter to absolute sovereignty. In this way, the interplay of the principles and institutions through which the peaceful coexistence of opposing interests and groups *within* nation-states could be assured – namely, law, democracy and the monopoly on the means of violence – could lead to the institutional pacifica-tion of the international order.

The objections to this internationalism have often been rehearsed, but they acquire particular force when applied to the United Nations at its present stage of development. The United Nations, as a global republic and global democracy in embryo, must be developed further through global law. However, this contradicts the hegemonic role that the USA claims for itself. There is only one shining star in the heavens of planetary order which is capable of founding and guaranteeing a global order – the USA, the sole superpower.

An important question then becomes: Will the Security Council become a rubber stamp for legitimating the US wars against terror and for world democratization – or will it not? Could institutionalized pacifism and internationalism acquire an authority of their own that is not exhausted in legitimizing the Americanization of the world? How can the state fragmentation of the cosmopolitan exercise of power be overcome without propagating an all-powerful world state? From this perspective, the importance of the second Gulf War resides in the fact that the USA was denied legal sanction, through the organized opposition of a heterogeneous faction of states composed of France, Germany, Russia and China (in which, however, conspicuous cosmopolitan motives were mixed with opposition rooted in a national-imperial power politics).

5.3   Self-critical cosmopolitanism, or the fear of utopia

The cosmopolitan outlook reveals how far removed the national outlook and methodological nationalism are from reality, and thereby opens up new opportunities and perspectives for critique. The precondition for its success is self-criticism. The one-dimensional project of global Americanization fails to grasp that there are plural modernities. Indeed, it fails to recognize that a global dictatorship of the American way is not only in open contradiction to the latter, but is itself a chief cause of global terror. Instead of American optimism, the Americans are now exporting American pessimism by infecting everyone else with their terror phobia. What is urgently required is a thorough self-demystification. The theory of the second modernity can sharpen the sense of reality, the global sense, for this. Everyday talk (and hence also action) in the West is haunted by a whole series of 'perverse concepts'. 'Disarming states' is no more a recipe for peace than the idea of conducting 'wars of disarmament'. Even the notion of 'just war' is a war in disguise, war-for-peace, military mobilization to end war. Even the concept of 'humanitarian intervention' is a kind of verbal tranquillizer designed to make those who swallow it numb to the fact that it amounts to a declaration of war-for-peace. Those who distinguish between police and global police think they are already in the clear because the concept of 'police' guarantees internal pacification by means of law and restraint in the use of force. But 'global domestic politics' involves different actors than national domestic politics. The role of the 'global policeman' is exercised by an alliance of states that does what states have always done – namely, wage war against states – only now under the guise of a 'police' operation.

The antinomy between law and war is invalid. For the right to ban war must be enforced by military means. One often hears the demand that disarmament should begin with the arms industry, not with states. An excellent idea! But who is supposed to enforce the disarmament, and hence the prohibition and criminalization, of the arms industry, and how? The demand is that states must be disarmed. But won't states and international organizations have to arm themselves in order to disarm states? Aren't 'police interventions' to disarm states wars, wars which moreover become 'just wars' with the blessing of cosmopolitan law? Doesn't talk of 'disarmament' require the (violent) annulment of the multiple monopolies on the means of violence of individual states? And mustn't the latter be replaced by a global centralized monopoly on the means of violence, which would in addition enjoy the legality and legitimacy of a global army euphemized into a 'world police force', at least under certain circumstances, against which resistance cannot be countenanced? What began as a call for cosmopolitanism mutates into an invitation to anti-cosmopolitanism, in the sense that the enlightened interests of others can and must be protected, if necessary against themselves.

These kinds of self-criticisms seem to confirm the criticisms of the idea of a global cosmopolitanism by national theories of politics and the state which loudly proclaim their universal validity. Are protectionism and nostalgia, postmodernism, indifference, cynicism, or at best irony, all that is left to ward off the tidal waves of new realities and the questions they inexorably pose?

No. The promise (not escape) of the cosmopolitan outlook goes beyond this. Translated into political terms, it confirms the thesis that we have thus far had only a deformed, half-hearted cosmopolitanism. The diagnosis of the crisis is: too little cosmopolitan outlook; and the cure: *more* cosmopolitan sense of reality.

The proposed models of a cosmopolitan world order are deformed and half-hearted because they promote a *shallow* cosmopolitanism. This book, by contrast, advocates a *deep* cosmopolitanism. The cosmopolitan idea has thus far been worked out only in a shallow and superficial way because, first, the theory of cosmopolitan politics has in essence been developed as moral philosophy and legal theory, not as political theory. Closely related to this is a second deficiency, namely, that the world of states was generally assumed to be invariant. The distinction between cosmopolitanism and the cosmopolitan outlook introduced in the first chapter can help us to overcome this problem. The detour through cosmopolitan realism is not in fact a detour. The reservoir of ideas of political and normative cosmopolitanism can never be developed in a merely *additive* manner, as the superstructure of an invariant state foundation. But this is precisely what is intended by shallow cosmopolitanism, whose ramifications we encounter in the fields of political (and normative) philosophy and theory.

But the deepening and radicalization of cosmopolitanism first sketched in this book with reference to specific topics would mean, second, that what shallow cosmopolitanism posits as invariant must itself be questioned and researched. Specifically, we must inquire to what extent reality itself breaks open the national–international axiomatics and to what extent an *inner cosmopolitanization* of international politics, of social inequalities, of society and the state in all its themes and problems can be empirically and theoretically uncovered and demonstrated.

Not just the weaknesses of the UN Charter or the birth defects of the Security Council are decisive in this regard, but also the inability and unwillingness of states, their governments and their populations to take advantage of the possibilities afforded by the idea of a cosmopolitan order to regulate their conflicts peacefully. Thus the decisive question is how and to what extent a self-transformation of the world of nation-states into cosmopolitan states is (or can be made) possible, actual and observable.

In other words, the cosmopolitan icing on the cake of an invariant world of states and societies leads to a dead end of false alternatives. Only when reality itself becomes cosmopolitan and this is publicly realized and reflected – hence only with the cosmopolitanization of memories, biographies and conceptions of social inequality and justice – will cosmopolitan politics create realistic options for action. If the 'shallow', abridged cosmopolitanism is in addition a *vertical* cosmopolitanism whose implementation is conceived from the top down, from the central power monopoly to the states to be disarmed, then 'deep' cosmopolitanism must be conceived as a *horizontal* cosmopolitanism. Here nation-states and national societies interact and interpenetrate beyond the distinction between the national and the international. The ideas of statehood and state sovereignty have not become superfluous. It is not enough to grant institutional recognition to global civil society and its actors. The ideas of the state and sovereignty must also be redefined and extended in a cosmopolitan direction.

6

Cosmopolitan Europe: Reality and Utopia

Over a century ago a young 24-year-old black American, W. E. B. Du Bois, crossed the Atlantic for Europe, his ship sailing in the opposite direction to the prison ship that brought his enslaved forebears to America to enrich the slave trade. Four hundred years after Columbus had opened the door to the flourishing transatlantic slave trade, this descendant of slaves and slave-holders, a student of history and philosophy at Harvard, had a prestigious scholarship that enabled him to continue his studies in Berlin. At the university in Berlin he sought to broaden his horizons by attending courses in politics, and especially in sociology; his unshakeable faith in the German tradition led him to hope that he would receive a lesson in emancipation from racism. The terms in which Du Bois described his experiences in Europe not only speak for many other black Americans, but also reawaken the memory of a cosmopolitan Europe:

Europe modified profoundly my outlook on life and my thought and feeling toward it, even though I was there but two short years with my contacts limited and my friends few. But something of the possible beauty and elegance of life permeated my soul; I gained a respect for manners. I had been before, above all, in a hurry. I wanted a world, hard, smooth and swift, and had no time for rounded corners and ornament, for unhurried thought and slow contemplation. Now at times I sat still. I came to know Beethoven's symphonies and Wagner's Ring. I looked long at the colors of Rembrandt and Titian. I saw in arch and stone and steeple the history and striving of men and also their taste and expression. Form, color, and words took new combinations and meanings. (Du Bois 1986: 586–7)

This intellectual love affair of a black American with a Europe which for him typified emancipation from racism also represents an expectation for the current self-understanding of a Europe which finds itself challenged internally by its eastwards expansion and externally by the tumult of a self-destructive civilization. How can it be that in Western Europe at this crucial historical juncture hardly any major intellectual voices can be heard vigorously defending the eastwards expansion of Europe against the timid, faint-hearted reservations of nationalists?

How is it possible that for a majority of people in very different countries the image of the European Union, which was created to liberate Europe from the grip of its war-torn history, oscillates between dutiful celebration and open hostility? How could the European self-criticism that fired the imaginations of conservative politicians such as Winston Churchill, Charles de Gaulle and Konrad Adenauer in the aftermath of the horrors of the Second World War, and the crimes against humanity perpetrated by the Nazi regime, end in an institutionalized failure of imagination? Will the spectrum of emotions from benign indifference to open, sometimes hateful rejection be sufficient to absorb the foreseeable fractures and breakdowns to which the project of European transformation exposes itself as it approaches the historic moment of eastwards enlargement?

More pointedly: Is there even a reality that deserves the name 'Europe', or is this merely an aspirational concept for an illusion which cannot stand up to critical examination? Could it be that the rallying idea of Europe is merely a front for the very opposite of all that Europe stands for, namely rejection of democracy, freedom, separation of powers, transparency and political accountability? Isn't the experiment of a European confederation of states condemned to failure just like all the other empires with similar ambitions that have gone before – from the empire of Charles V, Napoleonic hegemony and the Austro-Hungarian Empire, to the British Empire, the Soviet Union or, today, the USA? After all, why should something work for the European Union which world history has otherwise judged a failure? Is it not a remarkable sign of nostalgia and introversion that, in the age of globalization, the European Union is urgently preoccupied with its own affairs and is trying to give itself a political constitution while the world around it is disintegrating in a storm of terror and crises?

No – absolutely not! Indeed the very opposite is true. The critics fail to see the *reality* of Europe. Anti-Europeanism is based on a false image of Europe. It is trapped in the contradictions of the national self-misunderstanding that continues to hold Europe captive. By way of contrast, I shall outline a conception of cosmopolitan Europe in four theses by turning the tables on the critics: national realism is becoming false, a national *illusion* which has led our thought, action and research in and about Europe down a blind alley (cf. Beck and Grande 2004).

1   The European Union is not a club for Christians, a transcendental community of common descent

Only a non-anthropological, anti-ontological, radically open and procedurally determinate, in other words, a politically pragmatic, image of humanity and culture deserves the label 'European'. This becomes clear when we ask 'Where do you stand on Turkey?', which has become the critical question of

European politics. It divides opinion and ignites the conflict between the old national and a new cosmopolitan Europe.

All of a sudden, a European discourse of origins is on everyone's lips. Those who want to keep the Turks out discover that the roots of Europe lie in the Christian West. Only one who has always been a part of this 'occidental community of shared destiny' is 'one of us'. The rest are Europe's *excluded* others. According to this worldview, each person has a single homeland which he cannot choose; it is a birthright and it coincides with the geography of nations and their dominant stereotypes. Thus if a white person happens to meet an exotic-looking individual who speaks English with an Irish or an Oxford accent, this sort of territorial social ontology is thrown out of kilter, and the individual is 'grilled' until the appearance of the assumed consonance between passport, skin colour, accent, place of residence and place or origin is re-established.

In the corresponding literature – dubbed 'the Empire writes back' – this has acquired the derisive and deliberately ironic name of the 'where-are-you-from-originally' dialogue:

'Well', said Joyce relieved, 'you look very exotic. Where are you from, if you don't mind me asking?' 'Willesden', said Irie and Millat simultaneously. 'Yes, yes, of course, but where *originally*?' 'Oh', said Millat, putting on what he called a *budbud-ding-ding* accent. 'You are meaning where from am I *originally*.' Joyce looked confused. 'Yes, *originally*.' 'Whitechapel', said Millat, pulling out a fag. 'Via the Royal London Hospital and the 207 bus.' (Smith 2001: 319)

This debased, misguided and dangerous territorial understanding of culture haunts even the well-intentioned idea of 'cultural dialogue', as if 'Islam' and 'the West' each existed in its own exclusive space and must now at last enter into conversation with each other. Where in all this is 'Londistan' – *the* Islamic metropolis outside the Islamic world? Where are the Western Muslims, the Arab middle class, the oriental Christians, the Israeli Arabs, the second- and third-generation Muslim immigrants in every Western country, and so forth? What we have here, of course, is a kind of considerate exclusion. As the former chairman of the German Christian Democrats Wolfgang Schäuble put it, 'Surely it is in the interests of the Turks themselves not to repudiate their own roots or to relinquish their Turkish identity.' Those who are reinventing the Christian West in order to erect barriers around Europe are turning Europe into a religion, almost a race, and are turning the project of the European Enlightenment on its head.

In this way the political theory of Carl Schmitt, with its friend-and-foe categories, is insinuating itself into the debate over European identity, the idea being that you have to exclude those who are culturally different if you want to preserve your cultural identity. Since politics is not a matter of cultural hermeneutics but of self-fulfilling political prophecies, stereotypes of ethnic-religious belonging borrowed from the past in this way become cemented for the future.

The term 'cosmopolitan Europe' can be understood as precisely the negation of this sort of territorial social ontology which seeks to block all paths to the future. For one thing, the term 'cosmopolitan Europe' has an empirical meaning because it opens our eyes to the 'entangled modernities' (Shalini Randeria) in which we live, for example, that the Turks some people want to keep out are long since already inside. Turkey arrived on the European scene a long time ago, as a member of NATO, as a trading partner, as one pole of transnational forms of life. Moreover, large parts of Turkey are Europeanized. To members of the middle class living in the major cities of the Islamic world such as Istanbul, Beirut or Teheran, the customs and values of an Anatolian villager are no less alien than they would be to a middle-class resident of Paris or Berlin. Also, if you want to cling to the illusion that clear boundaries can be drawn between the European and Muslim worlds, you have to grant the EU a monopoly on Europeanness and ignore the overlapping spheres of identity constituted by Europe, the Atlantic alliance and NATO. To allow a Christian-occidental principle of ethnic descent to be resurrected from the mass graves of Europe is to fail to understand Europe's *inner cosmopolitanization*. It is to deny the reality of the roughly 17 million people living in the EU who cannot recognize this ethnic-cultural heritage of 'Europeanness' as their own, because they are Muslims or people of colour, for example, yet who understand and organize themselves culturally and politically as Europeans. The history of black Europeans and their contribution to the cultural dynamics and moral self-understanding of a cosmopolitan Europe remains to be written (Gilroy 2000: 339). The fact that Europe is a microcosm of global society is also misunderstood. In the world of the twenty-first century there is no longer a closed space called 'the Christian West' of which romantic historians such as Hans-Ulrich Wehler dream. With growing transnational interconnections and obligations, Europe is becoming an open network with fluid boundaries in which the outside is already inside.

There is no doubt that the current state of the European Union merits criticism. But where can we find suitable standards of criticism? In the national self-image, in laments over the loss of national sovereignty? No. The concept of a cosmopolitan Europe makes possible a critique of EU reality which is neither nostalgic nor national but radically European. It holds that much about the current state of the EU is un-European. That is why Europe is paralysed. The diagnosis of the crisis is 'too little Europe', and the cure, 'more Europe' – properly understood, that is, in a cosmopolitan sense!

That goes for both internal and external relations. It is utterly un-European to reduce Muslims to Islam. It is precisely because European values are secular values that they are not tied to any particular religion or heritage. No one would say: 'This person is Catholic and comes from Bavaria and therefore can't be a democrat.' Yet, in the eyes of many nationalistic Europeans, being a Muslim still so totally determines one's personality that it excludes the possibility of being a 'real' democrat. In this sense, the Western nationalist outlook is a fundamentalist outlook with paradoxical commonalities with the anti-modern fundamentalism of an Osama bin Laden. They mutually confirm each other in a sinister way. 'Europeanness', by contrast, means being able to combine in a single existence what appear to a narrow-minded ethnic mentality to be mutually exclusive characteristics; one can, after all, be a Muslim and a democrat, a socialist and a small businessperson, love the Bavarian landscape and way of life and support anti-immigrant initiatives. The European conception of what it means to be human does not presuppose the goodness of human beings, but is in a strict sense ahuman and anti-essentialist. It has cast off all pretentious concepts of the human and has shed the powerful, naïve assumptions of a moralizing metaphysics. Radical openness is a defining feature of the European project and is the real secret of its success. A European civil society arises only when Christians and Muslims, white- and black-skinned democrats, and so forth, struggle over the political reality of Europe. Europe without Muslim democrats would be a Christian, and hence an un-European, Europe.

The political union must be conceived as a cosmopolitan union of Europe, in opposition to the false normativity of the national. Paradoxically, hatred of the West arises not only and/or primarily because Muslims who want to live by the Qur'an reject human rights and democracy. The hatred that develops in those who are excluded as culturally different by Europeans results from just the opposite state of affairs, namely, that in its dealings with those deemed culturally different Europe forgets and denies its own values. It is a *truncated* Europe that sows the seeds of disappointment from which hatred springs. Many intellectuals and citizens in the Islamic world feel alarmed or resigned at the thought that democracy and human rights count for so little in their countries. They do not reproach the West for its standards, but for not applying them when it provides support for dictatorships, corrupt regimes or state terror. Navid Kermani writes:

Certainly those who sympathize with Osama bin Laden, the Taliban or Saddam Hussein are not limited to a few groups of extremists. But the despairing question one encounters far more often, from Rabat to Teheran to Jakarta, is why the West supported these political monsters for so many years. Those who blather on about the hatred of the Islamic masses towards the West should, just as a test, offer visas for sale in those cities; if the West were really so unpopular there, it would hardly be the case that young people in particular would sooner emigrate today than tomorrow.

Ultimately, Kant anticipated certain elements of a still incomplete Copernican turn in political theory when he maintained that the national foundations of modern societies are questionable because they did not take account of the consequences of actions for members of different cultures and nations. Thus

Kant recognized the need to reform and reformulate relations between the state and citizens within the framework of a cosmopolitan ethics and community.[1] He traced the image of a universal world community which is both individualized and globalized and in which individuals, as citizens of the world and citizens of nations, have become co-legislators. We are far removed from this goal. However it is depicted, Kant saw transitions and intermediate forms that accord more weight to cosmopolitan experiences and norms than to national experiences and identifications. And, for him, cosmopolitan realism consisted in acting 'as if' this were possible.

2   Cosmopolitan Europe is taking leave of postmodernity. Simply put: nationalistic Europe, postmodernity, cosmopolitan Europe

Cosmopolitan Europe was consciously initiated after the Second World War as the political antithesis to a nationalistic Europe and its moral and physical devastation. The British war prime minister, Winston Churchill, standing among the ruins of a destroyed continent in 1946, enthused: 'If Europe were once united . . . there would be no limit to the happiness, prosperity and glory which its three or four hundred million people would enjoy.' It was the charismatic statesmen of the Western democracies, in particular those among them who were involved in the active resistance, who reinvented Europe beyond the national cemeteries and mass graves, by drawing on the historical store of European ideas. Cosmopolitan Europe is a project born of resistance.

It is important to recognize this because two things converge in this project. First, resistance is ignited by the realization that European values can be perverted. The point of departure is accordingly not humanism, but antihumanism, that is, the bitter realization that totalitarian regimes are always based on some idea of the 'truly human', designed to separate, exclude, refashion or destroy those who did not want to accommodate themselves to this ideal. But if there is no longer any human substance to be saved, if we are dealing with a decentred quasi-subject of whom we can no longer say what it is, what it wants or even what is still inviolable about it – what is there left to preserve? Who can guarantee that it won't be abducted, tortured and killed? This is precisely where the sources of public protest and resistance are crucial. For they reflect the principles of human dignity nourished by the experience of compassion. The awareness of global norms that founds political action arises *post hoc*, as it were, as a side effect of the violation of these same norms.

Cosmopolitan Europe is a Europe which struggles morally, politically, economically and historically for *reconciliation*. In a decisive break with the past, fifteen hundred years of European warfare are to be brought definitively to an end. From the beginning, this so to speak groundless and foundationless reconciliation is less something preached idealistically than realized materialistically. The unlimited happiness of which Churchill spoke means in the first place a market without borders. It is to be realized as the profane creation of interdependencies in the political domains of security, economics, science and culture. The adjective 'cosmopolitan' stands for this openness limited by the critique of ethno-nationalism which clamours for recognition of cultural difference and diversity.

The dilemmas of an institutionalized cosmopolitanism are especially evident in the commemoration of the Holocaust. If one asks in which documents and negotiations its origins can be studied and documented, one answer would be the Nuremberg Trials of the perpetrators of the Nazi terror in Germany. This was the first international court. It is remarkable that it was a creation of legal categories and a judicial procedure *beyond* national sovereignty. This made it possible to capture the historical monstrosity of the systematic, state-organized extermination of the Jews in legal concepts and court procedures, and it can and must be interpreted as a primary source of the new European cosmopolitanism.

Article 6 of the *Charter of the International Military Tribunal* lays down three types of crimes – 'crimes against peace', 'war crimes' and 'crimes against humanity' – on the basis of which the Nazi criminals were prosecuted. Interestingly, 'crimes against peace' and 'war crimes' presuppose nation-state sovereignty, and hence conform to the logic of the national outlook, whereas 'crimes against humanity' contradict it by abrogating national sovereignty and seeking to formulate the cosmopolitan outlook in legal categories; and it is no coincidence that the prosecutors and judges who participated in the Nuremberg Tribunal were unable to come to grips with the historically new category of 'crimes against humanity'. After all, what was being introduced was not just a new law or a new principle but a new legal logic which broke with the existing nation-state logic of international law. I quote from Article 6c: 'Crimes against humanity: namely, murder, extermination, enslavement, deportation, and other inhumane acts committed against any civilian population, before or during the war; or persecutions on political, racial or religious grounds in execution of or in connection with any crime within the jurisdiction of the Tribunal, whether or not in violation of the domestic law of the country where perpetrated.'

The formulation 'before or during the war' clearly demarcates crimes against humanity from war crimes. This creates the notion of responsibility of individual perpetrators *beyond* the national legal context, in effect of responsibility towards the community of nations, towards humanity. If a state becomes criminal, individuals who serve it must expect to be prosecuted and condemned for their deeds before an international court. The formulation 'any civilian population' suspends the national principle according to which a person's obligations within national borders are total and freedom from obligations beyond those borders is equally total, and replaces it with the legal principle of cosmopolitan responsibility. The cosmopolitan legal principle protects civilian populations not only against violence from other hostile states (something already implied by the concept of 'war crimes') but, in a much more far-reaching and provocative sense, from the random acts of violence committed by sovereign states against their own citizens. Ultimately, a cosmopolitan legal ethics completely inverts relations of priority, so that the principles of cosmopolitan law *trump* national law. Crimes against humanity can neither be legitimated by appeal to national laws nor tried and condemned within the nation-state. In sum, the historically novel category 'crimes against humanity' abrogates the principles of national legislation and adjudication.

This raises questions to which there are no easy answers: Who are the victims of crimes against humanity – the Jews or humanity, hence everybody? Including the perpetrators? How can a crime be perpetrated against 'humanity' when 'humanity' is a concept to which no entity corresponds? Having proclaimed the death of the human subject, must we not now defend the rights of the dead under the banner of 'human rights'?

Cosmopolitan Europe expresses a genuinely European self-contradiction in a moral, legal and political sense. If the traditions from which colonialist, nationalist and genocidal horror originate are European, then so are the evaluative standards and legal categories in terms of which these acts are proclaimed as crimes against humanity before a global public. The victors could have simply court-martialled the elite responsible for the Nazi terror and executed them by firing squad, as Stalin and Churchill in fact first demanded. Or they could have been brought before national courts to be condemned in accordance with national law (as happened in the Eichmann trial in Jerusalem and the Auschwitz trials in Germany). Instead, they mobilized the European tradition of recognizing others and the right against the ethnic perversion of the law based upon it.

Reflection on the Holocaust in the social sciences has for good reasons given rise to a discourse of despair. According to Horkheimer and Adorno, the dialectic of enlightenment itself that generates perversion. This assumed causal relation between modernity and barbarism can also be discerned in Zygmunt Bauman's book *Modernity and the Holocaust* (1989). But this despairing farewell to modernity need not be the last word on the matter. Indeed, it is blind to the ways in which the creation of the European Union has inaugurated a struggle over institutions with the aim of confronting European horror with European values and methods. The Old World is reinventing itself.

In this sense, the commemoration of the Holocaust functions as a warning against the ubiquitous modernization of barbarism (Levy and Sznaider 2001). The negativity of modernity and European awareness of it is not merely a pose, an ideology of the tragic. It reflects the historical invention of a deviant modernity of nation and state which has developed the potential for moral, political, economic and technological disaster inexorably and without concern for its own destruction, like a kind of experimental chamber of horrors. The mass graves of the twentieth century – of the two world wars, the Holocaust, the atomic bombs dropped on Hiroshima and Nagasaki, the Stalinist death camps and genocides – testify to this. Yet there also exists an unreflected and unbroken link between European pessimism, the critique of modernity and *post*modernity, which perpetuates this despair – Jürgen Habermas is right about this. In other words, a paradoxical coalition exists between the national and the postmodern Europe. The theorists of post-modernity deny the possibility of combating the horror of European history with more Europe, with a radicalized, cosmopolitan Europe.

Both national modernity and postmodernity make us blind to Europe. Europeanization means struggling to find institutional responses to the bar-barism of European modernity and, by the same token, taking leave of a post-modernity that fails to grasp this. Cosmopolitan Europe is the institutionalized self-criticism of the European path. This process is incomplete; indeed, it cannot be completed. Moreover, it has only just begun, with the sequence Enlightenment, postmodernity, cosmopolitan modernity. Could this radical self-critique be what distinguishes the EU from the USA and from Muslim societies? Is this the secret of success which makes a self-critical Europe so attractive in the contest over definitions of the future and modernity in our one world? A cosmopolitan Europe is a historically rooted Europe which breaks with its history and draws the strength to do so from its own history, a Europe which is *self-critically* experimental. Hence, it is the Europe of reflexive mod-ernization in which the principles, boundaries and guiding ideas of national politics and society are up for discussion. As Daniel Levy and Natan Sznaider have argued, radical, self-critical European commemoration of the Holocaust does not destroy, but rather constitutes, the identity of Europe. Paradoxically formulated, it can enable Europe to find its continuity in its break with the past. In the commemoration of the Holocaust, the break with the past draws its power for the future. What is at stake is the institution of future-oriented forms of memory for a cosmopolitan self-critique of Europe *in opposition to* national founding myths and warrior myths. A similar challenge is posed, incidentally, by postcolonialism and also by the nascent revolutionary consequences of developments in human genetics, nanotechnology, and so forth.

3 Thinking of Europe in national terms not only fails to understand the reality and future of Europe; it also (re)produces the self-obstructions that have become characteristic of political action in Europe

This becomes apparent in the established canon of concepts of politics and the state: the reality of a cosmopolitan Europe can only be realized via *negation*, that is, through a radical self-critique of current concepts of politics and the state. The national outlook not only misunderstands the reality and future of Europe. It can see only two ways of interpreting European politics and integration, in terms either of a federal state (federalism) or of a confederation (intergovernmentalism). Both models are empirically false. Understood in normative and political terms, they deny the very thing at stake now and in the future: the Europe of diversity.

A national Greater Europe, a federal superstate, presupposes the disempowerment of European nations, their consignment to the museum; nation-states within a confederation, by contrast, jealously defend their sovereignty against the expansion of European power. From the national perspective, European integration must ultimately be conceived as an internalization of colonialism. Either us or them. What we give up, they gain. Either there is a single *state* of Europe (federalism), in which case there are *no* national member states; or else the national member states remain the masters of Europe, in which case there is *no* Europe (intergovernmentalism).

The same holds for the current debate over a European constitution. Great Britain, for example, does not have a constitution; yet it speaks (at times) with a genuinely European, genuinely democratic, cosmopolitan voice. This means that those who seek to create a *single* constitution for Europe would abolish Europe, hollow it out, rob it of its amiable, open-minded provincialities. However, choosing the option of no European constitution has the equally banal consequence that there can be no Europe. Trapped in the false alternatives of the national outlook, we are faced with a choice between no Europe – and no Europe! In other words, the reality of Europe arose and can be understood only in opposition to the established range of concepts. A political science deeply entrenched in methodological nationalism proceeds according to the motto 'the revolt of European reality against the leading concepts of political science must be crushed with all the means at the disposal of empirical research.' Yet this revolt of reality has a name, a concept – cosmopolitan Europe.

This can be seen from the legal *realities* of the EU. For Europeanization brings forth a new kind of both/and in which national legal and political cultures continue to exist and are simultaneously merged into a European legal culture. Cosmopolitanism means 'logic of inclusive oppositions'; that is what makes it so interesting for political theory and social theory. It is not a matter of negating or condemning self-determination but of liberating it from national solipsism and opening it up for the concerns of the world. A cosmopolitan Europe, then, opens our eyes for what has long been there already (at least inchoately) and must be affirmed and radicalized *against* the narrow-mindedness of the national outlook: a Europe of diversity. If one extends this to the concepts of politics and the state, a concept of the *cosmopolitan state* which mirrors the reality of Europe becomes possible.

The leading hypothesis of the cosmopolitan European confederation is that national world (civil) wars can be addressed by separating state from nation. Just as an areligious state allows citizens to practise a variety of religions, so too a cosmopolitan Europe would have to safeguard the coexistence of ethnic, national, religious and political identities and cultures across national borders through the principle of constitutional tolerance. Europe teaches us that the political evolution of the world of states and of concepts and theories of the state is by no means at an end.

The other side of the decline of the nation-state order is the opportunity it offers a European cosmopolitan state formation to re-model itself in the face of economic globalization, transnational terrorism and the political impacts of climate change. In view of the ominous aggregation of global problems which refuse to yield to national solutions, the only way politics can regain credibility is by making the quantum leap from a national to a cosmopolitan state. This is what is paradigmatically at stake in a cosmopolitan Europe: in an era of globalized problems that overwhelm people on a daily basis, to regain credibility, both in politics and in political science, in middle-range, regional forms and strategies of cooperation and in corresponding middle-range political theories. This also holds for Asia, America and Africa, but it is particularly true for the EU experiment. The old nation-state game is no longer viable. National realpolitik is becoming unreal. Or it is degenerating into a lose–lose game. Europeanization means a meta-power game. A power game over transforming the seemingly eternal rules of the national–international order has been under way for quite some time. Those who refuse to join in – how did Gorbachev put it? – will be the losers (Beck 2005).

The first principle of cosmopolitan realism is: *Europe will never be possible as a project of national homogeneity.* To build the common European house according to the national–international logic is neither realistic nor desirable; on the contrary, it is counterproductive. Only a cosmopolitan Europe which (as its founders intended) both overcomes and acknowledges its national tradition – overcomes it by acknowledging it (and hence excludes a national Greater Europe, but celebrates national diversity as an essential characteristic of Europe) – is both European (in the sense of non-national) and national, because it is plural-national, hence European.

The British behave as though Great Britain still existed; the Germans believe that Germany exists; the French think that France exists; and so on. But these state-organized national 'containers' have long since ceased to exist as empirical realities. In the cosmopolitan Europe a new realpolitik of political action is taking shape. At the beginning of the third millennium the circular maxim of national realpolitik – national interests must be promoted nationally – must be replaced by the maxim of cosmopolitan realpolitik: our politics is more successful at the national level the more European and cosmopolitan it becomes. The European question, the question of how a cosmopolitan Europe can become more dynamic and effective is: How can the 'vicious circle' of the national zero-sum game be replaced by the 'virtuous circle' of a European positive-sum game? How is it possible, if not to overcome national egoism, then at least to 'tame' it in a European manner? How could a *European* national self-interest develop? How can the exploitation of the European Union by national egoism be prevented?

Here, too, the concept of cosmopolitan realpolitik proves fruitful. The creation of interdependencies in every field of politics, the politics of interconnectedness which puts Europeanization on a permanent footing, is not a one-off form of cooperation which ultimately leaves the nation-states concerned untouched, as the intergovernmental perspective implies. Instead, Europeanization transforms state power and national sovereignty to their very core. Nation-states become *transnational* states, in a dual sense. On the one hand, national and European interests are fused in such a way that national interests can be Europeanized and pursued and maximized *as* European interests. On the other hand, the instrumentalization of Europe, the pursuit of an *in*-authentic cosmopolitanism, remains an option for *all* states. Every member government must anticipate that the other member states might well act in exactly the same way. It follows that the instrumentalization of the European common good is ever present as a threatened diminution of one's own 'national-European' interests.

Thus Europeanization, assuming it goes well, means that strategies develop for reflexive self-limitation by member states in their own interest. For pragmatic reasons, the latter do not make use of their latent sovereignty, abiding instead by the European rules laid down by the European institutions in order to maximize their own long-term national interests.

What paralyses Europe, however, is the fact that its intellectual elites are living a national lie. They complain about a faceless European bureaucracy and the farewell to democracy, yet tacitly base their complaints on the completely unrealistic assumption that there could be a way back to the idyll of the nation-state. Infatuation with the nation-state flies in the face of its own historicity, the disconcerting naïvety with which things are taken to be eternal and natural which were considered unnatural and absurd just two or three hundred years ago. This sort of intellectual protectionism, this self-delusion steeped in nostalgia, holds sway not only in the shabby enclaves of right-wing populism in Europe. It reigns – cutting right across the right–left distinction – even in the most highly educated and cultivated circles; even the most sophisticated political theories cling to the myth of the nation-state. Granted, the nation-state has not sunk into the grave of history. It no doubt still exists as a fact of state and international law. But in Europe, at the latest with the creation of a common currency, but also before this with the dissolution of internal borders and with the implementation of European law, its very essence has been transformed, 'Europeanized', 'cosmopolitanized'. More than 50 per cent of all decisions that shape our daily lives are taken not at the national level but in the European Union, so that there is no corner of so-called national societies left untouched by Europe.

Whenever what seemed eternal and certain begins to shift, the old certainties are trotted out even more militantly. So it is no surprise that there is a causal relationship between the successes of Europeanization and the rise of neonationalism and right-wing populism in Europe. While European nation-states are becoming caught up in processes of mutual absorption, combination and synthesis, the national imagination reigns more than ever in people's heads, as a sentimental ghost, a rhetorical habit, in which the fearful and bewildered seek a refuge and a future.

4   Cosmopolitan realism is not a utopia but a reality: it captures the experience of the Western alliance and the European Union and extends it for the age of global dangers

This Atlantic realism which can easily be forgotten can be illustrated by the greatest imaginable success of a resolute, militarily backed disarmament policy in world history, the collapse of the Warsaw Pact. Here a military alliance between nuclear powers dissolved almost without a whimper – and without a single shot being fired! 500,000 Russian soldiers peacefully withdrew from Central Europe; the Soviet Empire made a peaceful exit from the stage of world history; the Marxist–Leninist ideology with its pretension to total global power ended up in the dustbin of history; and the way was opened for the eastern enlargement of NATO and the EU – all, to repeat, without a single shot being fired! Could there be a more conclusive demonstration of the thesis that only both together, military power and the power of legitimate law and consensus, are capable of solving the virtually insoluble global problem of the threat of nuclear weapons?

In what sense is the EU an empire? The European states have definitively ended five hundred years of war, culminating in two world wars which devastated Europe, in order to form a new union which shares a currency and the aspiration to promote internal democratization and find broad commonalities in their foreign and security policies. Viewed historically, this undertaking among states with different cultures can only be described as revolutionary. For the first time in history states have learnt that their power is not diminished but increased by renouncing national sovereignty. All states must submit to an internal process of self-democratization and must protect human rights and civil liberties, with the result that a war between members has become unthinkable.

The member states view themselves as a gradually expanding cooperative of states which draws ever more actual and potential member states into its ambit. In this way the European Union exerts a new influence on the world stage. For the first time in history we are witnessing the rise of an empire founded on voluntariness and procedural agreement, hence *not* on military force. The contrast to the war-torn Europe of old could hardly be greater.

Does the USA symbolize the ultimate 'cosmopolitan nation'? Doesn't it provide a home for all ethnicities, world cultures and world religions and fuse them in a national unity? Yes, but strictly speaking America stands for a 'multicultural *nation*'. The distinction between multiculturalism and cosmopolitanism is essential for understanding this difference.[2] The highly apt metaphor of the 'melting pot' has been coined for American national multiculturalism. Commitment to difference extends only as far as is permitted by the commitment to national unity. From the beginning, the USA aspired not to a cosmopolitan America of *national difference*, but rather to a *national* America pledged to *overcoming* difference. The world cultures, world ethnicities and world religions to which America provides a home were supposed to be absorbed – that is, fused and dissolved – in the pathos of the nation.

Furthermore, the remarkable success of the American experiment of a multicultural nation is built on the circumstances of a country of immigration which are unique in a world of national and ethnic territorial states. The protocol of the American experiment is: How can immigrants, that is, deterritorialized groups, be reterritorialized by setting down national roots in a 'new land' and be fused into a nation? The European experimental protocol is: How can historically deeply rooted territorial ethnicities, nationalities and regional identities, whose conflicts have been deeply etched in people's memories in the blood-soaked language of violence, be opened up to new interrelations and involvements so that they develop into a cosmopolitan cooperative of states? The European Union is *not* a land of immigrants, a multi-ethnic national superstate, or a 'melting pot'. If America is the home of short history, Europe is the home of long history. The USA does not have historical institutions in the European sense: neither the Catholic Church nor the feudal system; neither the wars of religion nor the early capitalist class conflict between labour and capital and the mass political parties it brought forth; neither fascism, National Socialism, the Holocaust, Stalinism, nor the welfare state, which in its own way is also an answer to the questions posed by this insane European history. In a word, American national multiculturalism is built on a tabula rasa history, history light.

The American path of national multiculturalism is ruled out in Europe not just for historical reasons, but even more so for *logical* reasons, because the historical reality of many nations cannot be replaced by a single big nation. Thus Europe can be realized *only* as the cosmopolitan unity of the recognition and reconciliation of many national and regional histories, or not at all. Cosmopolitan Europe does not mean the extinction or dissolution of nations, just as the Peace of Westphalia did not mean the extinction or dissolution of different religions. On the contrary, it means that the principles of national, cultural, ethnic and religious toleration are institutionally anchored, preserved and guaranteed.

The triumphal procession of cosmopolitan Europe speaks the utterly clear language of the political surplus value which results from the cooperative fusion of the nation-states, and hence does not disempower them.

Nobody can escape the relations of responsibility of world risk society. As long as we Europeans are preoccupied only with ourselves, current global risks will continue to increase – also for Europe. If governments and peoples continue to confine themselves to hermetic national spaces, then ever more countries and cultures will sink into chaos and decline. Then it is only a matter of time before the rich and powerful nations are also endangered by global interdependencies. Not only the danger represented by Iraq and North Korea, but also the condition of Africa, for example, weighs on the conscience of the world. But we could relieve our conscience if the world community accepted this challenge. The solution to these problems does not lie in navel-gazing but in the cosmopolitan opening of Europe.

This task demands that we develop (conceptually, empirically and politically) a *cosmopolitan realism* that assimilates national realism with its well-founded scepticism, but which also opens it up for an age of global dangers and crises and reformulates it accordingly. The dangers threatening states today and for the foreseeable future are in principle two-faced: they transcend the boundaries between the national and international domains, but at the same time they relativize the asymmetries of power between states. Even the most powerful nation in the world is powerless in the face of these threats. Unilateralism is ineffective and counterproductive.

In order to consolidate and increase their power, states must (a) cooperate and (b) negotiate international rules and found corresponding international institutions. In other words, because states want to survive they have to cooperate. However, long-term cooperation transforms the self-definition of states to their core. Their egoistic drive to survive and extend their power compels them to unite and reform themselves – not rivalry, but cooperation maximizes national interests. Anti-cosmopolitanism is at the same time anti-national, because it fails to understand that, in an age of global interdependencies and dangers, there is only one way to pursue and maximize national interests, namely, the cosmopolitan way. We must make a distinction between a self-destructive way (autarchy) and a power-maximizing way of interweaving national interests, the latter being the internalization of cosmopolitanism by the nation and the state.

Here it becomes evident once again that the cosmopolitan outlook does not signify altruism or idealism but realism – in this case, the enlightened self-interest of transnational states. This can be read, in turn, as an example of the internal cosmopolitanization of national experiences and aspirations. The question concerning political cosmopolitanism, therefore, leads to the question: How can the horizontal cosmopolitanization of places, biographies, families, parents, education, economics, work, leisure, consumption, politics, and so forth, be observed, reinforced and raised to public awareness? But this is a further question which goes beyond the scope of this book, whose aim has been to understand the cosmopolitan outlook (see Beck and Grande 2004).

Notes

Chapter 1   Global Sense, Sense of Boundarylessness

1   On the distinction between globalization and cosmopolitanization see above, pp. 8ff.

2   On this see the outstanding book by Sigrid Thielking, *Weltbürgertum: Kosmopolitische Ideen in Literatur und politischer Publizistik seit dem achtzehnten Jahrhundert* (Thielking 2000), to which this chapter is also indebted.

3   The conception of the second modernity as the 'age of side effects' is set forth in Beck (1996); Beck, Bonss and Lau (2001); and Beck, Holzer and Kieserling (2001).

4   Cf. pp. 33ff. in this chapter and ch. 2, 2.8.

5   The dynamics of risk-cosmopolitanism will be explored further in section 3.1 and in ch. 5, pp. 149ff.

6   For the discussion concerning methodological nationalism see, among others, Martins 1974; A. D. Smith 1995; Beck 1999, 2000b; Gilroy 1993; Zürn and Wolf 2000; Scott 1998; Sassen 2000; Falk 1995; Taylor 1999; Shaw 2000b; Luard 1990; McNeill 1985.

7   One might ask: how influential is methodological nationalism in sociological *theory*? At a first glance, explicit references to 'national societies' are hard to find. This surely has to do with the fact that the most innovative sociological theorists of modern society employ a methodological universalism that has more or less completely internalized or sublimated methodological nationalism, to the point where it is no longer recognizable as such – more so in the case of Niklas Luhmann, less so in that of Claus Offe (2003) and Pierre Bourdieu. It remains to be demonstrated that the methodological universalism of Luhmann's systems theory, for instance, shares the underlying assumptions of methodological nationalism in its either/or logic of the binary code and the construction of system boundaries.

8   For a criticism see Levy and Sznaider 2001.

9   The fact that the history of Islam can look back on an early period of coexistence and toleration with others, specifically in the case of Muslim Spain, was already appreciated by Western scholars in the eighteenth and nineteenth centuries (Kohlhammer 2003). Thus Herder celebrated Arab Andalusia as the 'first Enlightenment' of Europe and regarded the Arabs as the 'educators of Europe'. However, this enthusiasm can easily obscure the fact that the Andalusian government was founded on a theocratic model of political domination. Christians

and Jews, who shared the religious heritage represented by the figure of Abraham, were accorded the status of alien minorities. Although they could rise in the social hierarchy, they remained second-class citizens, had to pay special taxes, and had to wear prescribed clothes. Moreover, there were outbreaks of violence, such as the murder of thousands of Jews in the year 1066 in Granada and the violent mass expulsion of Christians in 1126.

10   The following summarizes, with some minor changes of emphasis, what I have already expounded in greater detail in my book *Power in the Global Age* (pp. 24–34).

11   Quoted from Gilroy 2000: 241.

12   See also chapter 3 on the qualitative exploration of 'banal' cosmopolitanization.

Chapter 2   The Truth of Others

1   Thus there is a close connection in the USA between the popularity and political influence of communitarian currents and Huntington's slogan of the clash of cultures, which ascribes the intention of destroying civilization exclusively to non-Western societies and non-Christian faiths. Two interpretations are typically excluded in advance: nobody thinks it possible that barbarism could break out again in the West itself; and no serious attention is given to the fact that the seeds of conflict are nourished by the side effects of global interdependence.

2   Aside from nationality, the relationship between religiosity and cosmopolitanism is in need of clarification, a task which I cannot undertake here. The new importance assumed by religious membership is properly viewed as a reversion to earlier historical conditions, nor can it be dismissed as a mere reaction. Could it be that answers to the postmodern constellation are to be found here? Could it represent an attempt to find a synthesis or connection which is both transnational *and* rooted, namely, in the particular universalism of 'the Church'? Would the cosmopolitanization of religions then mean the decoupling of the binding power of religiosity from historical (national or ethnic) group membership?

Chapter 3   Cosmopolitan Society and its Adversaries

1   In response to the same question, Elisabeth Beck-Gernsheim (Beck-Gernsheim 2004) combines empirical data and analysis with a reflexive sociology, that is, a sociology of sociology, which reflects in a self-critical manner on its own position in the relation between us and them, natives and foreigners. This approach could acquire the 'penetrating character' that eludes the mere presentation of data. Nevertheless, to begin with we will here focus exclusively on the conceptual development of this empirical method of cosmopolitan realism, which is by no means a trivial matter. This is not to dispute the claim that the breakthrough of methodological cosmopolitanism can only be achieved in combination with a self-critical sociology of sociology; it was with this goal in mind that Beck-Gernsheim wrote and published her book simultaneously with this one, and it can be read as a methodological cosmopolitanism *from below*.

2   The claim is not, of course, that this holds for all human beings under all circumstances. On the preconditions of its coming to awareness, see pp. 33ff.

3   See chapter 1, section 3, above and section 3 of this chapter.

4 These points will be taken up again in chapter 4.
5 On the systematic distinction between domains and horizons of experience, see Koselleck 1985.
6 On the function of memory in the cosmopolitan age, see Levy and Sznaider 2001.

Chapter 4   The Politics of Politics

1 In what follows these ideas will be reinterpreted for the purposes of the analysis of the second modernity.
2 On the new forms of war in the cosmopolitan age, see also chapter 5.
3 Other, grimmer, future scenarios will be discussed in chapter 5.

Chapter 5   War is Peace

1 This pact was agreed between the USA and the other world powers in 1928 and denounces offensive wars; it was also invoked during the Nuremberg Trials as grounds for prosecuting the Nazi German elite.
2 The war on the Eastern front conducted by Nazi Germany already exhibited the characteristics of an unconstrained total war. The war against the Jews and other minorities in Eastern Europe marked the dissolution of old-style war between states. Cosmopolitan commemoration of the Holocaust (Levy and Sznaider 2001) acquires a corresponding paradigmatic significance. The Second World War was both at once: whether the distinctions and elementary rights of wars between states were respected or disregarded depended on the front and the enemy. The bombing of civilians and the associated debates currently being conducted should also be seen in this context.
3 Ref. III ZR 245/98, 26 June 2003.
4 There are clear parallels with the distinction between the technological and environmental dangers of the first and second modernity. Like the danger of war, the dangers and impacts of the industrial production of the first modernity (e.g., toxic emissions in ground water and in the atmosphere) were perceptible, were spatially, temporally and socially restricted, and could be tied to specific agents and agencies, whereas the 'immediacy', the visible presence of danger, no longer applies to the second modernity (exemplary in this regard was the invisible nuclear contamination of extensive areas of Eastern and Central Europe following the catastrophe in Chernobyl) (Beck 1992, 2002b).

Chapter 6   Cosmopolitan Europe

1 Habermas: the universal speech community, the basic norms of communicative action, lay down political goals for the 'postnational constellation'.
2 See above, chapter 2, section 2.7.

References and Bibliography

Abell, R., and Reyniers, M. (2000) On the Failure of Social Theory. *British Journal of Sociology*, 51(4): 739–50.

Adam, B. (1998) *Timescapes of Modernity*. New York and London: Routledge.

Adam, B. (2003) Reflexive Modernization Temporized. *Theory, Culture and Society*, 20(2): 59–78.

Adam, B. (2004) *Moderne Zeiten*. Frankfurt am Main: Suhrkamp.

Adam, B., Beck, U., and van Loon, J. (2000) *The Risk Society and Beyond*. London: Sage.

Agamben, G. (2003) Der Gewahrsam-Ausnahmezustand als Weltordnung. *Frankfurter Allgemeine Zeitung*, 19 April.

Ahlbrecht, H. (1999) *Geschichte der völkerrechtlichen Strafgerichtsbarkeit im 20. Jahrhundert: Unter besonderer Berücksichtigung der völkerrechtlichen Straftatbestände und der Bemühungen um einen ständigen Internationalen Strafgerichtshof.* Baden-Baden: Nomos.

Aksoy, A., and Robins, K. (2003) The Enlargement of Meaning: Social Demand in a Transnational Context. London, MS.

Albright, M. (1998) Speech on Human Rights, Atlanta, Georgia, 3 December: <http://www.usconsulate.org.hk/uscn/state/1998/1203.htm>.

Albrow, M. (1996) *The Global Age*. Cambridge: Polity.

Albrow, M. (1997) Auf Reisen jenseits der Heimat. In U. Beck (ed.), *Kinder der Freiheit*. Frankfurt am Main: Suhrkamp.

Amery, J. (1977) *Jenseits von Schuld und Sühne*. Stuttgart: KlettCotta.

Amit, V. (ed.) (2000) *Constructing the Field*. London: Routledge.

Appadurai, A. (1990) Disjuncture and Difference in the Global Cultural Economy. *Public Culture*, 2: 1–19.

Appadurai, A. (1991) Global Ethnospaces: Notes and Queries for a Transnational Anthropology. In R. Fox (ed.), *Recapturing Anthropology*. Santa Fe, NM: School of American Research Press.

Appadurai, A. (1995) The Production of Locality. In R. Fardon (ed.), *Counterworks: Managing the Diversity of Knowledge*. London: Routledge.

Appiah, K. A. (1992) *In my Father's House*. Oxford: Oxford University Press.

Appiah, K. A. (2001) African Identities. In S. Seidmann and J. C. Alexander (eds), *The New Social Theory Reader*. London: Routledge.

Archer, M. S. (1991) Sociology for One World: Unity and Diversity. *International Sociology*, 6(2): 131–47.

Archibugi, D., Held, D., and Köhler, M. (eds) (1998) *Re-imagining Political Community*. Cambridge: Polity.

Arendt, H., (1964) *Eichmann in Jerusalem: A Report on the Banality of Evil*. New York: Viking.

Arendt, H., and Jaspers, K. (1992) *Correspondence 1926–1969*. New York: Harcourt Brace Jovanovich.

Arnason, J. P. (1990) Nationalism, Globalization and Modernity. *Theory, Culture and Society*, 7: 207–36.

Bade, K. J. (ed.) (1992) *Deutsche im Ausland, Freunde in Deutschland*. Munich: Beck.

Ball, H. (1999) *Prosecuting War Crimes and Genocide: The Twentieth-Century Experience*. Lawrence: University Press of Kansas.

Barkan, E. (2000) *The Guilt of Nations: Restitution and Negotiating Historical Injustices*. New York: Norton.

Bauman, Z. (1989) *Modernity and the Holocaust*. Ithaca, NY: Cornell University Press.

Bauman, Z. (1990) *Thinking Sociologically*. Oxford: Blackwell.

Bauman, Z. (1991) *Modernity and Ambivalence*. Cambridge: Polity.

Beck, U. (1992) *Risk Society: Towards a New Modernity*. London: Sage.

Beck, U. (1996) Das Zeitalter der Nebenfolge und die Politisierung der Moderne. In U. Beck, A. Giddens and S. Lash (1996), *Reflexive Modernisierung*. Frankfurt am Main: Suhrkamp.

Beck, U. (1997) *The Reinvention of Politics: Rethinking Modernity in the Global Order*. Cambridge: Polity.

Beck, U. (1999) *World Risk Society*. Cambridge: Polity.

Beck, U. (2000a) *What Is Globalization?* Cambridge: Polity.

Beck, U. (2000b) *Freiheit oder Kapitalismus: Gesellschaft neu denken*. Frankfurt am Main: Suhrkamp.

Beck, U. (2002a) The Terrorist Threat: World Risk Society Revisited. *Theory, Culture and Society*, 19(4): 39–55.

Beck, U. (2002b) *Ecological Politics in an Age of Risk*. Cambridge: Polity.

Beck, U. (2003) Towards a New Critical Theory With Cosmopolitan Intent. *Constellations*, 4 (December).

Beck, U. (2005) *Power in the Global Age*. Cambridge: Polity.

Beck, U., and Beck-Gernsheim, E. (2002) *Individualization*. London: Sage.

Beck, U., and Grande, E. (2004) *Kosmopolitisches Europa*. Frankfurt am Main: Suhrkamp.

Beck, U., and Holzer, B. (2004) Wie global ist die Weltrisikogesellschaft? In U. Beck and C. Lau (eds), *Entgrenzung und Entscheidung: Was ist neu an der Theorie reflexiver Modernisierung?* Frankfurt am Main: Suhrkamp.

Beck, U., Bonss, W., and Lau, C. (2001) Theorie reflexiver Modernisierung – Fragestellungen, Hypothesen, Forschungsprogramme. In U. Beck and W. Bonss (eds), *Die Modernisierung der Moderne*. Frankfurt am Main: Suhrkamp.

Beck, U., Bonss, W., and Lau, C. (2004) Entgrenzung erzwingt Entscheidung. In U. Beck and C. Lau (eds), *Entgrenzung und Entscheidung: Was ist neu an der Theorie reflexiver Modernisierung?* Frankfurt am Main: Suhrkamp.

Beck, U., Giddens, A., and Lash, S. (1996) *Reflexive Modernisierung*. Frankfurt am Main: Suhrkamp.

Beck, U., Holzer, B., and Kieserling, A. (2001) Nebenfolgen als Problem soziologis-cher Theoriebildung. In U. Beck and W. Bonss (eds), *Die Modernisierung der Moderne*. Frankfurt am Main: Suhrkamp.

Beck, U., Levy, D., and Sznaider, N. (2004) Erinnerung und Vergebung in der Zweiten Moderne. In U. Beck and C. Lau (eds), *Entgrenzung und Entscheidung: Was ist neu an der Theorie reflexiver Modernisierung?* Frankfurt am Main: Suhrkamp.

Beck, U., Sznaider, N., and Winter, R. (eds) (2003) Globales Amerika? Bielefeld: transcript.

Beck-Gernsheim, E. (2000) *Juden, Deutsche und andere Erinnerungslandschaften*. Frankfurt am Main: Suhrkamp.

Beck-Gernsheim, E. (2004) *Wir und die Anderen*. Frankfurt am Main: Suhrkamp.

Beisheim, M., Zürn, M., et al. (1999) *Zeitalter der Globalisierung? Thesen und Daten zur gesellschaftlichen und politischen Denationalisierung*. Baden-Baden: Nomos.

Benford, G. (1999) *Deep Time: How Humanity Communicates Across Millennia*. New York: Avon.

Benjamin, W. (1991) Vom Weltbürgertum zum Großbürger. In idem., *Gesammelte Schriften*, Vol. 4. Frankfurt am Main: Suhrkamp.

Benn, G. (1989) *Essays und Reden*. Frankfurt am Main: Fischer.

Berger, P. L. (1963) *Invitation to Sociology*. Garden City, NY: Anchor.

Berlin, I. (1976) *Vico and Herder: Two Studies in the History of Ideas*. London: Hogarth Press.

Bernal, M. (1987) *Black Athena: The Afrocentric Roots of Classical Civilization*. New Brunswick, NJ: Rutgers University Press.

Bhabha, H. (1994) *The Location of Culture*. London: Routledge.

Billig, M. (1995) *Banal Nationalism*. London: Sage.

Bloch, E. (1985) Bodenständigkeit als Blasphemie. In idem., *Werkausgabe*, Vol. 5. Frankfurt am Main: Suhrkamp.

Bock, P., and Wolfrum, E. (eds) (1999) *Umkämpfte Vergangenheit: Geschichtsbilder, Erinnerung und Vergangenheitspolitik im internationalen Vergleich*. Göttingen: Vandenhoeck & Rupprecht.

Bohrer, K. H., and Scheel, K. (eds) (2000) Europa oder Amerika? Zur Zukunft des Westens. *Sonderheft Merkur*, 9/10 (September/October).

Bonilla, F., Melendez, E., Morales, R., and Torres, M. (eds) (1998) *Borderless Borders*. Philadelphia: Temple University Press.

Boyarin, D., and Boyarin, J. (1993) Diaspora: Generation and the Ground of Jewish Identity. *Critical Inquiry* 19(4): 693–726.

Brenner, N. (1998) Global Cities, Global States: Global City Formation and State Territorial Restructuring in Contemporary Europe. *Review of International Political Economy*, 5(2): 1–37.

Brenner, N. (1999) Beyond State-Centrism? Space, Territoriality, and Geographical Scale in Globalization Studies. *Theory and Society*, 28: 39–78.

Brenner, N. (2000) The Urban Question as a Scale Question: Reflections on Henri Lefebvre, Urban Theory and the Politics of Scale. *International Journal of Urban and Regional Research*, 24(2): 361–78.

Bretherton, C. (1998) Allgemeine Menschenrechte. In U. Beck (ed.), *Perspektiven der Weltgesellschaft*. Frankfurt am Main: Suhrkamp.

Brubaker, R. (1996) *Nationalism Reframed*. Cambridge: Cambridge University Press.

Bryceson, D., and Vuorela, U. (eds) (2002) *The Transnational Family: New European Frontiers and Global Networks*. Oxford: Berg.

Burawoy, M., Blum, J. A., George, S., Gille, Z., Gowan, T., et al. (2000) *Global Ethnography: Forces, Connections and Imaginations in a Postmodern World*. Berkeley: University of California Press.

Caglar, A. S. (2001) Constraining Metaphors and the Transnationalization of Spaces in Berlin. *Journal of Ethnic and Migration Studies*, 27(4): 601–13.

Caglar, A. S. (2002) Media Corporatism and Cosmopolitanism. In S. Vertovec and R. Cohen (eds), *Conceiving Cosmopolitanism*. Oxford: Oxford University Press.

Carens, J. H. (1978) Aliens and Citizens: the Case for Open Borders. *Review of Politics*, 49(2): 251–73.

Castells, M. (1997) *The Rise of the Network Society*. Oxford, and Cambridge, MA: Blackwell.

Castles, S. (2003) Towards a Sociology of Forced Migration and Social Transformation. *Sociology*, 37(1): 13–34.

Chakrabarty, D. (1992) Postcoloniality and the Artifice of History. *Representation*, 37: 1–26.

Chambers, I., and Curti, L. (eds) (1996) *The Postcolonial Question*. London: Routledge.

Cheah, P., and Robbins, B. (eds) (1998) *Cosmopolitics: Thinking and Feeling Beyond the Nation*. Minneapolis: University of Minnesota Press.

Cohen, J. L. (1999) Changing Paradigms of Citizenship and the Exclusiveness of the Demos. *International Sociology*, 14(3): 245–68.

Collier, P. (2003) *Breaking the Conflict Trap: Civil War and Development*. Oxford: Oxford University Press.

Comaroff, J., and Comaroff, J. (1992) *Ethnography and the Historical Imagination: Studies in the Ethnographic Imagination*. Boulder, CO: Westview Press.

Cox, K. R. (1997) *Spaces of Globalization: Reasserting the Power of the Local*. New York: Guilford.

Crossette, B. (1999) U.N. Chief Wants Faster Action to Halt Civil Wars and Killings. *New York Times*, 21 September.

Cwerner, S. B. (2000) Chronotolitan Ideal: Time, Belonging and Globalization. *Time and Society*, 9(2/3): 331–45.

Daase, C., Feske, S., and Peters, I. (eds) (2002) *Internationale Risikopolitik*. Baden-Baden: Nomos.

Dahrendorf, R. (1999) Whatever Happens to Liberty? *New Statesman*, 6 September, 25–7.

Delanty, G. (1996) *Inventing Europe: Idea, Identity, Reality*. Basingstoke: Macmillan.

Delanty, G. (1998) Social Theory and European Transformation: Is there a European Society? *Sociological Research Online*, 3, <http://www.socresonline/3/1/1.html>.

Deltson, E. (2000) 'Tourists', 'Russian-Pontics', and 'Native Greeks': Identity Politics in a Village in Northern Greece. *Anthropological Journal on European Cultures*, 9(2): 31–52.

Derrida, J. (2000) Jahrhundert der Vergebung. *Lettre*, 48.

Dewey, J. (1954) *The Public and its Problems*. Denver: Swallow.

Dicken, P. (1998) *Global Shift: Transforming the World Economy*. London: Paul Chapman.

Diner, D. (2003) *Gedächtnis-Zeiten: Über jüdische und andere Geschichten*. Munich: Beck.

Dirlik, A. (1997) *The Postcolonial Aura: Third World Criticism in the Age of Global Capitalism*. Boulder, CO: Westview Press.

Dirlik, A. (2000) *Postmodernity's Histories*. Lanham, MD: Rowman & Littlefield.

Dörr, S., and Faist, T. (1997) Institutional Conditions for the Integration of Immigrants in Welfare States: A Comparison of the Literature on Germany, France, Great Britain, and the Netherlands. *European Journal of Political Research*, 31(4): 401–26.

Doyle, M. W. (2000) Global Economic Inequalities. In P. Wapner and L. E. J. Ruiz (eds), *Principled World Politics*. Lanham, MD: Rowman & Littlefield.

Du Bois, W. E. B. (1986) Dusk of Dawn. In idem., *Writings*. New York: Library of America.

Dürrschmidt, J. (2000) *Everyday Lives in the Global City*. London: Routledge.

Eade, J. (1997) *Living the Global City: Globalization as Local Process*. New York: Routledge.

Eisenstadt, S. N. (2000) Multiple Modernities. *Daedalus*, 129(1): 1–29.

Enzensberger, H. M. (1992a) *Die Große Wanderung*. Frankfurt am Main: Suhrkamp.

Enzensberger, H. M. (1992b) Über die Schwierigkeit, ein Inländer zu sein. In idem., *Der Fliegende Robert*. Frankfurt am Main: Suhrkamp.

Eppler, E. (2002) *Vom Gewaltmonopol zum Gewaltmarkt?* Frankfurt am Main: Suhrkamp.

Esping-Andersen, G. (1990) *The Three Worlds of Welfare Capitalism*. Cambridge: Polity.

Espinoza, V. (1999) Social Networks Among the Poor: Inequality and Integration in a Latin American City. In B. Wellman (ed.), *Networks in the Global Village*. Boulder, CO: Westview Press.

Faist, T. (2000) *The Volume and Dynamics of International Migration and Transnational Social Space*. Oxford: Oxford University Press.

Faist, T. (2002) Jenseits von Nation und Post-Nation: Transstaatliche Räume und doppelte Staatsbürgerschaft. *Zeitschrift für Internationale Beziehungen*, 7(1): 109–44.

Falk, R. (1995) *Humane Governance*. Cambridge: Polity.

Favell, A. (1998a) A Politics that is Shared, Bounded, and Rooted? Rediscovering Civil Political Culture in Western Europe. *Theory and Society*, 27: 209–36.

Favell, A. (1998b) The Europeanisation of Immigration Politics. *European Integration Online Papers*, 2, <http//www.eiop.or.at/eiop/texte/1998–010.htm>.

Featherstone, M. (1993) Global and Local Cultures. In J. Bird et al. (eds), *Mapping the Futures: Local Cultures, Global Change*. London and New York: Routledge.

Featherstone, M. (2000) Technologies of Post-Human Development and Potential for Global Citizenship. In J. P. Nederveen Pieterse (ed.), *Global Futures: Shaping Globalization*. London: Zed Books.

Featherstone, M., and Lash, S. (eds) (1999) *Spaces of Culture: City, Nation, World*. London: Sage.

Feuchtwanger, L. (1932) Psalm des Weltbürgers. In idem., *Der jüdische Krieg*. Berlin: Propylaen.

Feuchtwanger, L. (1984) *Ein Buch nur für meine Freunde*. Frankfurt am Main: Fischer.

Feuchtwanger, L. (1993) *Erfolg: Drei Jahre Geschichte einer Provinz*. Berlin: Fischer.

Fine, R., and Cohen, R. (2002) Four Cosmopolitan Moments. In S. Vertovec and R. Cohen (eds), *Conceiving Cosmopolitanism*. Oxford: Oxford University Press, 137–64.

Fisch, J. (1992) *Reparationen nach dem zweiten Weltkrieg*. Munich: Beck.

Fouron, G., and Schiller, N. G. (2001) All in the Family: Gender, Transnational Migration, and the Nation State. *Identities*, 7(4): 539–82.

Fraser, N. (1997) *Justice Interruptus*. London: Routledge.

Fuchs, D., Gerhards, J., and Roller, E. (1993) Wir und die Anderen: Ethnozentrismus in den zwölf Ländern der europäischen Gemeinschaft. *Kölner Zeitschrift für Soziologie und Sozialpsychologie*, 45: 238–53.

Fukuyama, F. (1989) The End of History. *National Interest*, summer.

Gallini, C. (1996) Mass Exoticism. In I. Chambers and L. Curti (eds), *The Postcolonial Question*. London: Routledge.

Gane, N. (2001) Chasing the 'Runaway World': The Politics of Recent Globalization Theory. *Acta Sociologica*, 44(1): 81–9.

Gardner, K. (2002) Death of a Migrant: Transnational Death Rituals and Gender Among British Sylhetis. *Global Networks*, 2(3): 191–204.

Gardner, K., and Grillo, R. (2002) Transnational Households and Ritual: An Overview. *Global Networks*, 2(3): 179–90.

Gebesmair, A. (2000) *Musik und Globalisierung*. Vienna: Institut Mediacult.

Gerhards, J. (2003) Globalisierung der Alltagskultur zwischen Verwestlichung und Kreolisierung: Das Beispiel Vornamen. *Soziale Welt*, 2: 145–62.

Gerhards, J., and Rössel, J. (1999) Zur Transnationalisierung der Gesellschaft der Bundesrepublik: Entwicklungen, Ursachen und mögliche Folgen für die europäische Integration. *Zeitschrift für Soziologie*, 28: 325–44.

Gerhardt, V. (2003) Die Macht im Recht. *Merkur*, 7: 557–69.

Giddens, A. (1990) *The Consequences of Modernity*. Cambridge: Polity.

Giddens, A. (1994) *Beyond Left and Right*. Cambridge: Polity.

Gille, Z. (2001) Critical Ethnography in the Time of Globalization: Toward a New Concept of Site. *Cultural Studies – Critical Methodology*, 1(3): 319–34.

Gille, Z., and O'Riain, S. (2002) Global Ethnography. *Annual Review of Sociology*, 28: 271–95.

Gilroy, P. (1993) *The Black Atlantic*. Cambridge, MA: Harvard University Press.

Gilroy, P. (1996) Route Work: The Black Atlantic and the Politics of Exile. In I. Chambers and L. Curti (eds), *The Postcolonial Question*. London: Routledge.

Gilroy, P. (2000) *Against Race*. Cambridge, MA: Harvard University Press.

Ginsburg, F., and Rapp, R. (eds) (1998) *Conceiving the New World Order: The Global Politics of Reproduction*. Berkeley: University of California Press.

Göle, N. (2000) Snapshots of Islamic Modernities. *Daedalus*, 129(1): 91–117.

Goldring, L. (1998) The Power of Status in Transnational Social Fields. In M. P. Smith and L. E. Guarnizo (eds), *Transnationalism from Below*. New Brunswick, NJ: Transaction, 165–95.

Graf, O. M. (1949) *Die Eroberung der Welt*. Munich: Desch.

Graf, O. M. (1982) *Die Erben des Untergangs*. Frankfurt am Main: Fischer.

Grande, E. (2003) Reflexiver Kosmopolitismus. Discussion paper, Munich (January).

Grande, E., and Risse, T. (2000) Bridging the Gap: Konzeptionelle Anforderungen an die politikwissenschaftliche Analyse von Globalisierungsprozessen. *Zeitschrift für Internationale Beziehung*, 2: 235–67.

Gray, J. (2003) *Al-Qaeda and What it Means to be Modern*. London: Faber & Faber.

Gross, J. (2001) *Nachbarn: Der Mord an den Juden von Jedwabne*. Munich: Beck.

Gruen, E. (2002) *Diaspora: Jews Amidst Greeks and Romans*. Cambridge, MA: Harvard University Press.

Guillen, M. (2001) Is Globalization Civilizing, Destructive or Feeble? A Critique of Five Key Debates in the Social Science Literature. *Annual Review of Sociology*, 27: 235–60.

Gunaratna, R. (2002) *Inside Al-Qaeda: Global Network of Terror*. New York: Columbia University Press.

Gzesh, S., and Espinoza, R. (2002) Immigrant Communities Building Cross-Border Civic Networks: The Federation of Michoacan Clubs in Illinois. In S. Annheur, M. Glasius and M. Kaldor (eds), *Global Civil Society Yearbook 2002*. Oxford: Oxford University Press.

Habermas, J. (1996) Citizenship and National Identity. In idem., *Between Facts and Norms: Contributions to a Discourse Theory of Law and Democracy*. Cambridge: Polity.

Habermas, J. (2001) *The Postnational Constellation: Political Essays*. Cambridge: Polity.

Habermas, J. (2006) From Power Politics to Cosmopolitan Society. In idem., *Time of Transitions*. Cambridge: Polity.

Hacohen, M. H., and Popper, K. (1999) Jewish Identity and Central European Culture. *Journal of Modern History*, 71: 105–49.

Hahn, A. (1994) Die soziale Konstruktion des Fremden. In W. M. Sprondel (ed.), *Die Objektivität der Ordnungen und ihre kommunikative Konstruktion*. Frankfurt am Main: Suhrkamp.

Hall, S. (1991) The Local and the Global: Globalization and Ethnicity. In A. D. King (ed.), *Culture, Globalization and the World-System*. Basingstoke: Macmillan.

Hall, S. (1996) When Was 'the Post-Colonial'? Thinking at the Limit. In I. Chambers and L. Curti (eds), *The Postcolonial Question*. London: Routledge.

Hankel, G., and Stuby, G. (eds) (1995) *Strafgericht gegen Menschenrechtsverbrechen: Zum Völkerstrafrecht 50 Jahre nach den Nürnberger Prozessen*. Hamburg: Hamburger Edition.

Hannerz, U. (1992) The Global Ecumene as a Network of Networks. In A. Kuper (ed.), *Conceptualizing Society*. London: Routledge.

Hargittai, E., and Centeno, M. A. (2001) Defining a Global Geography. *American Behavioral Science*, 44(10): 1545–60.

Hartmann, M. (1999) Auf dem Weg zur transnationalen Bourgeoisie? Die Internationalisierung der Wirtschaft und die Internationalität der Spitzenmanager Deutschlands, Frankreichs, Großbritanniens und der USA. *Leviathan*, 27: 113–41.

Harvey, D. (1990) *The Condition of Postmodernity: An Inquiry into the Origins of Cultural Change*. Oxford: Blackwell.

Hedetoft, U. (2003) *The Global Turn*. Aarhus: Aalborg University Press.

Heine, H. (1997) *Sämtliche Schriften*, Vol. 3, ed. K. Briegleb. Munich: dtv.

Held, D. (1995) *Democracy and the Global Order*. Cambridge: Polity.

Held, D. (2000) Regulating Globalization? The Reinvention of Politics. *International Sociology*, 15(2): 394–408.

Held, D. (2003) From Execution to Cosmopolitan Multilateralism. In D. Held and M. Koenig-Archibugi (eds), *Taming Globalization*. Cambridge: Polity.

Held, D., McGrew, A., Goldblatt, D., and Perraton, J. (1999) *Global Transformations*. Cambridge: Polity.

Herrera Lima, G. F. (2001) Transnational Families: Institutions of Transnational Social Space. In L. Pries (ed.), *New Transnational Social Spaces*. London: Routledge, 77–93.

Hiebert, D. (2002) Cosmopolitan at the Local Level: The Development of Transnational Neighbourhood. In S. Vertovec and R. Cohen (eds), *Conceiving Cosmopolitanism*. Oxford: Oxford University Press.

Hilberg, R. (1961) *The Destruction of the European Jews*. Chicago: Quadrangle.

Hitzler, R. (1994) Mobilisierte Bürger. *Ästhetik und Kommunikation*, 85/86: 58f.

Holmes, D. R. (2000) *Integral Europe: Fast-Capitalism, Multiculturalism, Neofascism*. Princeton, NJ: Princeton University Press.

Hondrich, K.-O. (1994) Grenzen gegen die Gewalt. *Die Zeit*, 28 January: 4.

Horkheimer, M., and Adorno, T. W. (1993) *Dialectic of Enlightenment*. New York: Continuum.

Huntington, S. (1996) *The Clash of Civilizations and the Remaking of World Order*. New York: Simon & Schuster.

Isin, E. F. (2000) *Democracy, Citizenship and the Global City*. London: Routledge.

Jaspers, K. (1976) *The Origin and Goal of History*. Westport, CT: Greenwood Press.

Jaspers, K. (1978). *The Question of German Guilt*. Westport, CT: Greenwood Press.

Jessop, R. (1999) Reflections on Globalization and its Illogics. In C. Olds et al. (eds), *Globalization and the Asian Pacific: Contested Territories*. London: Routledge, 19–38.

Jonas, A. (1994) The Scale Politics of Spatiality. *Environment and Planning Society and Space*, 12(3): 257–64.

Jones, K. T. (1998) Scale as Epistemology. *Political Geography*, 17(1): 25–8.

Kagan, R. (2003) *Of Paradise and Power: America and Europe in the New World Order*. New York: Knopf.

Kaldor, M. (1998) *New and Old Wars*. Cambridge: Polity.

Kaldor, M. (2003) Das ohnmächtige Empire. In U. Speck and N. Sznaider (eds), *Empire Amerika: Perspektiven einer neuen Weltordnung*. Munich: DVA.

Kant, I. (1983) Idea for a Universal History with a Cosmopolitan Intent. In idem., *Perpetual Peace and Other Essays*, ed. T. Humphrey. Indianapolis: Hackett.

Kant, I. (1996) Towards Perpetual Peace: A Philosophical Project. In idem., *Practical Philosophy*, ed. M. Gregor. Cambridge: Cambridge University Press.

Kant, I. (1998) *Critique of Pure Reason*, ed. P. Guyer and A. Wood. Cambridge: Cambridge University Press.

Keane, J. (1998) *Civil Societies*. Cambridge: Polity.

Kearney, M. (1998) Transnationalism in California and Mexico at the End of Empire. In H. Donnan and T. M. Wilson (eds), *Border Identities: Nation and State at International Frontiers*. Cambridge: Cambridge University Press.

Kermani, N., and Lepenies, W. (2003) Verkannte Brüder. *Süddeutsche Zeitung*, 11 June.

Kertész, I. (2003) *Die exilierte Sprache*. Frankfurt am Main: Suhrkamp.

Kieserling, A. (1998) Massenmedien. Munich, MS.

King, A. D. (ed.) (1997) *Culture, Globalization and the World-System: Contemporary Conditions for the Representation of Identity*. Minneapolis: University of Minnesota Press.

Kline, S. (1995) The Play of the Market: On the Internationalization of Children's Culture. *Theory, Culture and Society*, 12: 103–29.

Kohlhammer, S. (2003) Ein angenehmes Märchen – die Wiederentdeckung und Neugestaltung des muslimischen Spanien. *Merkur*, 57: 595–608.

König, H., Kohlstruck, M., and Wöll, A. (eds) (1998) *Vergangenheitsbewältigung am Ende des zwanzigsten Jahrhunderts*. Opladen: Westdeutscher Verlag.

Koopmans, R., and Statham, P. (2001) *How National Citizenship Shapes Transnationalism: A Comparative Analysis of Migrant Claims-Making in Germany, Great Britain and the Netherlands.* Oxford: ESCR Transnational Communities Programme Working Paper WPTC-OI-IO, <www.transcommm.ox.ac.uk>.

Koselleck, R. (1985) *Futures Past.* Cambridge, MA: MIT Press.

Kotkin, J. (1993) *Tribes: How Race, Religion and Identity Determine Success in the New Global Economy.* New York: Random House.

Kritz, N. (ed.) (1995) *Transitional Justice: How Emerging Democracies Reckon with Former Regimes.* Washington, DC: US Institute of Peace.

Kyle, D. (2000) *Transnational Peasants.* Baltimore: Johns Hopkins University Press.

Lakatos, I. (1970) Falsification and the Methodology of Scientific Research Programmes. In I. Lakatos and A. Musgrave (eds), *Criticism and the Growth of Knowledge.* Cambridge: Cambridge University Press.

Landmann, M. (1978) Mein Judentum. In H. J. Schultz (ed.), *Mein Judentum.* Munich: Piper.

Lash, S. (1999) *Another Modernity.* Oxford: Blackwell.

Lash, S., and Urry, J. (2005) *Global Culture Industry: The Mediation of Things.* Cambridge: Polity.

Latour, B. (2001) *Das Parlament der Dinge.* Frankfurt am Main: Suhrkamp.

Latour, B. (2003) Is Remodernization Occurring – and if so, How to Prove it? *Theory, Culture and Society*: 20(1): 35–49.

Laube, H. (1973) *Das junge Europa*, Vol. 1. Frankfurt am Main: Athenäum.

Levitt, P. (2001) *The Transnational Villagers.* Berkeley: University of California Press.

Levy, D. (1999) The Future of the Past: Historiographical Disputes and Competing Memories in Germany and Israel. *History and Theory*, 38(1): 51–66.

Levy, D. (2002) The Transformation of Germany's Ethno-Cultural Idiom: The Case of Ethnic German Immigrants. In D. Levy and Y. Weiss (eds), *Challenging Ethnic Citizenship. German and Israeli Perspectives on Immigration.* New York: Berghahn.

Levy, D., and Dierkes, J. (2002) Institutionalizing the Past: Shifting Memories of Nationhood in German Education and Immigration Legislation. In J.-W. Mueller (ed.), *Memory and Power in International Relations.* Cambridge: Polity.

Levy, D., and Sznaider, N. (2001) *Erinnerung im globalen Zeitalter: Der Holocaust.* Frankfurt am Main: Suhrkamp.

Levy, D., and Sznaider, N. (2002) Memory Unbound: The Holocaust and the Formation of Cosmopolitan Memory. *European Journal of Social Theory*, 5(1).

Levy, D., and Sznaider, N. (2004) *Memory in the Global Age: The Holocaust.* Philadelphia: Temple University Press.

Lieberson, S. (2000) *A Matter of Taste: How Names, Fashions and Culture Change.* New Haven, CT, and London: Yale University Press.

Liebes, T., and Katz, E. (1993) *The Export of Meaning: Cross-Cultural Readings of Dallas.* Cambridge: Polity.

Lin, J. (1998) *Reconstructing Chinatown: Ethnic Enclave, Global Change.* Minneapolis: University of Minneasota Press.

Linklater, A. (1998) *The Transformation of Political Community.* Columbia: University of South Carolina Press.

Lipschutz, R. D. (1992) Reconstructing World Politics: The Emergence of Global Civil Society. *Millennium*, 21(3): 389–420.

Lobel, O. (2003) Family Geographies: Global Care Chains, Transnational Parenthood and New Legal Challenges in an Era of Labour Globalization. In J. Holder and C. Harrison (eds), *Law and Geography*. Oxford: Oxford University Press.

Loon, J. van (2000) Mediating Risks of Virtual Environments. In S. Allan, B. Adam and C. Carter (eds), *Environmental Risks and the Media*. London: Routledge.

Lopez, S. (2000) Contesting the Global City: Pittsburgh's Public Service Unions Confront a Neoliberal Agenda. In M. Burawoy et al., *Global Ethnography: Forces, Connections, and Imaginations in a Postmodern World*. Berkeley: University of California Press.

Luard, E. (1990) *The Globalization of Politics*. London: Macmillan.

Lübbe, H. (2001) *Ich Entschuldige Mich: Das neue politische Bußritual*. Berlin: Siedler.

Lugo, A. (2000) Theorizing Border Inspections. *Cultural Dynamics*, 12(3): 353–73.

Luhmann, N. (1975) Weltgesellschaft. In idem., *Soziologische Aufklärung*. Opladen: Westdeutscher Verlag.

Luhmann, N. (1994) Europa als Problem der Weltgesellschaft. *Berlin Debatte*, 2: 3–7.

Luhmann, N. (1999) Ethik in internationalen Beziehungen. *Soziale Welt*, 5(4): 373–82.

Maalouf, A. (2000) *In the Name of Identity*. Harmondsworth: Penguin.

McGrane, B. (1989) *Beyond Anthropology*. New York: Columbia University Press.

McNeill, W. H. (1985) *Polyethnicity and National Unity in World History*. Toronto: University of Toronto Press.

Mahler, S. J. (1998) Theoretical and Empirical Contributions Toward a Research Agenda for Transnationalism. In M. P. Smith and L. E. Guarnizo (eds), *Transnationalism from Below*. New Brunswick, NJ: Transaction, 64–100.

Malcomson, S. L. (1998) The Varieties of Cosmopolitan Experience. In P. Cheah and B. Robbins (eds), *Cosmopolitics: Thinking and Feeling Beyond the Nation*. Minneapolis: University of Minnesota Press.

Mann, T. (1983a) Betrachtungen eines Unpolitischen. In idem., *Reden und Aufsätze. Gesammelte Werke*, Vol. XII. Frankfurt am Main: Fischer.

Mann, T. (1983b) *Reflections of a Nonpolitical Man*. New York: F. Ungar.

Martins, H. (1974) Time and Theory in Sociology. In J. Rex (ed.), *Approaches in Sociology*. London: Routledge.

Mato, D. (1997) On Global and Local Agents and the Social Making of Transnational Identities and Related Agendas in 'Latin' America. *Identities*, 4(2): 167–212.

Mauss, M. (2000) *The Gift: The Form and Reason for Exchange in Archaic Societies*. New York: Norton.

Menivar, C. (2002) Living in Two Worlds? Guatemalan-Origin Children in the United States and Emerging Transnationalism. *Journal of Ethnic and Migration Studies*, 28(3): 531–52.

Meyer, J. W., Boli, J., Thomas, G. M., and Ramirez, F. O. (1997) World Society and the Nation-State. *American Journal of Sociology*, 103(1): 144–81.

Miller, D. (1995) *Worlds Apart: Modernity Through the Prisms of the Local*. London: Routledge.

Miller, D., and Slater, D. (2000) *The Internet: an Ethnographic Approach*. Oxford: Berg.

Mills, M. B. (1999) *Thai Women in the Global Labor Force: Consuming Desires, Contested Selves*. New Brunswick, NJ: Rutgers University Press.

Minow, M. (1998) *Between Vengeance and Forgiveness: Facing History After Genocide and Mass Violence*. Boston: Beacon Press.

Mohan, G., and Zack-Williams, A. B. (2002) Globalization from Below: Conceptualising the Role of the African Diasporas in Africa's Development. *Review of African Political Economy*, 92: 211–36.

Münkler, H. (2002) *Die neuen Kriege*. Reinbeck bei Hamburg: Rowohlt.

Nassehi, A. (1998) Die 'Welt'-Fremdheit der Globalisierungsdebatte. *Soziale Welt*, 49.

Nassehi, A., and Schroer, M. (2003) *Der Begriff des Politischen*. Baden-Baden: Nomos.

Neckel, S. (1994) Gefährliche Fremdheit. *Ästhetik und Kommunikation*, 85/86: 47.

Nederveen Pieterse, J. P. (ed.) (2000) *Global Futures: Shaping Globalization*. London: Zed Books.

Nederveen Pieterse, J. P. (2003) *Globalization and Culture*. Lanham, MD: Rowman & Littlefield.

Nietzsche, F. (1996) *Human, All too Human*. New York: Routledge.

Offe, C. (2003) Is There, or Can There be a 'European Society'? In I. Katenhusen and W. Lamping (eds), *Demokratien in Europa: Der Einfluss der europäischen Integration auf Institutionenwandel und neue Konturen des demokratischen Verfassungsstaates*. Opladen: Leske & Budrich.

Olick, J., and Levy, D. (1997) Mechanisms of Cultural Constraint: Holocaust Myth and Rationality in German Politics. *American Sociological Review*, 62: 921–36.

Ong, A. (1997) Chinese Modernities: Narratives of Nation and Capitalism. In idem., *Ungrounded Empires: The Cultural Politics of Modern Chinese Transnationalism*. New York: Routledge.

Ong, A. (1999) *Flexible Citizenship: The Cultural Logics of Transnationality*. Durham, NC: Duke University Press.

Orellana, M. F., Thorne, A. C., and Wan Shun, E. L. (2001) Transnational Childhoods: The Participation of Children in Processes of Family Migration. *Social Problems*, 48(4): 572–91.

Orwell, G. (1983) *1984*. Harlow: Longman.

Osier, M. (1997) *Mass Atrocity, Collective Memory, and the Law*. New Brunswick, NJ: Transaction.

Otter, Y. N. (2003) Islam und Europa. In Alfred Herrhausen Gesellschaft (ed.), *Europa leidenschaftlich gesucht*. Munich: Piper.

Ottoman, H. (1987) *Philosophie und Politik bei Nietzsche*. Berlin: de Gruyter.

Papadakis, Y. (2000) The Social Mapping of the Unknown: Managing Uncertainty in a Mixed Borderline Cypriot Village. *Anthropological Journal of European Cultures*, 9(2): 93–112.

Park, R. E. (1928) *The Marginal Man*. Chicago: University of Chicago Press.

Parrenas, R. S. (2002) The Care Crisis in the Philippines: Children and Transnational Families in the New Global Economy. In A. Hochschild and B. Ehrenreich (eds), *Global Woman: Essays on Women and Globalization*. New York: Nation Books.

Pauly, L., and Grande, E. (eds) (2005) *Complex Sovereignty: Reconstituting Political Authority*. Toronto: University of Toronto Press.

Perlmutter, H. V. (1992) On the Rocky Road to the First Global Civilization. In S. Hall, D. Held and T. McGrew (eds), *Modernity and its Futures*. Cambridge: Polity, 103–6.

Phillips, R. B., and Steiner, C. B. (1999) *Unpacking Culture: Art and Commodity in Colonial and Postcolonial Worlds*. Berkeley: University of California Press.

Portes, A. (2001) The Debates and Significance of Immigrant Transnationalism. *Global Networks*, 1(3): 181–93.

Portes, A., Guarnizo, L. E., and Landolt, P. (1999) The Study of Transnationalism: Pitfalls and Promises of an Emergent Research Field. *Ethnic and Racial Studies*, 22(2): 217–37.

Portes, A., Haller, W., and Guarnizo, L. E. (2002) Transnational Entrepreneurs: The Emergence and Determinants of an Alternative Form of Immigrant Economic Adaptation. *American Sociological Review*, 67: 278–98.

Pries, L. (ed.) (1997) *Transnationale Migration*. Baden-Baden: Nomos.

Randeria, S. (1998) Against the Self-Sufficiency of Western Social Sciences. Berlin, MS.

Randeria, S. (1999) Jenseits von Soziologie und soziokultureller Anthropologie. *Soziale Welt*, 50(4): 373–82.

Randeria, S. (2001) Local Refractions of Global Governance. Dissertation, Berlin.

Rawls, J. (1993) *Political Liberalism*. New York: Columbia University Press.

Riccio, B. (2000) The Italian Construction of Immigrant. *Anthropological Journal of European Cultures*, 9(2): 53–74.

Robertson, R. (1992) *Globalization: Social Theory and Global Culture*. London: Sage.

Robertson, R., and Khondker, H. H. (1998) Discourses of Globalization: Preliminary Considerations. *International Sociology*, 13(1): 25–40.

Robins, K., and Aksoy, A. (2001) From Spaces of Identity to Mental Spaces: Lessons from Turkish-Cypriot Cultural Experience in Britain. *Journal of Ethnic and Migration Studies*, 27(4): 685–711.

Rorty, R. (1998) Justice as a Larger Loyalty. In P. Cheah and B. Robbins (eds), *Cosmopolitics: Thinking and Feeling Beyond the Nation*. Minneapolis: University of Minnesota Press.

Rosenmayr, L. (1992) *Die Schnüre vom Himmel*. Vienna: Bohlau.

Rosenstrauch, H. (1988) *Aus Nachbarn wurden Juden*. Berlin: Transit.

Sahlins, M. (2000) *Culture in Practice: Selected Essays*. New York: Zone.

Said, E. W. (1978) *Orientalism*. New York: Pantheon.

Said, E. W. (1993) *Culture and Imperialism*. New York: Knopf.

Salih, R. (2000) Towards an Understanding of Gender and Transnationalism: Moroccan Migrant Women's Movements Across the Mediterranean. *Anthropological Journal of European Culture*, 9(2): 75–92.

Salih, R. (2002) *Gender in Transnationalism: Home, Longing and Belonging Among Moroccan Migrant Women*. London: Routledge.

Sassen, S. (2000) New Frontiers Facing Urban Sociology at the Millennium. *British Journal of Sociology*, 51(1): 143–60.

Sassen, S. (2003) Globalization or Denationalization? *Review of International Political Economy*, 10(1): 1–22.

Schein, L. (1998) Importing Miao Brethren to Hmong America: A Not-So-Stateless Transnationalism. In P. Cheah and B. Robbins (eds), *Cosmopolitics: Thinking and Feeling Beyond the Nation*. Minneapolis: University of Minnesota Press.

Schiffauer, W. G., Baumann, G., Kastoryano, R., and Vertovec, S. (eds) (2003) *Civil Enculturation: State, School and Ethnic Differences in Four European Countries*. Oxford: Berghahn.

Schiller, H. (1989) Disney, Dallas and Electronic Data Flows: The Transnationalisation of Culture. In C. W. Thomsen (ed.), *Cultural Transfer and Electronic Imperialism? The Impact of American Television Programs on European Television*. Heidelberg: Carl Winter.

Schiller, N. G. (1997) The Situation of Transnational Studies. *Identities*, 4(2): 155–66.

Schlögel, K. (2003) Tragödie der Vertreibungen: Über das Erfordernis, ein europäisches Ereignis neu zu erzählen. *Lettre*, 60: 78–83.

Schmitt, C. (1963) *Theorie des Partisanen*. Berlin: Duncker & Humblot.

Schwan, G. (1997) *Politik und Schuld: Die zerstörerische Macht des Schweigens*. Frankfurt am Main: Fischer.

Scott, J. C. (1998) *Seeing Like a State*. New Haven, CT: Yale University Press.

Shaw, M. (1994) The Theoretical Challenge of Global Society. In A. Sreberny-Mohammadi et al. (eds), *Media in Global Context*. London: Arnold.

Shaw, M. (2000a) Historical Sociology and the Global Transformation. In R. Parlan (ed.), *Global Political Economy*. London: Sage.

Shaw, M. (2000b) *Theory of the Global State: Globality as Unfinished Revolution*. Cambridge: Cambridge University Press.

Shaw, M. (2002) Post-Imperial and Quasi-Imperial: State and Empire in the Global Era. *Millennium*, 31(2).

Shriver, D. (1995) *An Ethic for Enemies: Forgiveness in Politics*. New York: Oxford University Press.

Simmel, G. (1958) Exkurs über den Fremden. In idem., *Soziologie: Untersuchungen über die Formen der Vergesellschaftung*. Berlin: Duncker & Humblot.

Sklair, L. (2001) *The Transnational Capitalist Class*. Oxford: Blackwell.

Smith, A. (1975) *The Wealth of Nations*, 2 vols. London: Dent.

Smith, A. D. (1995) *Nations and Nationalism in a Global Era*. Cambridge: Polity.

Smith, G., and Avishai, M. (eds) (1997) *Amnestie oder die Politik der Erinnerung in der Demokratie*. Frankfurt am Main: Suhrkamp.

Smith, M. (2001) *Transnational Urbanism: Locating Globalization*. Oxford: Blackwell.

Smith, M. P., and Guarnizo, L. E. (eds) (1998) *Transnationalism from Below*. New Brunswick, NJ: Transaction.

Smith, Z. (2001) *White Teeth*. London: Penguin.

Soyinka, W. (1999) *The Burden of Memory, the Muse of Forgiveness*. New York: Oxford University Press.

Soysal, L. (2002) Beyond the 'Second Generation'. In D. Levy and Y. Weiss (eds), *Challenging Ethnic Citizenship*. New York: Berghahn.

Speck, U., and Sznaider, N. (eds) (2003) *Empire Amerika: Perspektiven einer neuen Weltordnung*. Munich: DVA.

Spengler, O. (1934) *Decline of the West*. New York: Knopf.

Strange, S. (1996) *The Retreat of the State: The Diffusion of Power in the World Economy*. Cambridge: Cambridge University Press.

Stichweh, R. (2000) *Die Weltgesellschaft*. Frankfurt am Main: Suhrkamp.

Swaan, A. de (1995) Die soziologische Untersuchung der transnationalen Gesellschaft. *Journal für Sozialforschung*, 35: 107–20.

Szerszynski, B., and Urry, J. (2002) Cultures of Cosmopolitanism. *Sociological Review*, 50(4).

Sznaider, N. (1996) Pain and Cruelty in Socio-Historical Perspective. *International Journal of Politics, Culture and Society*, 10(2): 331–54.

Sznaider, N. (1998) The Sociology of Compassion: A Study in the Sociology of Morals. *Cultural Values*, 2(1): 117–39.

Sznaider, N. (2000a) *Über das Mitleid im Kapitalismus*. Munich: Bibliothek der Provinz.

Sznaider, N. (2000b) Compassion and Cruelty in Modern Society: The Case of the Holocaust. *Amsterdam Journal of Sociology*, 26(4): 487–506.

Sznaider, N. (2000c) *The Compassionate Temperament: Care and Cruelty in Modern Society.* Lanham, MD: Rowman & Littlefield.

Sznaider, N. (2000d): Cosmopolitanism as Civilizing Process. *International Journal of Politics, Culture and Society*, 14(2): 297–314.

Taylor, C. (1999) Two Theories of Modernity. *Public Culture*, 11(1).

Teitel, R. G. (2002) Humanity's Law: Rule of Law for the Global Politics. *Cornell International Law Journal*, 35(2): 355–87.

Thayer, M. (2001) Transnational Feminism: Reading Joan Scott in the Brazilian Sertao. *Ethnography*, 2(2): 243–72.

Therborn, G. (1995) Routes to/through Modernity. In M. Featherstone, S. Lash and R. Robertson (eds), *Global Modernities*. London: Sage.

Therborn, G. (2000) At the Birth of Second Century Sociology: Times of Reflexivity, Spaces, and Nodes of Knowledge. *British Journal of Sociology*, 51(1): 37–57.

Thielking, S. (2000) *Weltbürgertum: Kosmopolitische Ideen in Literatur und politischer Publizistik seit dem achtzehnten Jahrhundert*. Munich: Fink.

Tocqueville, A. de (1945) *Democracy in America*, 2 vols. New York: Vintage.

Tomlinson, J. (1999) *Globalization and Culture*. Cambridge: Polity.

Touraine, A. (1994) Der Staat zerbricht. *Die Woche*, 7 April: 23.

Trojanow, I. (2003) Europas vergessene Wurzeln. In Alfred Herrhausen Gesellschaft (ed.), *Europa leidenschaftlich gesucht*. Munich: Piper.

Tsing, A. (2000) The Global Situation. *Cultural Anthropology*, 15(3): 327–60.

Urry, J. (2000) *Sociology Beyond Societies*. New York and London: Routledge.

Vertovec, S. (2003) Migrant Transnationalism and Modes of Transformation. Oxford, MS.

Vertovec, S., and Cohen, R. (eds) (2002) *Conceiving Cosmopolitanism*. Oxford: Oxford University Press.

Wade, R. H. (2003) The Disturbing Rise in Poverty and Inequality. Is it all a 'Big Lie'? In D. Held and M. Koenig-Archibugi (eds), *Taming Globalization*. Cambridge: Polity.

Wallerstein, I. (1991) The National and the Universal: Can There be Such a Thing as World Culture?. In idem., *Geopolitics and Geoculture: Essays on the Changing World-System*. Cambridge: Cambridge University Press.

Wapner, P., and Ruiz, L. E. J. (2000) *Principled World Politics*. Oxford: Rowman & Littlefield.

Weiler, J. H. H. (1999) *The Constitution of Europe: 'Do the New Clothes Have an Emperor?' and Other Essays on European Integration*. Cambridge: Cambridge University Press.

Weizmüller, R. (1997) Zu den Folgen der Globalisierung für die nationalen Güter-, Finanz- und Arbeitsmärkte. *Aus Politik und Zeitgeschichte*, 33/34: 20–8.

Wiedernroth, E. (1992) Was macht mich so anders in den Augen der Anderen? In K. Oguntoye et al. (eds), *Farbe bekennen*. Frankfurt am Main: Fischer.

Wiese, L. (1916) Kosmopolitismus. *Die Schaubühne*, 12(2): 28–31.

Wong, D. (1992) Fremdheitsfiguren im gesellschaftlichen Diskurs. In J. Matthes (ed.), *Zwischen den Kulturen?* Göttingen: Schwartz.

Yanitsky, O. N. (2000) Sustainability and Risk: The Case of Russia. *Innovation*, 13(3): 265–77.

Young, R. (1990) *White Mythologies: Writing History and the West*. London: Routledge.

Zanetti, V. (2002) Nach dem 11. September: Paradigmenwechsel im Völkerrecht? *Deutsche Zeitschrift für Philosophie*, 50(3): 455–69.

Zangl, B. (2003) *Frieden und Krieg: Sicherheit in der nationalen und postnationalen Konstellation*. Frankfurt am Main: Suhrkamp.

Zolo, D. (1997) *Cosmopolis*. Cambridge: Polity.

Zürn, M. (1998) *Regieren jenseits des Nationalstaates*. Frankfurt am Main: Suhrkamp.

Zürn, M., and Wolf, D. (2000) Europarecht und internationale Regime. In E. Grande et al. (eds), *Wie problemlosungsfähig ist die EU?* Baden-Baden: Nomos.

Zweig, S. (1988) *Die Welt von gestern: Erinnerungen eines Europäers*. Frankfurt am Main: Fischer.

Index

- Inclusive differentiation
    (recogⁿ of differ)
- Cosmopolzn — not always voluntary;
    — a _fact_ of present day living,
            not a 'choice' but a side-effect.

- Cosmopolitanism
- Cosmopolitonisation ; banal cosmopolitenism .
  ^ institutionolised cosmopolitonism ?.
- The cosmopolitan outlook

- Methodological cosmopolitonism